# Dalit Women :
## Fear and Discrimination

# Dalit Women: Fear and Discrimination

Sneha Verma

MOHIT PUBLICATIONS
New Delhi - 110002 (India)

First Published : 2010



ISBN : 978-81-7445-522-2

*Published by :*
**MOHIT PUBLICATIONS**
4675/21, Ansari Road, Daryaganj-110002
Phone : 23255141; Fax. : 23284126

PRINTED IN INDIA

Published by Sangita Goel for Mohit Publications, New Delhi-02, Typeset by Abhijeet Typesetters and Printed at Nav Prabhat Printing Press Delhi.

# Preface

There are about 250 million Dalits in India. There is meagre improvement in the socio-economic condition of dalits in the past 50 years. Which that is not enough when compared to non-dalits. Of course, much more needs to be done. The urgent need is to have a national sample survey on dalits. Every fourth Indian is a dalit. There is no proper survey to give the correct number of dalit women in India. They are generally scattered in villages and they are not a monogamous group. About 75% of dalits live below poverty line. Economic backwardness of dalits is mostly due to injustice done to them by the high castes and also due to exploitation. From the time immemorial they worked like slaves, sold as commodities resulting in their social discrimination, economic deprivation and educational backwardness. To assess the position of dalit women in India this chapter is divided into various heads.

The situation of Dalit women in India needs special attention. They are one of the largest socially segregated groups anywhere in the world, and make up 2% of the world's total population. Dalit women are discriminated against three times over: they are poor, they are women, and they are Dalits. Dalit women constitute half of the ca. 200 million Dalit population, and 16.3 of the total Indian female population. The traditional taboos are the same for Dalit men and Dalit women. However, Dalit women have to deal with them more often. Dalit women are discriminated against not only by people of higher castes, but also within their own communities. Men are dominant in Dalit communities. Dalit women also have less power within the Dalit movement itself. Women are active in large numbers in the movement but most leadership positions in the organisations, local bodies and associations have until now been held by men.

The coaching programmes conducted by the Government for dalit women are beneficial in training many women to compete in the competitive exam. These programmes also do not reach the needy dalit women because they are cornered by the very few creamy dalit women. This should be monitored properly and the schemes should be reached by the most deprived and constantly struggling dalit women. Because these dalit women are neglected by socially advanced communities and also by the better off among the dalits, which leads to an unhealthy socio-economic condition. There should be some scientific basis to pick up the poorest and they should be equipped with facilities. There are some pre-examination coaching centres giving trainings for dalits which are doing very good service to train them in vocational line, for competitive exam, in medical and engineering field, railway recruitment boards, bank recruitment, etc.

Marginalisation and racial exclusion of dalits is a burning issue today. This book on dalits goes back into past and looks at the history of dalit alienation, fear and discrimination. Issues like racial conflict, racism and justice, relevance of human rights to dalits, caste and colour prejudices etc. find description in the book. Discrimination on different contexts finds its manifestations in physical segregation of communities, restrictions on resources like water and land, social prohibitions, restrictions on entry to religious places etc. The book enlightens us on such things in a country where Constitution guarantees equal rights and privileges to every Indian citizen.

*—Author*

# Contents

# CHAPTER 1

# Dalit Women in India

## Introduction

There are about 250 million Dalits in India. There is meagre improvement in the socio-economic condition of dalits in the past 50 years. Which that is not enough when compared to non-dalits. Of course, much more needs to be done. The urgent need is to have a national sample survey on dalits. Every fourth Indian is a dalit. There is no proper survey to give the correct number of dalit women in India. They are generally scattered in villages and they are not a monogamous group. About 75% of dalits live below poverty line. Economic backwardness of dalits is mostly due to injustice done to them by the high castes and also due to exploitation. From the time immemorial they worked like slaves, sold as commodities resulting in their social discrimination, economic deprivation and educational backwardness. To assess the position of dalit women in India this chapter is divided into various heads.

## Education

Till some years ago, many dalit women were ill treated and educationally backward inspite of the facilities for free education. The reasons for the high rate of illiteracy among dalit women are many.

The following are the main reasons:

1. Resistance from the family to send girls to schools.
2. Fear of insecurity in villages.

3. Lack of physical facilities like accommodation, school, transport and medical fac'lities.
4. The girls were forced to take care of the siblings when the parents are away at work.
5. Girls were forced to do domestic chores which prevent them from attending school.
6. Working to earn for the family prevent the girls from attending school.
7. Working with parents to earn their livelihood in beedi factories or other unorganized sector made them illiterate.
8. Because of the sick and unemployed parents girls were forced to work.
9. Many were forced to get married at young age, which stop schooling.
10. Social restriction is that the girls should stop education after marriage.
11. In some areas there are complaints from dalit women teachers of misbehaviors, blackmail and exploitation by the male staff of other high caste people.
12. Distance of schools from home.
13. Irrelevant content of the education system.
14. Fear of alienation of girls from their environment as a result of education are some of the other factors for low literacy level among SC girls. Even if the education improved the marriage prospects of the girls, the minus point is the increase in dowry. Therefore many parents wish to withdraw the girls from schools.

The present positions seems to be better with reference to the rate of literacy among dalits. The literacy rate is 31.48% for boys and 10.93% for girls. Dalits women belonging to the creamy layer of the society are better with good education and socially and economically they are well off like other high castes. They are fully aware of the welfare schemes provided by the Government and their percentage is very low when compared with the total dalit population. In rural areas, the first generation girls from SC needs the attention of Government and other organization. Mostly the teachers of the locality provide information to them about the welfare schemes. In many Dalit association executive position are occupied by male members whereas very poor representation is made by women in their pasts. The women are not properly informed about the Government schemes and there is an urgent need to get a feedback about the welfare schemes where lot of money is spent for the development of Dalits. The funds are not utilized properly for their upliftment. Many of the schemes go unnoticed because they are not popularized properly.

The coaching programmes conducted by the Government for dalit women are beneficial in training many women to compete in the competitive exam. These programmes also do not reach the needy dalit women because they are cornered by the very few creamy dalit women. This should be monitored properly and the schemes should be reached by the most deprived and constantly struggling dalit women. Because these dalit women are neglected by socially advanced communities and also by the better off among the dalits, which leads to an unhealthy socio-economic condition. There should be some scientific basis to pick up the poorest and they should be equipped with facilities. There are some pre-examination coaching centres giving trainings for dalits which are doing very good service to train them in vocational line, for competitive exam, in medical and engineering field, railway recruitment boards, bank recruitment, etc.

Here are some suggestions for the better implementation of the schemes to dalit women:

1. Competitive spirit should be instilled in the girls.
2. Selection and identification of the talented girls should be done correctly.
3. Identify the candidate at college level for coaching.
4. Result oriented teaching is necessary.
5. Group discussions, quiz, and seminars to instill confidence.
6. Teacher : Student ratio 1:20 or below.
7. Monitoring by the teacher after class hours.
8. Loan facility.

Financial aid for uniform for girls, maps, charts, examination grant, laboratory facilities, library facilities should be provided for them special coaching should be given for meritorious dalit girls to compete for IAS and IPS. Hostel facilities for dalit girls at all levels of education starting from primary school up to higher education should be provided reservation policy especially for girls should be allotted in both admission and employment. There is an increased awareness in recent years among dalit women about their rights and about the Government welfare schemes about higher education. This should be augmented by information technology, which should reach even to the remote rural citizen.

### Higher Education

The UGC has given reservation for seats in colleges for SC students 25%, ST 7.5%, which is highly beneficial. Also relaxation in marks for 5% is given to all dalit students in admission. Financial assistance in the form of fellowships is given to dalits. Rs. 3,600/- is given per JRF to continue research studies at the University level. There are special SC/ST cells at the University for effective implementation of the Government orders and to improve the condition of University level dalit students. There are some of the suggestions for effective implementation of the various welfare schemes for the dalit students.

1. The communication gap between the educational institution and the social welfare department should be reduced.
2. District wise computer database of the male and female dalit students is very essential to provide necessary facilities to them.
3. Pamphlets with details about the welfare schemes should be distributed to the students.
4. Supply of books to the dalit students.
5. Incentive scholarship should be given to deserving and meritorious girls to encourage them for higher education.

## Gender Equality

Female infanticide is more prevalent among the uneducated dalit families. Educational development among SC women is very marginal because only girls were not sent to school because of the responsibilities at home.

Therefore the gender discrimination starts at the very early stage in the life of a dalit girl. Normally girl children are retained at home to look after the siblings. Another thing is the compulsory marriage of the girls at very early age after which the education is stopped. Generally in the male-dominated society, polygamy is allowed and more so in many dalit families. Because of this the position of the women deteriorated. Joint family system, polygamy, property structure, early marriage, and permanent widowhood were hurdles for the development of all women in early period. But in the twentieth century, after the Mahatma Gandhian movement to educate women, slowly changes occurred in the position of women. But here, rural women were more blessed than urban women because divorce and remarriage were allowed for them. Mainly Sudras (i.e. low caste people) allowed divorce and remarriage for their women.

## Occupation

The occupation of many SC women can be divided in the following heads:

1. Agriculture labourer.
2. Marginal Cultivators.
3. Fisherwomen.
4. Traditional artisans.
5. Leather Workers.
6. Weavers.
7. Scavengers and sweepers.
8. Midwifery.
9. Beedi factories and unorganised sectors.

The Work Participation Rate (WPR) of SC population is said to be for males 22.25% and for females 25.98%. The contribution of SC women to the economic development of our country is significant especially in the agricultural sector. They are exploited by the higher caste landlords. They are paid very marginal salary for the hard work in the field for the whole day. In leather industries the tanning process is considered to be an unclean job which is done only by socially backward class. Traditional artistes get very more benefit because the middleman exploits them. The condition of scavenger and sweepers is very deplorable and they the most vulnerable sectors among SC. The working condition is very poor and the remuneration is also very poor.

### Family Role

Because of the girls remain uneducated, they got married very early. Marriage in the high reproductive stage with high fertility rate, children care more. Because of the unlimited family, the burden fell on the young girls which affected their health. They were not able to assist in family matters to their husbands. But now the situation is different. The girls manage to plan their family, educate the children, assist the husbands in family matters and office going and professional girls improve the economic conditions. On the whole the family becomes socially developed because of the education of the girls. Education among women increased intercaste marriages, which is definitely a sign of development. Government also encourages intercaste marriages among dalits and highcaste by incentives.

## Protection From Ill-treatment

Most women are ill-treated even today among tribals. Ministry of welfare GI (1993–94) Annual report had recorded 18,014 crimes against SCs (murder, rape, etc.). Disputes on land, minimum wage for SC workers bonded labourers, in debatedness – problem. SC/ST under privileged, regarded less then humanbeings assigned lowest of the low status in society. Scavenging: is no other country scavenging is amalgamated with the evil structure of caste.

### Untouchability and Ill-treatment

1. Non-access to temples, places of worship.
2. Non-access to hotels and eating-places.
3. Not available – barber services for SC/ST Tamil Nadu.
4. Not allowed in gramsabha sittings – Tamil Nadu.
5. Discrimination in educational institution, public health services.
6. Not allowed to participate in social ceremonies – Tamil Nadu.
7. General untouchability – Tamil Nadu.
8. Enforcement of removal of carcasses – Tamil Nadu.
9. Not access to public cremation / burial ground / public pathways/roads.

10. Not allowed in residential premises of high caste.
11. Access to Dharmasalas – denied.

Untouchability is acute in villages. There is a gradual change in rural areas because they have become aware of their rights. Spread of education, improvement in economic conditions, welfare measures.

## Measures to be Taken for Upliftment

### Basic Common Needs

The following facilities should be provided:

1. Nutrition: Malnutrition in female children high infant mortality should be corrected.
2. Health: Unclean surroundings – proper accommodation should be provided.
3. Family welfare: SC – women get married very soon high fertility – affect health.
4. Safe drinking water.
5. Electricity in village.
6. Essential goods and medicines.
7. Retail outlets not available.
8. Fair price shops – necessary.

### Slum Improvement at the Government Base

1. Conservation of assets of SC.
2. Provide land to SC women.
3. Train them in new fields for employment.
4. Ensure minimum wages.
5. Compulsory education up to 35 years.
6. Introduce new employment facilities.
7. Self-employment program for women.
8. Modernizing existing traditional activities.
9. Liberate the women from scavenging work – alternative arrangement for dignified work.
10. Eradicate social untouchability.
11. Provide minimum basic facilities.

12. Positive discrimination. i.e. policy of reservation should be continued both in Government and public sector.
13. Fee excemption, age relaxation for direct recruitment – separate interview.
14. Atrocity control room:

Close watch, monitoring of atrocities against dalit women.

## Present Position

The present position is better because of education, literacy rate for boys 31.48%, girls 10.93%. Now they have lot of self respect, aware of their rights, organisations to voice their feelings. The creamy layer is well aware of the Government welfare schemes. Among SC dalits executive positions in associations are occupied only by men, very poor representation by women. Feedback about the welfare programme is very essential.

## Dalit Women Begin a Quest for Dignity

Women activists of India have brought into sharp focus the case of 38-year-old Muthumari, a dalit woman of Keela Urappanur village of Madurai district, who was forced to drink a mixture of human excreta and water by an enraged mob of so-called upper caste people. To add to it, a bucketful of excreta was dumped on Muthumari, her husband Pitchai and other members of the family. This clear example of discrimination based on caste and gender cannot be ignored, say these women with a vision. It all happened on September 22, 2003, when Raju, a man belonging to one of the higher castes, took for granted the fact that dalit women could be sexually exploited, as through the decades they have been dehumanised and deprived and yet have no right to complain. Thus Raju had waylaid Muthumari, a grass-cutter, when she was returning home after a day of tedious work and grabbed her hand, trying to molest her. In a sudden impulse to defy this old social order that dalit women have to put up with the sexual greed of men from the upper castes, Muthumari fought off the molester and threatened to lodge a complaint with the village panchayat (local court).

Infuriated by this challenge of a dalit, who he thought would be meek and submissive, Raju, along with about 15 of his so-called higher caste people, later barged into Muthumari's house, dragged and attacked her, tore her blouse and abused her, pointing out that dalits were lesser humans. He then forced her to drink the mixture of human excreta and water, whilst more excreta was dumped on her and her family. This humiliation has left Muthumari feeling that her womanhood is diminished and her dignity has been trampled on. Weeping profusely, she says, "I'm unable to eat anything after the incident; I would have committed suicide but for my two sons."

Whilst this gross atrocity has sent shock waves through the nation, the Joint Action Council of Dalit Women's Organisation (JAC), comprising the Women Development Resource Centre, the Women's Watch, the Federation of Dalit Women's Empowerment and the Federation of Dalit Women's Panchayat Representatives, met urgently to pass a resolution to fight class/caste oppression.

The JAC has appealed to the National Human Rights Commission and the National Commission for Scheduled Castes and Scheduled Tribes to conduct an in-depth probe into this incident and has demanded immediate action against Raju and the other perpetrators under Section 3(i), (ii), (iii) and (x) of the SC/ST (Prevention of Atrocities Act). It has also sought adequate compensation for the victim and has insisted on protection of all dalit women in the southern districts. Apart from the JAC, the People's Watch Madurai and the People's Union for Human Rights have sent a fact-finding team to Keela Urappanur village to bring out a contextual analysis of the Muthumari incident.

Meanwhile, the Collector of Madurai, B Chandra Mohan and the Superintendent of Police Avi Prakash Sinha both met Muthumari and obtained feedback from her, assuring her that appropriate action would be taken. The first step towards victory to the women's organisations was when the molester Raju was arrested and remanded to judicial custody.

Thus Muthumari's degradation has provoked the quest for human dignity among the dalit women of India. These justice-seeking women are sure to reach their aspired goal of fighting against all atrocities, under one banner and a common platform to create a new humanity and end the subjugation of women from the lower castes.

## Dalits and Religion

*Hindu Dalits (Harijans):* Many Dalits continue to debate whether they are 'Hindu' or 'non-Hindu'. Missionaries have initiated several Dalit organizations. In some regions of India and Nepal, missionaries have been successful among the Dalits, both in Eastern India and Nepal, many Dalits have come under the combined influence of Maoists and the missionaries, even attacking and murdering Hindus. Traditionally, Hindu Dalits or Harijans have been barred from many activities that were seen as central to Vedic religion and Hindu practices of orthodox sects. Among Hindus each community has followed its own variation of Hinduism. The wide variety of practices and beliefs observed in Hinduism makes any clear assessment difficult.

Some of the movements in Hinduism have welcomed Dalits into their fold. The Satnami movement was founded by Guru Ghasidas a Dalit himself. In addition, other Hindu groups have reached out to the Dalit community in an effort to reconcile with them, with productive results. On August 2006, Dalit activist Namdeo Dhasal engaged in dialogue with the Rashtriya Swayamsevak Sangh in an attempt to "bury the hatchet".

In addition, the "Pandaram" are an order of Dalit Hindu priests (a task traditionally reserved for the Brahmins) based largely in Nepal and parts of South India. These Pandaram priests maintain the same tradition as the Brahmin priests, including using Sanskrit for the rituals (a language traditionally reserved for the Brahmins). They perform religious ceremonies from weddings to death rituals. They are not generally as well trained as the Brahmin priests, but are highly respected within their community and are addressed reverentially. Also, Hindu temples are increasingly more receptive to Dalit priests, such as Suryavanshi Das, the Dalit priest of a notable temple in Bihar. Another popular Harijan includes Babaji Palwankar Baloo, who joined the Hindu Mahasabha and was both a politician and a cricketer. He was an independence fighter.

However, extremist far-right militia groups such as the Ranvir Sena, largely run by upper-caste landlords in backward areas of the Indian state of Bihar, oppose equal treatment of Dalits and have resorted to violent means to suppress them. The Ranvir Sena is considered a terrorist organization. On the other side, extremist groups run by small minority of Dalits such as the "Dalit Panthers Movement" have committed violent acts against Brahmins and middle-caste people. In Pakistan, a predominantly Muslim nation, more than 60% of the 1. 4 million Hindu minority are Dalits.

*Muslim Dalits (Arzal):* Muslim society in India can also be separated into several caste-like groups. Descendants of indigenous lower-caste converts are discriminated against by "noble", or "ashraf", Muslims who can trace their descent to Arab, Iranian, or Central-Asian ancestors. There are several groups in India working to emancipate them from upper-caste Muslim discrimination. The Dalit Muslims are referred to by the Ashraf and Ajlaf Muslims as Arzal or "ritually degraded". They were first recorded in the 1901 census as those "with whom no other Muhammadan would associate, and who are forbidden to enter the mosque or to use the public burial ground". They are relegated to "menial" professions such as scavenging and carrying night soil. Babasaheb Ambedkar, a renowned Dalit activist and the framer of the Constitution of India, wrote about the Dalit Muslims and was extremely critical of their mistreatment by upper-caste Muslims quoting that "Within these groups there are castes with social precedence of exactly the same nature as one finds among the Hindus". In Pakistan, there are estimated to be 6.8 million Mayazurs (bonded labourers) in Punjab and another 7.5 million in Sindh. Although the Pakistani Supreme Court has ruled bonded labour unconstitutional and the National Assembly has passed laws prohibiting it, these laws remain largely unenforced due to the influence of large landlords. Furthermore, the AIBMM is striving to achieve the SC status for India's Muhajirs.

*Sikh Dalits:* Master Tara Singh himself helped uplift the Sikh Dalits. K.P. Singh a Dalit activist in UP was himself a Sikh. Kanshi Ram himself was of Sikh background although converted because he found that Sikh society did not respect Dalits and so became a neo-Buddhist. The Mazhabi are one Dalit of the Punjabi Dalits that are treated as outcastes from mainstream Sikh society and not allowed to enter Sikh temples. Jivan Singh, a friend of Guru Gobind Singh was a Dalit.

*Christian Dalits:* Converts to Christianity (facilitated by the influence of missionaries) have historically retained the caste system in their communities though many Christian leaders publicly reject caste. Joseph D'Souza, President of the All India Christian Council, has publicly pushed for a complete rejection of caste through partnership with Dalits across the country. A 1992 study of Catholics in Tamil Nadu showed that Dalit Christians face segregated churches, cemeteries, services and processions. They also face economic and social hardships due to the discrimination by upper-caste priests and nuns. One famous Dalit activist with the nom-de-plume of Bama Faustina has written books that provide a first-hand account of the discrimination against them by nuns and priests in South India.

## Dalits and Neo-Buddhism

In Maharashtra, Uttar Pradesh and a few other regions, Dalits have come under the influence of the neo-Buddhist movement initiated by Ambedkar. Some of them have come under the influence of the Neo-Buddhist and Christian Missionaries and have converted away from Hinduism into religions such as Christianity and Buddhism in what they have been told is an "attempt to eliminate the prejudice they face". Activists such as Udit Raj have claimed that such conversion will solve all discrimination problems faced by Dalits. Such claims have been criticized as "fragile at best". The conversion attempts have also been criticized by Hindu advocacy groups as "unhelpful" as Casteism is a complex dynamic that extends across all religions in India. However, the Constitution of India guarantees religious freedom and their right to choose their religion, although controversies related to mass-conversions have led to laws being passed against them in some states in India. Since then, several Christian converts have reconverted back into Hinduism as the conversions did not award them the financial rewards that the missionaries lured them with.

CHAPTER

# 2 Background Information on Dalit Women in India

In India and other countries in South Asia, people have been systematically discriminated against on the basis of their work and descent for centuries. Over 200 million people are Dalits, also known as untouchables or outcasts. They experience violence, discrimination, and social exclusion on a daily basis. Economic growth in India has been strong over the past decade. However, the caste disparities are increasing.

## Dalit Women

The situation of Dalit women in India needs special attention. They are one of the largest socially segregated groups anywhere in the world, and make up 2% of the world's total population. Dalit women are discriminated against three times over: they are poor, they are women, and they are Dalits. Dalit women constitute half of the ca. 200 million Dalit population, and 16.3 of the total Indian female population.

The traditional taboos are the same for Dalit men and Dalit women. However, Dalit women have to deal with them more often. Dalit women are discriminated against not only by people of higher castes, but also within their own communities. Men are dominant in Dalit communities. Dalit women also have less power within the Dalit movement itself. Women are active in large numbers in the movement but most leadership positions in the organisations, local bodies and associations have until now been held by men.

## Human Rights of Dalit Women

India is a democracy and is a Party to most of the major human rights treaties. These treaties provide the same rights for men and for women. Because India is also a Party to the Convention on the Elimination of All Forms of Discrimination Against Women (CEDAW), the Government has an extra obligation to make sure that women can realise their rights. It is generally accepted in international law that governments have to do more than just pass legislation to protect human rights. The Government of India has an obligation to take all measures, including policy and budgetary measures, to make sure that women can fulfil their rights. It also has an obligation to punish those who engage in caste-based violence and discrimination. The government of India, as a modern country with a growing economy, has the means to fulfil its obligations.

## Civil and Political Rights

India is a Party to the International Covenant on Civil and Political Rights. Based on this treaty, the Government of India has an obligation to make sure that Dalit women can enjoy a whole range of human rights, such as the right to life, freedom from torture or cruel, inhuman or degrading treatment or punishment, freedom from slavery, the right to be equal before the court, the right to recognition as a person before the law, the right to privacy, the right to marry only with free and full consent, and the right to take part in public affairs. The life and dignity of Dalit women depends on the realisation of these human rights. However, they are breached systematically. An essential precondition for the realisation of civil and political rights of Dalit women is registration. Article 24 (2) of the Covenant provides that every child shall be registered immediately after birth. In India, 46 % of all children are not registered. There is also no system of registration of marriages. This is not only a barrier for the realisation of civil and political rights; it also prevents the protection of Dalit girls from sexual exploitation and trafficking, child labour and forced and early marriages.

## Economic, Social, and Cultural Rights

India is also a Party to the International Covenant on Economic,

Social and Cultural Rights (ICESCR). This treaty not only identifies a range of economic, social and cultural rights, but it also requires that all people have these rights, without discrimination. The treaty also discusses the ways in which states must work to realise the rights. The rights outlined in the ICESCR include the right to work and to just and favourable conditions of work, and to form trade unions, the right to social security, protection of the family, the right to an adequate standard of living, including food, housing and clothing, and the right to health. Dalit women hardly enjoy any of these human rights.

## Millennium Development Goals and Dalit Women

In 2000, 189 countries accepted the Millennium Declaration and agreed to take the necessary action in order to attain eight specific goals: the Millennium Development Goals (MDGs). The realisation of human rights of Dalit women will have a major positive effect on the realisation of the MDGs. Dalit women are extremely poor, and make up 2% of the world's population. In India, 60 million children do not attend primary school; the majority of these children are Dalit girls. India's child mortality rate is one of the highest in the world and with its vast population and a rate of 540 maternal deaths per 100,000 live births, India accounts for more than 20 % of all global maternal deaths. A greater availability and accessibility of healthcare for women, including Dalit women, is needed.

## Violence against Dalit Women

Certain kinds of violence are traditionally reserved for Dalit women: extreme filthy verbal abuse and sexual epithets, naked parading, dismemberment, being forced to drink urine and eat faeces, branding, pulling out of teeth, tongue and nails, and violence including murder after proclaiming witchcraft, are only experienced by Dalit women. Dalit women are threatened by rape as part of collective violence by the higher castes. However, sexual assault and rape of Dalit women and girls also occur within their own communities. For Dalit men, the suppression and rape of women could be a way to compensate for their own lack of power in society. The Devadasi system of temple prostitution is the most extreme form of exploitation of Dalit women. Dalit girl children are forced to prostitution. The majority of cases of violence against Dalit women are not registered. The lack of law enforcement leaves many Dalit women unable to approach the legal system to seek redress. Women are often also unaware of the laws and their ignorance is exploited by their opponents, by the police, and by the judiciary system. Even when cases are registered, the lack of appropriate investigation, or the judge's own caste and gender biases, can lead to acquittal.

## Action by Dalit Women

Dalit women have been active throughout history, though often this has not been recorded. They were actively involved in the anti-caste and anti-untouchability movements in the 1920s. Today they are the strongholds of the Dalit movements in thousands of Indian villages. They continue to play a critical role in the movements for land rights. They are making their mark as independent thinkers and writers in the literary world and visionary leaders in the Panchayati Raj institutions. However, they are unable to put an end to the structural discrimination and exclusion. Violence and impunity are used to keep them in their place.

### Getting Organised as Dalit Women

Since the late 1980s, therefore, Dalit women have increasingly felt and articulated the need for a separate platform – created, developed and controlled by themselves – through which they could forge their own identity, fight for their rights and find solutions to their particular problems as Dalits and as women. Conscious that the call for a separate platform could be interpreted as a divisive move by both Dalit men and non-Dalit women, the proponents of such a special forum emphasise that their initiative must not be mistaken for a separatist movement. Rather they assert that there is need for strong alliances between the Dalit movement, the women's movement and the Dalit women's movement if their common vision of social, economic and political equality and justice for all is to be realised. The National Federation of Dalit Women (NFDW) was launched by Dalit women themselves and committed itself to undertake several tasks to bring about positive changes in the lives of Dalit women, such as legal action against caste based atrocities, political empowerment of Dalit women, economic empowerment against growing pauperisation, building self-confidence and leadership.

## The Status of Dalit Women in India's Caste Based System

In Ancient India (3200-2500 B.C.), the caste system was non-existent since even the most learned men were good householders and had varied occupations. The women of ancient India were just as superior as men in learning, education, and intellect. The choice for her mate was according to her own wishes and marriage was practiced after the coming of age. She attended parties, competitions, and religious functions as she wished. The remarriage of young widows was also a common practice (Thind).

The creation of a number of Hindu religious books including the *Manusmriti, Atharva Vedas, Vishnu smriti,* and many others like these and their strict compliance by the Brahmans (upper priestly hindu caste), led to a society in which equality between men and women was far from existent (Agarwal). Dr. B. R. Ambedkar, an architect of the Indian constitution, also makes it very clear in his article titled "The rise and fall of Hindu woman" that the root cause of suffering for women in India are these so called Hindu religious books (Thind; Agarwal). Books like the Manusmriti divide people into a stratified caste system and promotes inequality between men and women (Thind; Agarwal). According to the *Manusmriti*, women have no right to education, independence, or wealth. It not only justifies the treatment of dalit women as a sex object and promotes child marriage, but also justifies a number of violent atrocities on women as can be seen in the following verses (Agarwal; *Manusmitri*):

A man, aged thirty years, shall marry a maiden of twelve who pleases him. Or a man of twenty-four a girl of eight years of age. If (the performance of) his duties would otherwise be impeded, he must marry sooner. (*Manusmitri* IX.94)

By a girl, by a young woman, or even by an aged one, nothing must be done independently, even in her own house." (*Manusmriti* V.147) Her father protects (her) in childhood, her husband protects (her) in youth, and her sons protect (her) in old age; a woman is never fit for independence. (*Manusmriti* IX.3)

Women have no right to study the Vedas. That is why their Sanskaras are performed without Veda Mantras. Women have no knowledge of religion because they have no right to know the Vedas. The uttering of the Veda Mantras is useful for removing sin. As women cannot utter the Veda Mantras, they are as unclean as the untruth. (*Manusmriti* IX.18) A Brahman, Kshatriya, or Vaishya Man can sexually exploit any shudra woman. (*Manusmitri* IX.25)

Even the killing of a dalit woman is explicitly justified as a minor offence for the Brahmins: equal to the killing of an animal (*Manusmitri*). If the killing of an untouchable was justified as a minor offence, you can imagine the treatment they received throughout their lives.

In a male dominated society, Dalit women suffered unimaginable oppression, not only through caste, but gender too, from which there was no escape. The laws in the *Manusmriti* and other Vedic scriptures close all economic, political, social, educational, and personal channels through which Dalit women could be uplifted. The horrendous Laws in the *Manusmriti* were incorporated into Hinduism because they were favourable only to the Upper castes, which form the majority of India. Even today, in modern times, we see the severe oppression and exploitation of Dalit women. The Laws of the Manusmriti have a devastating effect on the level of education reached by Dalit women.

According to the National Commission for Scheduled Castes and Scheduled Tribes 2000, approximately 75% of the Dalit girls drop out of primary school despite the strict laws of the Government of India, which hold reservations for Dalit children. Despite showing keen academic aptitude, reasons for this early drop out from the education system is poverty or to escape humiliation, bullying and isolation by classmates, society, and even their teachers (Thind).

There are large numbers of reported atrocities on Dalit women that can be found recorded in various newspaper articles, journals, and government reports in India. The majority of the stories we read and hear are of bright young Dalit girls who are punished by the upper caste teachers in rural area of India, for daring to score good grades. Feeling rejected most girls in this situations drop out of school and have nowhere to turn but towards manual scavenging and other repulsive jobs (*News Archives*). According to the National Commission for Scheduled Castes and Scheduled Tribes, the majority of the educated people are of the upper caste, many of which may practice caste-based discrimination. Therefore, Dalit girls feel discouraged to enter education and we see the lowest literacy rate for Dalit girls compared to the Total population of educated upper caste girls. The Annual Report of University Grant Commission for 1999-2000, shows that Dalits in general have very low participation rates in higher education.

The main reasons for the very low literacy rate among Dalit women could be some or all of the following:

The Lack of educational resources especially in rural areas. Privatization of schools and colleges.

Extreme poverty, because of which they cannot afford the expensive fees for the private schools.

The demand for an increase in the Dowry for educated girls. Humiliation and bullying by the high caste students and teachers.

Since only a small percentage of the total population of Dalit women are educated, the fate of the majority is very grim. According to India's Ministry of Labour, 85% of the Dalit women have the most formidable occupations and work as agricultural labourers, scavengers, sweepers, and disposers of human waste. Many of these women work for minimal wages under the upper caste landlords, since it is proposed that by the National Commission for SC/ST that 85% of the Dalits are landless (*News Archives*). When the Dalit women refuse to work for ridiculously low wages or fail to follow their harsh orders it results open violence, humiliation, beatings, rape, and jail. There are also a number of cases where the houses of Dalit women have been burnt down (Agarwal; *News Achives*).

In one particular case, a four months pregnant agricultural labourer, from the southern part of India, was stripped naked and beaten, in front of the whole village and her family by the upper caste landlord. Later, she was retained in jail, where the police beat her. This resulted in the miscarriage of her baby (*News Archives*). In another case, a school student in Gujarat made a mistake of joining the dancing in the main square of her village, in which most of the participants were of the upper caste. The upper caste boys pulled her out and threatened to rape her. For interfering, her mother was slapped. In the hope for justice, she forced her parents to file a complaint to the police against her assailants. Her mother was constantly threatened by the upper caste families for complaining to the police. Feeling deeply humiliated by no justice and rumours of rape, the girl committed suicide (*News Archives*).

There are many cases like these, all of which cannot be discussed here. The worst exploitation of dalit women involves a lifetime of suffering, torture, and rape (Thind n.pag). Justified by the Vedic scriptures, the *Devdasi system* (also known as temple prostitution) was introduced by the High caste Hindus, and it still exists in some parts of India (Thind; Agarwal; Narula). According to the *Human Right Watch Report* in 1992, an estimated 50,000 girls were sold every year to Hindu organizations that are involved in the Devdasi system. These girls are called the "female servants of god" and are sexually exploited. After a lifetime of living as a prostitute and servant, the women in their later years are sold to brothels, where they are further tortured and often die of neglect or AIDS (Thind; *News Archives*). The Devdasi system and Child marriage are also justified by Hindu Scriptures (Thind; Agarwar; *News Archives*).

The 1992-93 Annual report from the Ministry of Welfare shows 1,236 reported cases of rape on Dalit women and the National Commission for SC/ST shows that approximately 10,000 cases of human right violations on Dalits are reported every month. But what is even more disturbing, is that only one out of ten of the cases are reported annually whilst, nine go unreported. In addition to this, according to the Human Right watch Report, approximately 115 million children are in slavery and 2.6 million children are held as bonded labourers (Narula). After fifty-five years of India's independence and despite the excellent laws in place to protect Dalit women, they are still suffering unimaginable atrocities from the high caste Hindus. It is believed that thousands of these cases go unreported and unpublicized because the poor Dalits that live in rural areas, who are the worst victims, have no control on power, wealth, justice, police and the media (Thind n.pag). The only way these Dalit women can escape the viscous cycle of poverty, abuse and oppression is through education. Through education more Dalit women can come to know their basic human rights and they can then raise an even stronger voice against abuse and exploitation from the upper castes (Thind; Agarwar).

Many Dalit Non-Government Organizations (NGO's), both in India and abroad, have been involved in raising the plight of India's 250 million untouchables. One of the most important tasks of these Dalit NGO's is to bring the plight of Dalit people to the attention of the International community and to document and publicize human right violations. As the poorest of the poor, Dalit women lack the means and the opportunity to defend themselves at home or to make their problems known outside of rural India. Many Dalit women have formed NGO's through which they collectively fight against abuse from the upper classes. Such Dalit women abandon tears and embrace the shield of confidence in the hope of equality.

## Women's Rights Overview

Dalit women constitute 80.5 million people—8 out of every 100 citizens in the country—and approximately 48% of the total Dalit population, 16% of the total female population and 8% of the total Indian population. Vulnerably positioned at the bottom of the caste, class and gender hierarchies, Dalit women are India's worst victims of discrimination, deprivation, exploitation, and violence. Not only do Dalit women face endemic violence and discrimination (due to both caste and patriarchy), but the vast majority of crimes against them go unreported, unregistered and un-punished.

In November 2006, NCDHR took part in (and helped to organize) the first-ever International Conference on the Human Rights of Dalit Women, held at The Hague. Determined to "transform their pain into power," Dalit women from India, Pakistan, Bangladesh, Sri Lanka, and Nepal presented shocking and heart-breaking testimonials about the violence perpetrated against them and the impunity that followed. In connection with this conference, NCDHR published a two-volume study entitled *Dalit Women Speak Out: Violence Against Dalit Women in India*, the culmination of over five years of research, which presents an analytic overview of the systemic violence—rape, murder, physical assault and verbal abuse & humiliation—faced by Dalit women in India along with 500 Dalit women's own narratives of the violence they personally experienced. The study and conference demonstrated how violence on Dalit women is intentionally used to maintain the oppression of the Dalit community by the dominant castes, while also demonstrating systematic patterns of impunity: In less than 1% of incidents in the study were perpetrators ever convicted in courts!

The available data on the situation of Dalit women presents quite a disturbing picture: An average of three Dalit women are raped everyday. A disproportionate number of the atrocities and human rights violations registered annually under the SC/ST (Prevention of Atrocities) Act are against women. The unemployment rate of Dalit women is 4.0% against 0.97% among non-Dalits in rural areas and 3.3% against 1.98% for non-Dalits in urban areas. The literacy rate of Dalit women is just 23.8% compared to that of 39.3% among non-Dalits. Due to discrimination, poverty, and gender role ideology, Dalit women have a drop out rate of 53.96% at the primary school level. The poverty rate among Dalit women is 36.2% against 21.6% among non-Dalit women. 94% of Dalit women are engaged in the unorganized, self-employed sector (farm/wage workers, domestic helpers, etc.), marked by overwork, low wages, non-payment of equal wages, and absence of social security or maternity benefits.

Dalit women face violence and exploitation not only from the dominant castes, but also at home within their own families and Dalit communities. Regardless of the context, when a Dalit woman defends her dignity and demands her basic human rights, if her position contradicts traditional caste, gender, and cultural norms, she is not given support and often becomes the target of violence. Statistics on Dalit women's access to justice show the extent of the problem. NCDHR's study and other reports show that perpetrators are punished in less than 1% of the cases. In other words, the perpetrators of crimes against Dalit women go completely free in more than 99% of the crimes committed, and are even seen to further threaten and punish the same survivors. The study further reveals that in 39% of the instances of violence the survivors did not seek legal redress for fear of bringing dishonour to their family, for lack of human or financial support, or because they did not trust that they would get justice. In 27% of the instances of violence, the victim's appeal for justice to the village panchayat or administration was thwarted by pressure and threats from the perpetrators. In 18% of the instances, the police thwarted justice by threatening, refusing to file the complaint, forcing an extra-legal compromise, or making false counter cases.

Despite the gravity of the situation, there are very little efforts or mechanisms by the Indian state or other movements or organizations to protect Dalit women or support their quest for justice. NCDHR aims in its work to create awareness among the national and international community regarding the unique plight of Dalit women and to expose the failure of the state to protect and promote Dalit women's rights. Our long term goal is to build effective monitoring and legal mechanisms to support women who face violence, to train and support Dalit women's rights defenders, to build alliances with other movements, and to ensure the effective functioning of the justice and administrative systems to destroy the culture of impunity.

### Dalit Women's Movement

The interface of the severely imbalanced social, economic and political power equations in caste and patriarchy impacts Dalit women uniquely, very distinct from the experience of other women and even Dalit men. These forces combine to expose them to increased physical and sexual violence and increased exploitation of their labour. All these combined together keep Dalit women from having access and control over assets and resources. It does not recognize their social and economic contribution. It limits their choices and opportunities, placing them on the bottom rung in all development indicators. This process of exclusion and discrimination inculcates the disrespect and indignity of Dalit women at the hands of all men and also of non-Dalit women.

*In recent years a sea of change has taken place and Dalit women have started asserting for their rightful place in Indian society.* The role played by thousands of Dalit women in running the panchayats across the country has turned out to be an amazing success story of political awareness and mobilization beyond any conceivable imagination. It has dealt a striking blow to the caste system and the values of patriarchy. In this process of being empowered they have paid heavy prices too, but their resilience is tremendous and quite laudable. At every level of the caste hierarchy and patriarchal system, the Dalit Women's movement is quite active in mobilizing the unheard voices and in turning them into a powerful agent of change. NCDHR—via projects and platforms such as AIDMAM and DWAJ—has joined in and seeks to advance the vital concerns of this Movement for Dalit Women's Human Rights.

## AIDMAM – All India Dalit Mahila Adhikar Manch (All India Dalit Women's Rights Platform)

The All India Dalit Mahila Adhikar Manch (AIDMAM) is a common platform for Dalit women committed to challenging the nexus of patriarchy, caste, age-old social customs and traditions, class oppression, exploitation and, most of all, marginalization of Dalit women in the family, community, and nation they live in. AIDMAM is part of NCDHR's campaign for Dalit Women's Rights and has the membership and solidarity of non-Dalit Women, Dalit Men, social activists and other human rights defenders committed to the cause of protecting and promoting the rights of Dalit Women under the leadership of Dalit Women. AIDMAM's objective is to hold the state accountable for its failure to prevent violence against Dalit women and to take up advocacy at the state, national and international levels.

## DWAJ – Dalit Women's Access to Justice and Dignity

Dalit Women Access to Justice and Dignity (DWAJ) is a project of UNDP and Department of Justice, Govt. of India under the Strengthened Access to Justice in India (SAJI) program. The project was initiated with vision that Dalit women can and should have equitable and effective access to justice delivery mechanisms to protect themselves from violence, exploitation and atrocities and to live with dignity. Currently the DWAJ project, which is run with the support of NCDHR and other organizations, concentrates on two districts in the each of the states of Andhra Pradesh (Ranga Reddy and East Godavari) and Rajasthan (Jaipur and Pali).

Specific Objectives of DWAJ:

- To capacitate 80 Dalit Women to access the Criminal Justice System. These eighty (80) women are Panchayat leaders/ NGO volunteers/lawyers/doctors/law students/ Dalit and Women leaders and are to be capacitated on: (1) relevant laws and justice delivery systems; (2) how to conduct fact-findings; and (3) providing support to victims/survivors, filing cases, and doing case follow-ups.
- To improve the implementation of mechanisms in favour of women from poor and vulnerable backgrounds.
- To initiate a dialogue and build an interface between victim/ survivors and duty bearers for better implementation of the rule of law.

The DWAJ project was initiated in November 2006 and works to identify cases related to violence against Dalit women, identify human rights defenders, organize and conduct training for HR defenders, conduct fact finding, organize round table conferences with various law enforcement agencies/commissions, and sensitize and bring pressure on the Police, Revenue and Judicial systems to address the issues, access penal and pecuniary justice to the victims/survivors.

## Rural Dalit Women and Work

For Dalit women, their daily agricultural, artisan and domestic work is shaped by and experienced through their gender and their caste. Because of their low-caste status and their economic vulnerability, Dalit women have functioned as handmaidens to the community's changing economic needs. Over the past century, they have experienced significant change in the kinds of work they perform, the groups for whom they work, and the types and quantities of remuneration they receive. The history of Dalit women's labour has been a gradual replacement of primarily artisan-related production with a variety of paid agricultural and nonagricultural work. The negative consequences of becoming free labourers in the agricultural economy include the breakdown of secure inter caste patron-client relationships and their replacement by informal and daily-wage labour in the context of increasing poverty. These are balanced against the positive social consequences of such changes for Dalit women, which include economic power in their homes and their communities, and which are tied to their role in acquiring rental land-called maatya-for farming. A complex of many factors contribute to a woman's assertions of maatya-based power, including but not limited to family composition, land availability, the woman's own political, cultural and social skills, and the support of her sons.

In the context of social contracts involving the material dimensions of life in the mountain farming communities of the Far West, gender changes have wrought changes in labour allocation and labour value in rural Nepal. The socioeconomic forces influencing these labour transformations operate locally, regionally, and internationally. The effects of labour transformations are present in those practices that serve to reproduce the social order of caste and gender hierarchy, as well as those practices that attempt to contest those hierarchies. To understand the present conditions of Dalit women's labour, we must first remember that historically, gender and caste relations have changed over time. While one could argue that caste restrictions have 'relaxed' over the past half-century in Nepal, other changes in Nepal's social history render caste relations ever more class (as wealth and education) controlled.

The most significant causes of change in Dalit women's productive work in the more recent period are male migration to India, competition from mass-produced goods, decreased supply of raw materials used in Dalit artisan production, decreased land market with consequent decreased formal and informal land ownership and increased land rental, changed norms for women's work, and an influx of outsiders into the area. While covering each of these factors individually is an extensive project (and I refer the reader to my full-length ethnography on the topic, On the Edge of the Auspicious: Gender and Caste in Nepal-1998), a brief discussion of a few of the more immediately dynamic factors will provide a glimpse of the social vibrancy of ever-changing rural agricultural life and the place of Dalits in it.

First, the influence of male migration is experienced daily in people's adjustment to the lack of employment opportunities and an increasingly absent male work force. Today, women whose husbands are in India must take on work for riti and non-riti patrons to maintain their households' position in the patronage system. Second, after the mid-last century opening of Nepal's border with India, Dalit commodities have had to compete with Nepalese, Chinese and Indian mass-produced imports that have replaced many locally made products. Over the past two decades, Dalit families have been forced to depend less on harvest payments and other customary clothing and cash subsidies from high castes because decreased demand for their goods has resulted in lower traditional payments. The artisans most affected by these imports are the SARKI leatherworkers. In addition to competition from international market forces, there are internal barriers to Dalit artisan production, particularly the recent limitations placed by the government, and the impact of environmental degradation, the supply of raw materials that black smiths, basket weavers, potters, and carpenters use in their work.

According to elderly villagers, in the past untouchable women were more involved in caste-specific commodity and service production, for a limited number of families, than they are now. Their work was narrowly defined by their family's position in the riti-bhagya system. Female leatherworkers, seamstresses, basket weavers, and goldsmiths who were skilled in artisan production worked with their husbands and other adult household members to meet local needs. Dalit families owned little or no land, and the economic strength of the traditional exchanges in the riti-bhagya system precluded the need for Dalit households to provision themselves in ways other than artisan production. If Dalit women did work for non-patron landowners, it was not outside their patron circles and was limited to work for the local rulers. In the contemporary period in Bajhang, untouchable female artisans are, like their husbands, experiencing competition from mass-produced goods from India, China and urban Nepal. Women are compelled to shift their productive activities from artisan to agriculturally related work on their own small rented plots or on the land of patron landowners. Today, women in one region allocated only 9 percent of their time to artisan work, while three times that amount of time was spent in agricultural production, usually on a patron's land. The list is long of the work that Dalit women do in rural Nepal. Such work includes artisan production like potting, weaving bamboo baskets, sewing clothes, and doing all the preliminary preparatory work for these, as well as the finishing work, such as delivering the products. Agricultural and daily domestic work that Dalit women do in addition to artisan work includes: threshing rice, wheat and millet, chopping wood, carrying heavy sacks of grain from the threshing floor to the home for storage, hauling slate for roofing, collecting firewood, carrying water, digging fields and preparing them for planting, carrying manure to the fields, and even house construction. The only job now unconditionally monopolized by men is sloughing.

What is important to remember is that a large percentage of Dalit women's work is done for patron families, and their contribution to maintaining good and reliable relations with the patrons is enormous. The rural economy of the far west integrates marked differences between women and men of low caste, in the allocation of time to productive activities; still, the complementarity of those differences leads to sustained subsistence provisioning in the Dalit household. We see these work arrangements most clearly in family farm production, riti-bhagya based labour, and wage labour. While Dalit women in the communities studied spent most of their productive time in agriculturally related work (68 percent), their husbands spent nearly the equivalent amount of time working in artisan production and outside income generating work (74 percent). This indicates flexibility and complimentarity of women's and men's work in family provisioning greater than that found in upper caste households (where men's leisure time was found to be more than two times that of the women in the family)

## Untouchability and Violence against Dalits

The so-called Scheduled Castes (SCs) of India, erstwhile Untouchable communities and presently termed Dalits by most movements and political bodies in the country, number 167.2 million people (2001 census). In addition, there are at least 42 million Muslim, Sikh and Christian Dalits who in one form or another are vulnerable to discrimination and also to different and particular form of backlash violence.

## Untouchability a Crime

The Constitution of India not only guarantees equality, liberty, fraternity, justice and basic human rights as Fundamental Rights but also prohibits the practice of Untouchability in any form. Through the efforts Dr. B.R. Ambedkar, the iconic leader of Dalits, who led the Dalit liberation movement and was the Chairperson of the Constitution Drafting Committee, the Constitution has made Untouchability a crime and provided safeguards against it. Article 17 of the Constitution abolished Untouchability and its practice in any form is forbidden. Article 25(2b) of the Constitution provides that Hindu religious institutions of a public character shall be open to all classes and sections of Hindus. This provision is contrary to the traditions of some sects of Hinduism that prohibits Scheduled Caste members from entering temples. Two important legislations were enacted to give effect to these articles. The Protection of Civil Rights Act, 1955 punishes the preaching and practice of Untouchability. Scheduled Castes and Scheduled Tribes (Prevention of Atrocities) Act 1989 criminalizes certain acts against members of the Scheduled Castes and Scheduled Tribes such as traffic in human beings, *'begar (free labour)'* and forced labour in any form.

A related law, the Bonded Labour System (Abolition) Act, 1976 provides for a special program for identifying bonded labourers, and for their liberation and rehabilitation. While this law does not specifically mention Scheduled Castes, it is especially significant to them because the majority of bonded labourers belong to the Scheduled Castes. Article 24 of this law provides that no child below the age of fourteen years shall be employed to work in any factory or mine or engaged in any hazardous employment. The Child Labour (Prohibition and Regulation) Act, 1986 complements this law. The practice of requiring Dalits to clean/ remove human feces by hand continues despite the prohibition of manual scavenging by the Employment of Manual Scavengers and Construction of Dry Latrines (Prohibition) Act, 1993.

## Rampant Untouchability Despite Law

A recent study on Untouchability in rural India, covering five hundred sixty five villages in eleven States, found that public health workers refused to visit Dalit homes in 33% of villages, and

Dalit children sat separately while eating in 37.8% of government schools. Dalits were prevented from entering police stations in 27.6% of villages, did not get mail delivered to their homes in 23.5% of villages, and were denied access to water sources in 48.4% of villages.

## Backlash Violence against those Challenging Untouchability

Police statistics averaged over the past five years show that every week: thirteen Dalits are murdered, five Dalits' homes or possessions are burned, six Dalits are kidnapped or abducted; every day: three Dalit women are raped, eleven Dalits are beaten up; and for every eighteen minutes a crime is committed against a Dalit. This is despite the fact that many Dalits do not report crimes for fear of reprisals by the dominant castes. Despite twenty-seven officially registered atrocities being committed against Dalits every day, the police often prevents Dalits from entering police stations, neglect their cases and even partake in torture.

## Impunity and Wilful Negligence

The state machinery, especially the police, exhibits gross negligence of the plight of Dalits resulting in impunity. In a query raised by the Chief Justice of the High Court of Andra Pradesh on a Public Interest Litigation case filed by Sakshi Human Rights Watch to the State Police Department, it admitted to 14,452 cases with delayed filing of charge sheet beyond the stipulated period of thirty days as per the SC/ST POA Act. This means insurmountable impunity resulting in denial of justice to the victims of violence.

## Multiple Forms of Discrimination and Violence

The discrimination against the Dalits takes different forms such as:

*Dalit Women:* They face double discrimination on the basis of caste and gender in all spheres of life and are subjected with impunity to gross violations of their physical integrity, including sexual abuse by dominant castes; they are socially excluded and economically exploited. The practice of *'divine prostitution' (Jogini/ Devadasi systems)* continues even today despite laws prohibiting this menace affecting the Dalit women.

*Communities involved in manual scavenging:* Of the more the 1.2 million manual scavengers, over 95% are Dalits. They are compelled to undertake this inhuman and degrading task under the garb of 'traditional occupation'. The practice of manual scavenging is illegal and unconstitutional and a blot on the face of humanity. But it still continues.

*Exclusion from political participation:* Many reports from across the country reveal that Dalits' exercise of their legitimate and rightful claim to representation (namely participation or leadership in the electoral process) is met with violence.

*'Discrimination by Default':* The 2005 Asian Tsunami demonstrated that all levels of authority involved in responding to the tragedy practiced Untouchability. Aid was distributed through caste panchayats, and those who called themselves traditionally as 'fisherfolk by birth' were given priority on receiving aid. These organizations proved efficient in distributing aid in their community, but excluded some people including Dalits regardless of loss or suffering. This was done through coercion as well as simple exclusion. Higher authorities or donors did nothing to ensure equitable distribution.

*Education:* Untouchability in schools has contributed to drop-out and illiteracy levels for Dalit children far beyond those of the general population, with the 'literacy gap' continuing between Dalits and non-Dalits and literacy rates for Dalit women remaining as low as 37.8% in rural India (2001 Census). Teachers have been found to maintain discriminatory attitudes and practices that underlie caste relations in society.

*Nutrition:* Half of India's Dalit children are undernourished, 21% are 'severely underweight', and 12% die before their 5$^{th}$ birthday.

*Exclusion from budget:* The Government of India has a potentially powerful mechanism for the economic empowerment of Dalits known as Special Component Plan (SCP). The spirit of the Plan has been consistently thwarted in its application and implementation by most of the departments at the Central and States levels, by diverting on an average Euro 2,000 million (2.7 billion US dollars) every year during the past five-year plan period.

***Labour market:*** Like other sectors Dalits also face discrimination in the labour market. This is clearly exhibited in exclusion of Dalits from employment by 'higher caste'; exclusion of 'low caste' from certain types of jobs/work due to notion of pollution and purity associated with Untouchability; selective inclusion in employment but with unequal treatment reflected (i) in lower wages (lower than wages given to other labourers), (ii) in terms and conditions with respect to hours of work, (iii) different behavior by employers towards low caste laborer /worker in the work place, and (iv) compulsive and forced work governed by traditional caste related obligations.

***Economic exclusion and discrimination:*** Through differential pricing in sale, purchase and hiring activities ranging from raw materials to finished goods Dalits are disadvantaged. They are also denied the sale or purchase of land for agriculture and non-agricultural use.

**Persistent denial in the United Nations**

While the situation of the Dalits still warrants special and urgent measures and interventions by various bodies of the state and the civil society, the state is still in a dilemma in its commitment to challenge the precipitation of the mindset of Untouchability and the resulting caste-based discrimination. While, at the time of Independence and thereafter, the Indian state did recognize and take constitutional and legislative remedies to correct the injustices caused, gross gaps in their implementation result in impunity. This mindset is also reflected in the actions of India at the United Nations (UN) and its various bodies that could have addressed the situation of discrimination and exclusion. It declined to address the issue in the World Conference against Racism, Racial Discrimination, Xenophobia and Relate Intolerance (WCAR) held in Durban, South Africa from 31 August-8 September 2001.

**Dalits Betrayed**

There is a strong comfort level in society and the state that crimes against Dalits do not need to be punished. This attitude of impunity is rooted in social and cultural values and persists in society despite the constitutional provisions against it. Protecting the rights of marginalized and vulnerable people is probably the most overlooked and disregarded area of human rights in India. However there is a clear departure from this *denial* through a realistic acknowledgment of the situation. Manmohan Singh, the President of India, at an international conference on Dalits and Minorities in New Delhi on the 27 November 2006 drew the parallel between social and caste injustices saying it was modern India's failure that millions of Dalits were still fighting prejudice. He explained: Even after 60 years of constitutional and legal protection and support, there is still social discrimination against Dalits in many parts of our country. Dalits have faced a unique discrimination in our society that is fundamentally different from the problems of minority groups in general. The only parallel to the practice of untouchability was apartheid.

## Dalit Movement in Tamil Nadu

The Dalit movement in Tamil Nadu has long and chequered history. Iyothee Thass, Erattaimalai Srinivasan, M.C.Rajah, N.Sivaraj and L.Elayaperumal Vai. Balasundaram were some of the stalwarts associated with the movement at various stages. The founder of the Self-Respect Movement and the Dravidar Kazhagam, ' Periyar' E.V.Ramasami, who was also among the early champions of the Dalit cause.

One of the earliest organized endeavours for the Dalit cause was perhaps a memorandum submitted to the Governor of Madras Presidency in the early 1890s on the horrifying living conditions of Paraiyars, one of the two principal social groups among Dalits, in the then Chengalpat district. Following this, Paraiyars and other sections of Dalits were assigned what was termed ' Panchama land'. Over the years this land was grabbed by caste – Hindu usurpers in violation of the provision against the transfer of its ownership. A hundred years later, in 1994, a movement was launched in the same district to restore the land to its rightful owners. This agitation, in which two people died in police firing, marked the beginning of the present phase of the Dalit movement in the state.

In the 1990s, the Dalit response was to get organized. The regional movements demonstrated the strength arising from numbers and unity, but also brought out some inherent limitations.

First, of course was the fact they did not have the resources, the personnel and leadership to build up and sustain large-scale movements. Of the three, leadership was the most crucial. It is in this context that the services of K.Krishnasamy and Thirumavalavan have to be appreciated, the former a medical practitioner and the later a well placed government official. Both of them gave part time help to aggrieved fellow Dalit initially, later they became leaders of Dalit Movements and have since emerged as political personalities. Their sustained effort and personal sacrifices have succeeded in mobilizing Dalits, enthusing more Dalits to devote time for the movements, and generated resources to make the movements fairly well established in the state. The DPI, one of the large dalit political movements in Tamilnadu since the 1990s has been remarkably active in taking up the issues of caste atrocities on dalits in the northern parts of the state. Its powerful protests against caste oppression and adherence to Periyar's radical social values were once well known. The conflicts between Dalits and Thevars, a caste Hindu social group, the southern districts are not new in the state and Dalits have mostly been at the receiving end. A significant out come of the confrontation between Dalits and caste Hindus in different parts of the state for nearly a decade is the emergence of two principal organizations, Puthiya Thamizhagam led by Dr.K.Krishnasamy and Viduthalai Siruthaigal of Thol. Thirumavalavan

## Dalit Women Movement in Tamil Nadu

Tamil Nadu Dalit women movement was launched during the year 1997 by SRED (Society for Rural Education and Development) human-rights organization who worked among women for 20 years to promote their rights. During those past period they start organizing women into groups and then as a federation. In the latter stage, they start coordinating at the groups into movements or one forum called Tamil Nadu women's forum that concentrate on promoting rights among common grass root women. Then while working among dalit women, they realized need for separate movement for dalit women with the focus of dalit and especially to protect their rights. With the help of various NGOs in Tamil Nadu they organized dalit women and start highlighting the issues of dalit wherever they find. Thirty voluntary leaders from 30 districts of Tamil Nadu coordinate together and take this movement to the grass roots. This movement is open for dalit women who can address their issues and atrocities where this movement fights for the rights and justice. This movement is active in 16 districts of Tamil Nadu and takes issues of violence against dalits, untouchable practices, discrimination, atrocities against them and the denial of livelihood rights.

Tamil Nadu Women's Forum (TNWF) is a state level imitative for women's rights and gender justice. TNWF was started in 1991 in order to train women for more leadership, to strengthen women's movement and to build up strong people's movement. This movement is also collaborated with some of the dalit parties like Viduthalai siruthaigal ( Dalit panthers of India-DPI). However, the transformation of the DPI from a political movement to a party seems to have led to a dramatic dilution of its radicalism. Importantly, dalit women despite their very active participation in politics, continue to lack of recognition and respect even within the dalit movement. When Parliament enacted the constitution (73rd) Amendment Act in 1993, the move was hailed as a breakthrough in bringing about a vibrant system of participatory democracy at the grassroots level and a paradigm shift in the process of development, for the first time it provided for statutory reservation of elected posts in local bodies for women, besides the Scheduled Castes (Dalits) and the Schedule Tribes. Caste Hindu leaders challenged the reservation of elected offices in local bodies for Dalits. In the elections, Dalits were prevented from filing nominations in several villages where Panchayat president ship were reserved for them. A large number of elected Dalit and women Panchayat presidents suffered humiliation at the hands of the Vice Presidents and co-members and even government officials. For rural women and Dalits most of whom were elected to these posts for the first time, it was uphill task.

## Women Movement against poverty and violence (MAPOVI)

Women MAPOVI is coordinated body of grass root women organizations or federations from all over Tamil Nadu. Grass root women become members of these federations by participating in a sangam in their respective village in respective districts. In the pursuit of village development each federations has become a local radical force for social and political change concerning the role of women. Each federation was organized with the efforts of concern NGOs who believe that empowerment of women can bring total empowerment of their society. Federation identified their own leaders to lead their federation and these women have themselves become empowered to act as role models and provide leadership among other women. As a result of their growing consciousness many federations joined together, networked to find joint solutions to common problems mainly the issues of poverty and violence. Many coordinated campaigns and joint public actions taken by Women MAPOVI and the social problems that they had been fighting against are the poverty and violence among women. Movement has succeeded in many issues due to various lobby actions. For instance the public meeting and the rally conducted by Tamil Nadu Anti liquor movement (TALM) in Aundipatti on 5.02.2002 against the introduction of cheap liquor by the state in Tamil Nadu has certainly strengthened the movement. Because, the loud protest of the women, has reached the government and the political parties and they withdraw the cheap liquor in Tamil Nadu during the month of April 2002.

To conclude, Dalit women, despite their very active participation in politics, continue to lack of recognition and respect even within the Dalit Movement. Though there are some women organization fighting for the rights of dalits and to uplift dalit women they joined together as Dalit Women Movement without a strong political support even within their dalit political parties. However, Dalit Women Movement in Tamil Nadu has been playing a significant role through Tamil Nadu Women's Forum and with the support of dalit political parties against all forms of discrimination and for their rights. It seems to be there is positive changing situation for the empowerment of Dalit women in Tamil Nadu, albeit slowly.

CHAPTER 3

# Dalit Women : the Downtrodden of the Downtrodden

The Dalits of India are perhaps the world's foremost example of a community whose rights are violated. Over 200 million are dalits also known as Untouchables or outcastes Despite the existence of Constitutional rights and other affirmative action that is meant to address the issues, today their predicament can be described in terms of a lost humanity and a dispossessed community who live in segregated conditions. Notwithstanding the democratic values, caste hierarchy continues to dominate feudal system of Indian Society. Dalits and particularly Dalit Women, are often offended, discriminated, deprived of human dignity and have been subject to inhuman treatment and ugly form of untouchability, illiteracy, poor health, lack/denial of education, alienation in labour market. All these have unfolded into abject poverty among them and dehumanising way of living.

## Dalit Women: They are Poor; They are women; They are Dalits

Dalit women in India suffer from three oppressions: gender, as a result of patriarchy; class, from being from the poorest and most marginalized communities; and caste, from coming from the lowest caste, the 'untouchables'. Although discrimination on the basic of caste is against the Indian constitution and prohibited by many laws, its practice is still widespread, especially in rural India. In India around 66 million women are Dalits, and 48 percent of the total Dalit population. Of the 16.3 percent of Dalit women population in India, 81.4 percent live in rural areas. They, along with their male counterparts, constitute a sizeable social group that continues to suffer from Descent based discrimination arising out of the caste system.

Descent based discrimination based on caste imposes social exclusion on persons belonging to Dalit castes, and their physical separation from the dominant castes in housing patterns, strict enforcement of the prohibition of interdining at public places, seating arrangements in educational institutions, particularly in schools and forces the performance of degrading occupation life manual scavenging and carrying of night soil by women. Sexual control and systematic rape of Dalit women by men of the dominant castes, forced prostitution in the name of religion through Devadasi system are all violation of human dignity. Therefore, Dalit's perpetually live in situation of threat and fear, which is apparent when their houses and property are destroyed/burnt or Dalit women are raped and killed, so on so forth because they are voiceless.

Dalit women not only grapple with the discrimination due to caste hierarchy and untouchability but they live in poverty coupled with political, legal and religio-cultural discrimination. Access to resources such as land, water is out of reach to these women. Henceforth, Dalit women end up working as bonded agricultural labourers with low/under paid wages, inspite of their knowledge and skills in farming. The extreme perennial economic deprivation has also resulted in illiteracy, malnourishment, poor health conditions, besides this they are also overworked, oppressed and victimized by a number of factors, including patriarchal attitude within the family and community.

## Dalit Women as Victims of Caste Hierarchy and Atrocities

Dalit Women's day-to-day struggle is one of existence, survival and justice. The everyday discrimination is dotted by mental and physical violence. Eternally, the principles of 'high and low', 'purity and pollution' has not left any scope for changing Dalit women's status. Thus any move by Dalit women to question the system, or challenge inequality to change the life situation has resulted in retaliation with abuses such as beating, rape, naked parading, labelled as witches and harassed for murder. This further

implicates in punishing the whole community by burning of houses, destruction of properties, valuables, crops etc. The crux of the Dalit Women's struggles for survival is rooted in her being at the lowest rung of the Caste hierarchy.

## Uttar Pradesh Leads in Atrocities

According to recent figures tables in Parliaments by the National Commission for Scheduled Bastes and Scheduled Tribes, the number of cases of atrocities against Dalits registered in 2000, stood at 23,742 cases (including 1,034 cases of rape). Dalit women are estimated to be the first victims, in close to 75 percent of these cases. The State of Uttar Pradesh leads in the number of cases registered under the Scheduled Castes / Scheduled Tribes (Prevention of Atrocities) Act 1989, followed by Rajasthan, Madhya Pradesh, Andhra Pradesh, Tamil Nadu, Karnataka, Gujarat and Bihar. Violence therefore, forms the core result of gender-based inequalities, and intensified by caste discrimination. Women are gang raped, forced into prostitution, stripped, paraded around naked, and made to eat excrement, even murdered for no crime of theirs. They are victims of worst form of degradation such as manual scavenging.

## Dalit Women as Manual Scavengers.

Thousands of women manual scavengers are forced to earn their living scavenging, cleaning dry latrines, by using metal pans and a short broom to scoop up the night soil. The excreta is carried in baskets on their heads. The dehumanized practice has killed dignity of women at the same time these women believe that without this job they will be nowhere to their livelihoods.

## Devadasi System: Prostitution in the Name of Religion

In the name of religion, thousands of untouchable female children between six and eight years are forced to become maidens of God (ritualized prostitution in temples). Once dedicated, the girls are unable to marry and are raped by temple priests and upper-caste men, eventually auctioned secretly into urban brothels for prostitution. It is estimated by NGOs that each year 5,000 to 15,000 girls are secretively auctioned to brothels.

### Social Ostracism and Exclusion

Branded untouchables for no fault of theirs, their physical mobility is restricted, they are forbidden to use natural resources such as drinking water, community land etc. They are also prohibited from using the main roads in the villages, from entering temples; their children are prevented from attending schools. In fact they are pushed out of the mainstream community life. This kind of exclusion is much more evident in villages as compared to cities.

### Dalit Assertiveness

One of the more significant developments in the post independence period is the rising Dalit consciousness and activism. While this is still confined to a relatively small section of Dalits, achievements in creative writing, cultural expression on the Dalit experience, a search for ideology and identity, a growing organized socio-political strength, are in evidence. Among the Dalit masses a new wave of assertiveness is noticeable on all fronts. Therefore, Dalits are becoming less willing to accept social, cultural an economic subjugation and claiming for dignified Human Rights. Many observe and belive that this assertiveness is the result of the middle and upper caste backlash.

## The Vision and the Role of Dalit Women in Liberation

Gender division reinforces and sustains caste distinctions; and the gender ideology legitimizes not only the structure of patriarchy but also the element of Caste hierarchy. Yet another dimension of ideology is that lower caste women are considered inferior and sexually loose. The role of Dalit women is crucial and it is in the centre of Dalit liberation and identity; in the larger framework of Dalit movement and struggle. Henceforth, women's position in the Dalit vision is more than an equal partner with men and this must form the main path of alternative consciousness. In essence, the Dalit vision and alternative consciousness is primarily feminist, non-patriarchal, non-hierarchical and positively ecological. Dalit women all over the country need to stand up for freedom, inalienable right to human dignity and equal status with men and others in the society. To conclude, Dalits demand liberation. The model of development pursed in independent India and especially in the current period of unfettered liberalization and globalization, is essentially hostile to their dignified existence. The system should recognize the right of Dalits to live. Dalit women should get priority over all other issues. According to Dr. Babasaheb Ambedkar, there are two enemies, iof Dalits, "Caste ideology and capitalism". We therefore, look forward for powerful assertion, alternatives and a socialist perspective based on justice and equality. Build a new perspective towards emancipation of Dalits and Dalit women. According to Dr. Ambedkar "battle is in the fullest sense of spiritual". It is a battle for freedom, it is the battle for the reclamation of human personality".

Therefore, Dalits women's vision emerges from their emotions, struggles, aspirations and experiences, which has its roots in untouchability and violence, which are very specific in nature to Dalit womanhood. Their suffering encourages them to have common cause with other oppressed and marginalized of the marginal for transforming the society as a whole. The NFDW intend

- To build the Dalit Women's organization strongly and to establish alliances across other discriminated communities globally and other social movements.
- Political representation and participation of women, particularly from Dalit communities, in all decision-making bodies to be enhanced, eventually planning to establish a political academy for women in India.
- Developing new and young women leadership.

"We Dalit women pledge ourselves to liberate all our people from the continuing bondage of poverty deprivation, suffering, and other discrimination".

## 'Hidden Apartheid' of Discrimination Against Indian Dalits

India has systematically failed to uphold its international legal obligations to ensure the fundamental human rights of Dalits, or so-called untouchables, despite laws and policies against caste discrimination, the Centre for Human Rights and Global Justice and Human Rights Watch said in a new report released today. More than 165 million Dalits in India are condemned to a lifetime of abuse simply because of their caste.

The 113-page report, "Hidden Apartheid: Caste Discrimination against India's 'Untouchables'," was produced as a "shadow report" in response to India's submission to the United Nations Committee on the Elimination of Racial Discrimination (CERD), which monitors implementation of the International Convention on the Elimination of All Forms of Racial Discrimination (ICERD). The committee will review India's compliance with the convention during hearings in Geneva on February 23 and 26.

On December 27, 2006 Manmohan Singh became the first sitting Indian prime minister to openly acknowledge the parallel between the practice of "untouchability" and the crime of apartheid. Singh described "untouchability" as a "blot on humanity" adding that "even after 60 years of constitutional and legal protection and state support, there is still social discrimination against Dalits in many parts of our country."

"Prime Minister Singh has rightly compared 'untouchability' to apartheid, and he should now turn his words into action to protect the rights of Dalits," said Professor Smita Narula, faculty director of the Centre for Human Rights and Global Justice (CHRGJ) at New York University School of Law, and co-author of the report. "The Indian government can no longer deny its collusion in maintaining a system of entrenched social and economic segregation."

Dalits endure segregation in housing, schools, and access to public services. They are denied access to land, forced to work in degrading conditions, and routinely abused at the hands of the police and upper-caste community members who enjoy the state's protection. Entrenched discrimination violates Dalits' rights to education, health, housing, property, freedom of religion, free choice of employment, and equal treatment before the law. Dalits also suffer routine violations of their right to life and security of person through state-sponsored or-sanctioned acts of violence, including torture. Caste-motivated killings, rapes, and other abuses are a daily occurrence in India. Between 2001 and 2002 close to

58,000 cases were registered under the Scheduled Castes and Scheduled Tribes (Prevention of Atrocities) Act – legislation that criminalizes particularly egregious abuses against Dalits and tribal community members. A 2005 government report states that a crime is committed against a Dalit every 20 minutes. Though staggering, these figures represent only a fraction of actual incidents since many Dalits do not register cases for fear of retaliation by the police and upper-caste individuals.

Both state and private actors commit these crimes with impunity. Even on the relatively rare occasions on which a case reaches court, the most likely outcome is acquittal. Indian government reports reveal that between 1999 and 2001 as many as 89 percent of trials involving offenses against Dalits resulted in acquittals.

A resolution passed by the European Parliament on February 1, 2007 found India's efforts to enforce laws protecting Dalits to be "grossly inadequate," adding that "atrocities, untouchability, illiteracy, [and] inequality of opportunity, continue to blight the lives of India's Dalits." The resolution called on the Indian government to engage with CERD in its efforts to end caste-based discrimination. Dalit leaders welcomed the resolution, but Indian officials dismissed it as lacking in "balance and perspective." "International scrutiny is growing and with it the condemnation of abuses resulting from the caste system and the government's failure to protect Dalits," said Brad Adams, Asia director at Human Rights Watch. "India needs to mobilize the entire government and make good on its paper commitments to end caste abuses. Otherwise, it risks pariah status for its homegrown brand of apartheid."

Attempts by Dalits to defy the caste order, to demand their rights, or to lay claim to land that is legally theirs are consistently met with economic boycotts or retaliatory violence. For example, in Punjab on January 5, 2006 Dalit laborer and activist Bant Singh, seeking the prosecution of the people who gang-raped his daughter, was beaten so severely that both arms and one leg had to be amputated. On September 26, 2006 in Kherlanji village, Maharashtra, a Dalit family was killed by an upper-caste mob, after the mother and daughter were stripped, beaten and paraded through the village and the two brothers were brutally beaten. They were attacked because they refused to let upper-caste farmers take their land. After widespread protests at the police's failure to arrest the perpetrators, some of those accused in the killing were finally arrested and police and medical officers who had failed to do their jobs were suspended from duty.

Exploitation of labour is at the very heart of the caste system. Dalits are forced to perform tasks deemed too "polluting" or degrading for non-Dalits to carry out. According to unofficial estimates, more than 1.3 million Dalits – mostly women – are employed as manual scavengers to clear human waste from dry pit latrines. In several cities, Dalits are lowered into manholes without protection to clear sewage blockages, resulting in more than 100 deaths each year from inhalation of toxic gases or from drowning in excrement. Dalits comprise the majority of agricultural, bonded, and child labourers in the country. Many survive on less than US$1 per day.

In January 2007 the UN Committee on the Elimination of Discrimination against Women concluded that Dalit women in India suffer from "deeply rooted structural discrimination." "Hidden Apartheid" records the plight of Dalit women and the multiple forms of discrimination they face. Abuses documented in the report include sexual abuse by the police and upper-caste men, forced prostitution, and discrimination in employment and the payment of wages.

Dalit children face consistent hurdles in access to education. They are made to sit in the back of classrooms and endure verbal and physical harassment from teachers and students. The effect of such abuses is borne out by the low literacy and high drop-out rates for Dalits. The Centre for Human Rights and Global Justice and Human Rights Watch call on CERD to scrutinize the gap between India's human rights commitments and the daily reality faced by Dalits. In particular, CERD should request that the Indian government:

- Identify measures taken to ensure appropriate reforms to eliminate police abuses against Dalits and other marginalized communities;

- Provide concrete plans to implement laws and government policies to protect Dalits, and Dalit women in particular, from physical and sexual violence;
- Identify steps taken to eradicate caste-based segregation in residential areas and schools, and in access to public services; and,
- Outline plans to ensure the effective eradication of exploitative labour arrangements and effective implementation of rehabilitation schemes for Dalit bonded and child labourers, manual scavengers, and for Dalit women forced into prostitution.

"International outrage over the treatment of Dalits is matched by growing national discontent," Smita Narula said. "India can't ignore the voices of 165 million citizens."

"Hidden Apartheid" is based on in-depth investigations by CHRGJ, Human Rights Watch, Indian non-governmental organizations, and media sources. The pervasiveness of abuses against Dalits is corroborated by the reports of Indian governmental agencies, including the National Human Rights Commission, and the National Commission on Scheduled Castes and Scheduled Tribes. These and other sources were compiled, investigated, and analyzed under international law by NYU School of Law's International Human Rights Clinic.

CHAPTER

4

# Indian Dalit Face Violence, Fear and Discrimination

More than 160 million people in India are considered "Untouchable"—people tainted by their birth into a caste system that deems them impure, less than human. India's Untouchables are relegated to the lowest jobs, and live in constant fear of being publicly humiliated, paraded naked, beaten, and raped with impunity by upper-caste Hindus seeking to keep them in their place. Merely walking through an upper-caste neighbourhood is a life-threatening offense.

Nearly 90 percent of all the poor Indians and 95 percent of all the illiterate Indians are Dalits, according to figures presented at the International Dalit Conference that took place May 16 to 18 in Vancouver, Canada.

## Violence against Dalit Women

Violence against Dalit women presents clear evidence of widespread exploitation and discrimination against these women, who are subordinated in terms of power relations to men in a patriarchal and caste-dominant society. Examples of such demeaning social customs include the devadasi and jogini system of forced prostitution, and the practice of manual scavenging. A written statement calling for international recognition of this issue has been sent to the Human Rights Council by Cordaid and Minority Rights Group International with the support of IDSN and Justice and Peace Netherlands.

The Universal Periodic Review of Bangladesh, which took place in February 2009, also included conclusions and recommendations to ensure that women's rights are protected and implemented. These recommendations, which will be considered at the 11th Council session, would greatly benefit the human rights of marginalised groups, in particular Dalit women, in Bangladesh. The Government is therefore urged to respond positively to them and, if possible, explain how they could be implemented to help realize the human rights of Dalit women.

## High Commissioner's visit to Nepal and India

During the High Commissioner's visit to Nepal and India in March 2009, Ms. Navi Pillay urged the respective governments to effectively address the issue of caste-based discrimination, both as a national and an international human rights problem. This is the strongest support ever shown by the principal human rights official of the UN to the global fight against caste-based discrimination, which was reaffirmed during the Durban Review Conference where she said in a press conference on 21 April that "she personally felt that "related intolerance" [in the DDPA] would cover discrimination on the basis of caste, class and social status." In response to the High Commissioner's presentation of her report at the session, Council members may welcome the High Commissioner's commitment to addressing this human rights issue, and encourage her to continue to promote this field of concern under her mandate. Together with Norwegian NGOs, IDSN has also requested that Norway, which was recently elected as a new Council member, make caste discrimination one of its main priorities.

## Lack of Enforcement, Not Laws

Enforcement of laws designed to protect Dalits is lax if not non-existent in many regions of India. The practice of untouchability is strongest in rural areas, where 80 percent of the country's population resides. There, the underlying religious principles of Hinduism dominate. Hindus believe a person is born into one of four castes based on karma and "purity"-how he or she lived their past lives. Those born as Brahmans are priests and teachers; Kshatriyas are rulers and soldiers; Vaisyas are merchants and traders; and Sudras are labourers. Within the four castes, there are thousands of sub-castes, defined by profession, region, dialect, and other factors. Untouchables are literally outcastes; a fifth group that is so unworthy it doesn't fall within the caste system. Although based on religious principles practiced for some 1,500 years, the system persists today for economic as much as religious reasons.

Because they are considered impure from birth, Untouchables perform jobs that are traditionally considered "unclean" or exceedingly menial, and for very little pay. One million Dalits work as manual scavengers, cleaning latrines and sewers by hand and clearing away dead animals. Millions more are agricultural workers trapped in an inescapable cycle of extreme poverty, illiteracy, and oppression. Although illegal, 40 million people in India, most of them Dalits, are bonded workers, many working to pay off debts that were incurred generations ago, according to a report by Human Rights Watch published in 1999. These people, 15 million of whom are children, work under slave-like conditions hauling rocks, or working in fields or factories for less than U.S. $1 day.

## Crimes Against Women

Dalit women are particularly hard hit. They are frequently raped or beaten as a means of reprisal against male relatives who are thought to have committed some act worthy of upper-caste vengeance. They are also subject to arrest if they have male relatives hiding from the authorities. A case reported in 1999 illustrates the toxic mix of gender and caste. A 42-year-old Dalit woman was gang-raped and then burnt alive after she, her husband, and two sons had been held in captivity and tortured for eight days. Her crime? Another son had eloped with the daughter of the higher-caste family doing the torturing. The local police knew the Dalit family was being held, but did nothing because of the higher-caste family's local influence.

There is very little recourse available to victims. A report released by Amnesty International in 2001 found an "extremely high" number of sexual assaults on Dalit women, frequently perpetrated by landlords, upper-caste villagers, and police officers. The study estimates that only about 5 percent of attacks are registered, and that police officers dismissed at least 30 percent of rape complaints as false. The study also found that the police routinely demand bribes, intimidate witnesses, cover up evidence, and beat up the women's husbands. Little or nothing is done to prevent attacks on rape victims by gangs of upper-caste villagers seeking to prevent a case from being pursued. Sometimes the policemen even join in, the study suggests. Rape victims have also been murdered. Such crimes often go unpunished.

Thousands of pre-teen Dalit girls are forced into prostitution under cover of a religious practice known as devadasis, which means "female servant of god." The girls are dedicated or "married" to a deity or a temple. Once dedicated, they are unable to marry, forced to have sex with upper-caste community members, and eventually sold to an urban brothel.

## Resistance and Progress

Within India, grassroots efforts to change are emerging, despite retaliation and intimidation by local officials and upper-caste villagers. In some states, caste conflict has escalated to caste warfare, and militia-like vigilante groups have conducted raids on villages, burning homes, raping, and massacring the people. These raids are sometimes conducted with the tacit approval of the police.

In the province Bihar, local Dalits are retaliating, committing atrocities also. Non-aligned Dalits are frequently caught in the middle, victims of both groups. "There is a growing grassroots movement of activists, trade unions, and other NGOs that are organizing to democratically and peacefully demand their rights, higher wages, and more equitable land distribution," said Narula. "There has been progress in terms of building a human rights movement within India, and in drawing international attention to the issue." In August 2002, the UN Committee for the Elimination of Racial Discrimination (UN CERD) approved a resolution condemning caste or descent-based discrimination. "But at the national level, very little is being done to implement or enforce the laws," said Narula.

## Crime Against Dalits

Statistics compiled by India's National Crime Records Bureau indicate that in the year 2000, the last year for which figures are available, 25,455 crimes were committed against Dalits. Every hour two Dalits are assaulted; every day three Dalit women are raped, two Dalits are murdered, and two Dalit homes are torched. No one believes these numbers are anywhere close to the reality of crimes committed against Dalits. Because the police, village councils, and government officials often support the caste system, which is based on the religious teachings of Hinduism, many crimes go unreported due to fear of reprisal, intimidation by police, inability to pay bribes demanded by police, or simply the knowledge that the police will do nothing.

"There have been large-scale abuses by the police, acting in collusion with upper castes, including raids, beatings in custody, failure to charge offenders or investigate reported crimes," said Narula. That same year, 68,160 complaints were filed against the police for activities ranging from murder, torture, and collusion in acts of atrocity, to refusal to file a complaint. Sixty two percent of the cases were dismissed as unsubstantiated; 26 police officers were convicted in court.

Despite the fact that untouchability was officially banned when India adopted its constitution in 1950, discrimination against Dalits remained so pervasive that in 1989 the government passed legislation known as The Prevention of Atrocities Act. The act specifically made it illegal to parade people naked through the streets, force them to eat feces, take away their land, foul their water, interfere with their right to vote, and burn down their homes. Since then, the violence has escalated, largely as a result of the emergence of a grassroots human rights movement among Dalits to demand their rights and resist the dictates of untouchability, said Narula.

### Lack of Enforcement, Not Laws

Enforcement of laws designed to protect Dalits is lax if not non-existent in many regions of India. The practice of untouchability is strongest in rural areas, where 80 percent of the country's population resides. There, the underlying religious principles of Hinduism dominate. Hindus believe a person is born into one of four castes based on karma and "purity"—how he or she lived their past lives. Those born as Brahmans are priests and teachers; Kshatriyas are rulers and soldiers; Vaisyas are merchants and traders; and Sudras are labourers. Within the four castes, there are thousands of sub-castes, defined by profession, region, dialect, and other factors.

Untouchables are literally outcastes; a fifth group that is so unworthy it doesn't fall within the caste system. Although based on religious principles practiced for some 1,500 years, the system persists today for economic as much as religious reasons.

Because they are considered impure from birth, Untouchables perform jobs that are traditionally considered "unclean" or exceedingly menial, and for very little pay. One million Dalits work as manual scavengers, cleaning latrines and sewers by hand and clearing away dead animals. Millions more are agricultural workers trapped in an inescapable cycle of extreme poverty, illiteracy, and oppression. Although illegal, 40 million people in India, most of them Dalits, are bonded workers, many working to pay off debts that were incurred generations ago, according to a report by Human Rights Watch published in 1999. These people, 15 million of whom are children, work under slave-like conditions hauling rocks, or working in fields or factories for less than U.S. $1 day.

## Crimes Against Dalit Women

Dalit women are particularly hard hit. They are frequently raped or beaten as a means of reprisal against male relatives who are thought to have committed some act worthy of upper-caste vengeance. They are also subject to arrest if they have male relatives hiding from the authorities. A case reported in 1999 illustrates the toxic mix of gender and caste.

A 42-year-old Dalit woman was gang-raped and then burnt alive after she, her husband, and two sons had been held in captivity and tortured for eight days. Her crime? Another son had eloped with the daughter of the higher-caste family doing the torturing. The local police knew the Dalit family was being held, but did nothing because of the higher-caste family's local influence. There is very little recourse available to victims. A report released by Amnesty International in 2001 found an "extremely high" number of sexual assaults on Dalit women, frequently perpetrated by landlords, upper-caste villagers, and police officers. The study estimates that only about 5 percent of attacks are registered, and that police officers dismissed at least 30 percent of rape complaints as false.

The study also found that the police routinely demand bribes, intimidate witnesses, cover up evidence, and beat up the women's husbands. Little or nothing is done to prevent attacks on rape victims by gangs of upper-caste villagers seeking to prevent a case from being pursued. Sometimes the policemen even join in, the study suggests. Rape victims have also been murdered. Such crimes often go unpunished. Thousands of pre-teen Dalit girls are forced into prostitution under cover of a religious practice known as *devadasis*, which means "female servant of god." The girls are dedicated or "married" to a deity or a temple. Once dedicated, they are unable to marry, forced to have sex with upper-caste community members, and eventually sold to an urban brothel.

## Resistance and Progress

Within India, grassroots efforts to change are emerging, despite retaliation and intimidation by local officials and upper-caste villagers. In some states, caste conflict has escalated to caste warfare, and militia-like vigilante groups have conducted raids on villages, burning homes, raping, and massacring the people. These raids are sometimes conducted with the tacit approval of the police. In the province Bihar, local Dalits are retaliating, committing atrocities also. Non-aligned Dalits are frequently caught in the middle, victims of both groups.

"There is a growing grassroots movement of activists, trade unions, and other NGOs that are organizing to democratically and peacefully demand their rights, higher wages, and more equitable land distribution," said Narula. "There has been progress in terms of building a human rights movement within India, and in drawing international attention to the issue."

In August 2002, the UN Committee for the Elimination of Racial Discrimination (UN CERD) approved a resolution condemning caste or descent-based discrimination. "But at the national level, very little is being done to implement or enforce the laws," said Narula.

## Systemic Discrimination, Violence and Impunity

The caste system declares Dalit women to be intrinsically impure and 'untouchable', therefore socially excluded. In class terms, the vast majority of Dalit women are poor; many are landless daily wage labourers who are systematically denied access to resources. As women, they are subjugated by patriarchal structures. Due to this intersectional discrimination, Dalit women are specifically targeted for daily, egregious acts of violence, in particular for sexual violence, including the Devadasi system of forced and ritualised prostitution. On account of their 'impure' caste and poverty, Dalit women comprise the majority of manual scavengers, that is, labourers who clean human excrement from dry toilets. When they assert fundamental rights, Dalit women are targeted for punitive violence by dominant castes. Due to patriarchal notions of community honour residing in women, dominant caste violence against Dalit women functions to punish the entire Dalit community and teach Dalits a lesson of obedience to caste norms. Moreover, Dalit women are discriminated against not only by dominant castes on account of their caste, class and gender, but also by their own communities on account of their gender. Dalit women have less power within the Dalit community in general.

When considering discrimination and violence against Dalit women, one can state that impunity is *the key problem* Dalit women face today – not only while seeking legal and judicial redress for violence, but also while attempting to access and enjoy their fundamental rights and freedoms. Perpetrators enjoy virtual immunity from prosecution for violence against Dalit women, as the police, who themselves often harbour caste prejudices, wilfully neglect to enforce the law. Not only the police, but perpetrators and their communities use their political, social and economic power to silence Dalit women, thereby denying them access to justice. The nature of collusion between state and dominant caste actors is such that the modern rule of law has no place in the hierarchical order of socio-economic and political power relationships, as caste-based power supersedes state-derived executive authority.

### Dalit Women's Assertion

Dalit women today are not simply passive victims; the current mood is not one of mere acceptance, but one of determination to 'transform their pain into power'. In fact, they have been active throughout history, though often this has not been recognised and recorded. They have been actively involved in the anti-caste and anti-untouchability movements.

Today they are the strongholds of the Dalit movements in thousands of South Asian villages, and are often at the forefront of struggles for basic human rights. They continue to play a critical role in the movements for land and livelihood rights and against untouchability, pointing to the potential for their self-emancipation, given adequate support.

They are making their mark as independent thinkers and writers in the literary world by critiquing dominant caste ideologies. They participate today as visionary leaders in the local governance institution by asserting their rights. While they continue to struggle against structural discrimination and exclusion, violence and impunity are systematically unleashed by dominant castes to keep them in their place.

While recognising the gendered nature of caste discrimination for Dalit women, these women have turned their 'suffering' into one of 'resistance', actively participating shoulder to shoulder with men in their communities in the anti-caste and anti-untouchability movements. They have simultaneously contributed to the welfare of their families, sustained their communities given their labour for producing food and wealth for their countries. In this regard, Dalit women build their identities on a culture of resistance against the hegemonic culture of the caste system, expressing their defiance and revolt against the caste, class and gender discrimination that oppresses them. This assertion of distinct identity and simultaneous forging of a collective identity in multiple struggles marks the Dalit women's movement in various ways.

## Dalit Women and Human Rights

The countries where caste discrimination persists are party to most of the relevant human rights instruments: the Universal Declaration on Human Rights and treaties such as the International Covenant on Civil and Political Rights (ICCPR), the International Covenant on Economic, Social and Cultural Rights (ICESCR) and the International Convention on the Elimination of All Forms of Racial Discrimination (ICERD). These treaties provide equal rights for men and women. As these countries are also party to the Convention on the Elimination of All Forms of Discrimination Against Women (CEDAW), governments have a specific obligation to make sure that women can realise their human rights. It is generally accepted in international legal standards that governments have to do more than just pass laws to protect human rights. Governments have an obligation to take all measures, including policy and budgetary measures, to make sure that women can fulfil and enjoy their fundamental rights. Equally importantly, governments must *implement* these laws, policy measures and programmes to fully discharge their obligations under international law. This includes an obligation to exercise due diligence in punishing those who engage in caste-based discrimination and violence.

### Millennium Development Goals and Dalit women

In 2000, one hundred and eighty-nine countries accepted the Millennium Declaration and agreed to take the necessary action in order to attain eight specific goals: the Millennium Development Goals (MDGs). The realisation of human rights of Dalit women will have a substantial positive effect on the realisation of the MDGs. This is because Dalit women are extremely poor, and make up two percent of the world's population. In India, for example, 60 million children do not attend primary school; a disproportionate number of these children are Dalit girls.

### International Conference on Dalit Women's Rights

Over the years Dalit women's organisations and movements have increasingly voiced their specific concerns and asserted their separate identity, calling for solidarity from the International Community. The Fourth World Conference on Women in Beijing in 1995 saw for the first time international recognition given to the discrimination faced by Dalit women. Dalit women also played a crucial role in the World Conference Against Racism in South Africa in 2001, where Dalit issues were brought to the fore of the international attention. Following the National Conference on Violence against Dalit Women in Delhi on 7 and 8 March 2006, Justitia et Pax Netherlands, Cordaid, and CMC as members of the Dalit Network Netherlands (DNN), in collaboration with the National Campaign on Dalit Human Rights (NCDHR, India), the National Federation of Dalit Women (India), the ALL India Dalit Women's Rights Forum (India), Feminist Dalit Organisation (FEDO, Nepal), the International Dalit Solidarity Network (IDSN) and other Dalit and Women's rights organizations, responded to the request of Dalit women and organised the International Conference on the Human Rights of Dalit Women on 20 and 21 November 2006 in The Hague, The Netherlands.

*Focus of International Conference*

Caste, class and gender discrimination prevents Dalit women from enjoying their basic human rights, particularly to dignity, equality and development. Atrocities and violence against Dalit women are both a means of sustaining systemic discrimination, as well as a reaction when particularly untouchability practices and caste norms are challenged or not adhered to. Impunity for this discrimination and violence is then used as a means to preserve the existing caste and gender disparities. Before Dalit women can enjoy their human rights, and before the Millennium Development Goals can be achieved, discrimination, violence and impunity must stop. Therefore we, the participants of The Hague Conference on Dalit Women's Rights, call upon the respective governments in Nepal, India, Pakistan, Bangladesh and Sri Lanka to take seriously the voices of Dalit women as they explain their specific situation, to support them in asserting their rights and to ensure Dalit women and girls are brought on par with the general population in terms of overall development (e.g. poverty reduction) within a period of five years. We call upon the international community to undertake and support every possible measure to fight the widespread discrimination, violence and impunity committed against Dalit women.

## Discrimination and Exploitative forms of Dalit Labour

Allocation of labour on the basis of caste is one of the fundamental tenets of the caste system. Within the caste system, Dalits have been assigned tasks and occupations that are deemed ritually polluting for other caste communities. Throughout this report, Human Rights Watch has documented the exploitation of agricultural labourers who work for a few kilograms of rice or Rs. 15 to Rs. 35 (US$0.38 to $0.88) a day. A sub-group of Dalits is condemned to labour even more exploitative. An estimated forty million people in India, among them fifteen million children, are bonded labourers. A majority of them are Dalits. According to government statistics, an estimated one million Dalits are manual scavengers who clean public latrines and dispose of dead animals; unofficial estimates are much higher. In India's southern states, thousands of Dalit girls are forced into prostitution before reaching the age of puberty.

Bondage is passed on from one generation to another. Scavenging and prostitution are hereditary occupations of "untouchable" castes. Dalits face discrimination when seeking other forms of employment and are largely unable to escape their designated occupation even when the practice itself has been abolished by law. In violation of their basic human rights, they are physically abused and threatened with economic and social ostracism from the community for refusing to carry out various caste-based tasks.

## Bonded Labour

"Bonded labour" refers to work in slave-like conditions in order to pay off a debt. Due to the high interest rates charged and the abysmally low wages paid, the debts are seldom settled. Bonded labourers are frequently low-caste, illiterate, and extremely poor, while the creditors/employers are usually higher-caste, literate, comparatively wealthy, and relatively more powerful members of the community. The Bonded Labour System (Abolition) Act, 1976 abolishes all agreements and obligations arising out of the bonded labour system. It aims to release all labourers from bondage, cancel any outstanding debt, prohibit the creation of new bondage agreements, and order the economic rehabilitation offreed bonded labourers by the state. It also punishes attempts to compel persons into bondage with a maximum of three years in prison and a Rs. 2,000 (US$50) fine. However, the extent to which bonded labourers have been identified, released, and rehabilitated in the country is negligible.

Most agricultural labourers interviewed for this report were paid between Rs. 15 and Rs. 25 (US$0.38 to $0.63), or two to three kilograms of rice, per day, well below the minimum wage prescribed in their state. Women were consistently paid less than men. Many labourers owed debts to their employers or other moneylenders. Under the Bonded Labour System (Abolition) Act, 1976, payment of less than minimum wage for the purposes of working off a debt amounts to bondage. The act's definition of the "bonded labour system" includes "any system of forced, or partly forced labour under which a debtor enters, or has, or is presumed to have, entered, into an agreement with the creditor to the effect that (v) by reason of his birth in any particular caste or community, he would (1) render, by himself or through any member of his family, or any person dependent on him, labour or service to the creditor, or for the benefit of the creditor, for a specified period or for an unspecified period, either without wages or for nominal wages.... Nominal wages are defined as wages which are less than (a) the minimum wages fixed by the Government, in relation to the same or similar labour, under any law for the time being in force; and (b) where no such minimum wage has been fixed in relation to any form of labour, the wages that are normally paid, for the same or similar labour to the labourers working in the same locality.

## Caste and Employment Discrimination

In traditional Indian society, the fourfold varna theory describes a broad functional division of labour. Though the caste system has not prevented occupational mobility for caste Hindus, many "untouchable" communities have been forced to continue their occupations as leather workers, disposers of dead animals, or manual scavengers, and to perform other tasks deemed too ritually polluting for upper castes. The constitutional abolition of "untouchability" meant that caste Hindus could no longer force

Dalits to perform any "polluting" occupation. Yet sweeping, scavenging, and leatherwork are still the monopoly of the scheduled castes, whose members are threatened with physical abuse and social boycotts for refusing to perform demeaning tasks. Migration and the anonymity of the urban environment have in some cases resulted in upward occupational mobility among Dalits, but the majority continue to perform their traditional functions. A lack of training and education, as well as discrimination in seeking other forms of employment, have kept these traditions and their hereditary nature alive.

## Manual Scavenging

Manual scavenging is a caste-based occupation. Dalit manual scavengers exist under different caste names throughout the country, such as the Bhangis in Gujarat, the Pakhis in Andhra Pradesh, and the Sikkaliars in Tamil Nadu. Members of these communities are invariably placed at the very bottom of the caste hierarchy, and even the hierarchy of Dalit sub-castes. Using little more than a broom, a tin plate, and a basket, they are made to clear feces from public and private latrines and carry them to dumping grounds and disposal sites. Though long outlawed, the practice of manual scavenging continues in most states.

Those working for urban municipalities are paid Rs. 30-40 a day (less than US$1), and those working privately are paid Rs. 5 (US$0.13) a month for each house they clean. Even those working for municipalities rarely get paid and are offered little health benefits for a job that entails many health hazards. In cities scavengers are actually lowered into filthy gutters in order to unclog them; they are fully immersed in human waste without any protective gear. In Bombay, children made to dive into manholes have died from carbon monoxide poisoning. In many communities, in exchange for leftover food, scavengers are also expected to remove dead animal carcasses and deliver messages of death to the relatives of their upper-caste neighbors. Their refusal to do so can result in physical abuse and ostracism from the community.

A social worker in the Dhandhuka taluk of Ahmedabad district, Gujarat, explained the relevance of caste to this work: Bhangis are the section of Dalits that do this work. The funds come from the government. In villages, the cleaners and who they clean for are always divided by caste... At all levels, villages and municipalities, Bhangis are the workers and they always work for upper castes.

In a 1997 report, the National Commission for Safai Karamcharis claimed that manual scavengers are "totally cut off from the mainstream of progress" and are "still subjected to the worst kind of oppression and indignities. What is more pathetic is the fact that manual scavenging is still largely a hereditary occupation. *Safai karamcharis* are no doubt the most oppressed and disadvantaged section of the population." The commission is a statutory body set up pursuant to the National Commission for Safai Karamcharis Act, 1993. Safai karamcharis are defined as those persons engaged in, or employed for, manually carrying human excreta or any sanitation work.

Martin Macwan is founder-director of Navsarjan, an NGO that has led the campaign to abolish manual scavenging in the western state of Gujarat. In an interview with Human Rights Watch he claimed that when Navsarjan had attempted to rehabilitate scavengers it was difficult to find alternative employment for them, and even more difficult to convince scavengers that they were able to take on, or were "worthy of performing," different occupations.

Members of the Bhangi community in Gujarat are paid by state municipalities to clean the gutters, streets, and community dry latrines. In an article in *Frontline,* a safai karamchari of Paliyad village, Ahmedabad district, complained that in the rainy season, the "water mixes with the faeces that we carry in baskets on our heads, it drips onto our clothes, our faces_ When I return home, I find it difficult to eat food. The smell never leaves my clothes, my hair. But in the summer there is often no water to wash your hands before eating. It is difficult to say which [season] is worse."

Human Rights Watch spoke to members of the Bhangi community in Gujarat's Ahmedabad district. The Bhangis lived in a residential area called Bhangivas separate from the Dharbars, Rajputs, and Vanniyas who constitute the caste Hindus in the area. The Bhangis were primarily employed as manual scavengers. They were also responsible for removing dead cats and dogs and were given Rs. 5 (US$0.13) or small amounts of food for doing so.

Forty-year-old Manju, a manual scavenger employed by the urban municipality, described her daily routine and wages:

In the morning I work from 6:00 a.m. to 11:00 a.m. cleaning the dry latrines. I collect the feces and carry it on my head to the river half a kilometer away seven to ten times a day. In the afternoon I clean the gutters. Another Bhangi collects the rubbish from the gutters and places it outside. Then I come and pick it up and take it one kilometer away. My husband died ten years ago since then I have been doing this. Today I earn Rs. 30 a day (US$0.75). Nine years ago I earned Rs. 16 (US$0.40), then Rs. 22 (US$0.55), and for the last two years it has been Rs. 30. But the payments are uncertain. For the last two months we have not received anything. Every two months they pay, but there is no certainty. We are paid by the Nagar Palika municipality chief officer.

Like many others, Manju's health had suffered as a result of her occupation: "I have often gotten sick: fevers, headaches, breaking and spraining hands and feet, fatigue, and dizziness. It is all dirty work." Several other Bhangi women interviewed complained of similar ailments. Most looked considerably older than their stated age. In addition to the above mentioned diseases of the poor, manual scavengers also tend to suffer from respiratory infections, gastro-intestinal disorders, and trachoma, a chronic contagious bacterial conjunctivitis commonly resulting in blindness. Human Rights Watch spoke to several workers with vision problems and to sixty-five-year-old Bachubhai Chaganbhai, who suffered from tuberculosis. He claimed that the illness was due to "working as a cleaner. I used to clean openlatrines. Because of this work I am sick. I stopped working five years ago and have been sick with TB ever since."

Because Bachubhai was a "permanent" worker, he received Rs. 1,500 (US$37.50) pension per month. He used to earn Rs. 2,000 (US$50) a month, or approximately Rs. 65 (US$1.63) a day. Activist Martin Macwan explained that [b]eing permanent means that you have an appointment letter. You also get health benefits but not much; you get to visit government dispensaries, which are not in good shape. But the state government has to give grants to the state municipalities depending on the number of permanents that are employed, so the municipalities try to keep them as casual labourers instead. But the number of hours they work is usually the same.

Despite the similarity in work and hours spent, casual labourers are paid only Rs. 34 (US$0.85) a day while permanent labourers were paid Rs. 80 (US$2). Most casual labourers never achieve permanent status, even after years of employment. Leelaben, another scavenger interviewed by Human Rights Watch, had been cleaning the latrines in Birla High School for over twenty years, "Still they have not made me permanent," she said. "I used to get paid Rs. 15 (US$0.38) a month, now I get paid Rs. 200 (US$5) a month."

The situation of private workers, mostly women working in upper-caste households, is even bleaker. In the Bhangivas residential area, in July 1998, there were a total of thirty private workers; the rest were employed by the municipality. Many private workers were paid only Rs. 3 (US$0.08) a day.

An activist in the southern state of Andhra Pradesh, who has been working for the rehabilitation of cleaning workers for the past fourteen years, described a similar pay scale in his state:

Private cleaners receive Rs. 5 to 10 a month for each house they clean [US$0.12 to $0.25]. They clean up to ten to fifteen houses a day, many of which have six or more family members. Those employed by urban municipalities are paid Rs. 2,000 to Rs. 2,500 [US$50-$63] a month but are only paid once every four to six months. Some are permanent, and some are casual. There are no health benefits, no gloves, no masks, no utensils. The majority are women.

A survey conducted by Safai Karmachari Andolan, an NGO movement for the elimination of manual scavenging, found over 1,650 scavengers in ten districts in Andhra Pradesh. Many were also engaged in underground sewage work. The survey also revealed that 98 percent of manual scavengers in the state belonged to scheduled castes.

A third category of cleaning workers are responsible for cleaning the railway systems. In Andhra Pradesh they are paid Rs. 300 (US$7.50) a month with very few benefits. In Gujarat, they are paid Rs. 12 (US$0.30) a day "for unlimited hours of work. They are told they can stop working when the train comes, but in India you never know when the train will come."

An activist working with the Sikkaliar (Dalit) community of Tamil Nadu described the community's economic exploitation and the tasks that its members are forced to perform. His village had 200 Thevar families. Seventy Sikkaliar families lived in a separate government-built colony. Those who worked as scavengers and removed dead animals from the village received Rs. 150 (US$3.75) per month for their services.

Social discrimination against scavengers is rampant. Most scavengers live in segregated rural colonies and are unable to make use of common resources. According to an Andhra Pradesh activist:

In one toilet there can be as many as 400 seats which all have to be manually cleaned. This is the lowest occupation in the world, and it is done by the community that occupies the lowest status in the castesystem. Even other scheduled-caste people won't touch the safai karamcharis [cleaning workers]. It is "untouchability" within the "untouchables," yet nobody questions it.

Human Rights Watch was taken to various tea stalls to witness the separate tea tumbler system in which scavengers are made to wash and handle their own tumblers so that glasses reserved for caste Hindus are not "polluted."

When we are working, they ask us not to come near them. At tea canteens, they have separate tea tumblers and they make us clean them ourselves and make us put the dishes away ourselves. We cannot enter temples. We cannot use upper-caste water taps. We have to go one kilometer away to get water.

Despite their appalling work conditions, manual scavengers are unable to demand higher wages or sanitary instruments for use in the collection of human excreta: "When we ask for our rights from the government, the municipality officials threaten to fire us. So we don't say anything. This is what happens to people who demand their rights." According to Macwan, in Ranpur town, Ahmedabad district, women who arrived late for work were made to clean men's urinals as punishment, "even if the men were still inside." Another social worker active in Gujarat added that Bhangis were forced to deliver messages of death to upper-caste family relatives; "They will be boycotted and beaten so they cannot say no."

Human Rights Watch spoke to an activist working to organize Sikkaliars in the Theni district of southern Tamil Nadu. He works with fifty Sikkaliar families in a Thevar-dominated area. The interview revealed that apart from having to perform degrading tasks, the Sikkaliars are also subject to physical and sexual abuse as well as restrictions on their right to vote.

Sikkaliars have to bury the Thevars' dead animals, and women have to collect waste. They only get meals for their work, even for burying animals. Sometimes Sikkaliars take the dead animal's meat and divide it among themselves. The Thevars harass women labourers, particularly young ladies. Once a girl attains puberty, she is harassed by Thevar men. If anyone opposes it, they will be severely punished. Sikkaliars depend on Thevars, and because there is no other support they often leave for other villages out of fear when fighting occurs. They are doing scavenger work as well as [agricultural] laborer work for which they are paid less than minimum wage. They clean the latrines, the bathrooms, the drains, and they do cremation work. If not they are severely punished by the Thevars. The children are not able to go to school.

The activist also described how Dalits are unable to freely exercise their constitutionally guaranteed right to vote. During the February 1998 elections, Sikkaliars were forced to vote according to the demands of the Thevar community or risk losing the little income they had: "Because Thevars are in the majority, they will come inside the voting booth and tell them who to vote for. If they don't act according to instructions, then they don't get employment, or they will be beaten."

Thevars treat Sikkaliars as slaves so they can utilize them as they wish. They exploit them sexually and make them dig graveyards for high-caste people's burials. They have to take the death message to Thevars. These are all unpaid services. Maybe they give them Rs. 10 [US$0.25] for the message. There are also very meager wages for grave digging. Still they have to do these things or they will be thrown out of the village. The activist referred to the women in his village as "sexual slaves" and claimed that Thevar men frequently enter Dalit houses at night to rape the women: "Dalit people have anger against Thevar people in mind. Thevars use their women, but Dalits cannot do anything." According to R. Balakrishnan, director of the Tamil Nadu chapter of the National Commission for Scheduled Castes and Scheduled Tribes, the raping of Dalit women exposes the hypocrisy of the caste system: "No one practices untouchability when it comes to sex."

## The Devadasi System: Ritualized Prostitution

The practice of *devadasi,* in which a girl, usually before reaching the age of puberty, is ceremoniously dedicated or married to a deity or to a temple, continues in several southern states including Andhra Pradesh and Karnataka. Literally meaning "female servant of god," devadasis usually belong to the Dalit community. Once dedicated, the girl is unable to marry, forced to become a prostitute for upper-caste community members, and eventually auctioned into an urban brothel. The age-old practice continues to legitimize the sexual violence and discrimination that have come to characterize the intersection between caste and gender. The patrons of the devadasis are generally from the higher castes because those from the devadasis own castes are too poor to afford to [pay] for the rituals_ In many cases a patron kept many girls and the number of girls used to be a yard stick of the status of that man. This system of patronage has given way to [a system of] commercial prostitution in the populated big cities.

Activists involved in the Dalit women's movement explain that the nexus between caste and forced prostitution is quite strong and that the devadasi system is no exception. Most Indian girls and women in India's urban brothels come from lower-caste, tribal, or minority communities. Like other forms of violence against women, ritualized prostitution, activists believe, is a system "designed to kill whatever vestiges of self-respect the untouchable castes have in order to subjugate them and keep them underprivileged." By keeping Dalit women as prostitutes, and by tying prostitution to bondage in rural areas, upper-caste men reinforce their declaration of social and economic superiority over the lower castes.

According to the Ambedkar Centre for Justice and Peace, a Canada-based NGO: Thousands of untouchable female children (between 6 and 8 years) are forced to become maidens of God (Devadasis, Jogins, a Hindu religious practice in Andhra Pradesh, Karnataka State, Maharashtra, Orissa State, to mention only a few). They are taken from their families, never to see them again. They are later raped by the temple priest and finally auctioned secretly into prostitution and ultimately die from AIDS. It is estimated by NGOs that 5,000 to 15,000 girls are auctioned secretly every year.

In an interview with Human Rights Watch, the head of an NGO active in Karnataka explained that in her state the girl is offered to the Goddess Yellamma in a village ceremony:

Earlier it was for priests, but now it is for high-caste men. They used to live in the temples_ now anyone can use them including lorry drivers_ Dreadlocked hair is taken as a sign from the Goddess Yellamma that the girl is meant to be a devadasi. In a festival, a marriage ceremony takes place between the girl and god. The eldest lady of the devadasi community ties the mangal sutra [marriage necklace]. In some ceremonies the girl wasparaded almost naked. The girl is then given some money but still works in the fields. She lives separately in the village and is used by all the men, including Dalit men. In 1992 the Karnataka state government passed the Karnataka Devadasi (Prohibition of Dedication) Act and called for the rehabilitation of devadasi women. Like many laws aimed at protecting women and lower castes, the act suffers from a lack of enforcement. Moreover, the police themselves have been known to use devadasis. As the Karnataka activist explained, the law works to the disadvantage of women because it criminalizes their actions and not the actions of their patrons. Police will even go so far as to demand sex as a bribe: "They will threaten to file charges under the act if the woman says no." Their perceived status in society, as women who are supposed to serve men sexually, also makes it more difficult for devadasis to approach the police for help: "When a devadasi is raped, it is not considered rape. She can be had by any man at any time."

In reviewing India's third periodic report to the U.N. Human Rights Committee, submitted under Article 40 of the International

Covenant on Civil and Political Rights (ICCPR) in July 1997, the Human Rights Committee regretted "the lack of national legislation to outlaw the practice of Devadasi, the regulation of which is left to the states," and added that "it appears that the practice continues and that not all states have effective legislation against it." The committee emphasized that the practice was incompatible with the ICCPR and recommended that "all necessary measures be taken urgently" toward its eradication.

## The Relationship between Scavenging and Debt Bondage

When interviewed in early 1998, thirty-year-old Parsotambhai, a mother of three in Ahmedabad district, Gujarat, earned Rs. 10 (US$0.25) a month for each house she cleaned. She also received small amounts of food once a day and complained that there was too much work. Others voiced similar complaints:

They give one person too much work so they have to take their family members, even their children, at night to finish the work; otherwise they would get fired. It takes four people to do the work that they give one person. None of the children are really studying. Girls sometimes study up to fifth standard, boys up to seventh.

Given the insignificant amounts of remuneration and the need to engage several family members in work assigned to one, it comes as little surprise that many families borrow money from their upper-caste neighbors and consequently going into bondage. Their poverty is so acute that Macwan has even documenteda Bhangi practice of separating non-digested wheat from buffalo dung to make *chappatis* (flat bread). One scavenger commented:

There is no health care, no benefits from the government. We cannot live on what we get paid, but we have to. We also have to take loans from the upper caste. They charge 10 percent in interest per month. We have no clothes, no soap, no wages, and no payments on time.

### Failure to Implement Protective Legislation

The Employment of Manual Scavengers and Construction of Dry Latrines (Prohibition) Act, 1993 punishes the employment of scavengers or the construction of dry (non-flush) latrines with imprisonment for up to one year and/or a fine as high as Rs. 2,000 (US$50). Offenders are also liable to prosecution under the Scheduled Castes and Scheduled Tribes (Prevention of Atrocities) Act, 1989. In 1992 the government launched a national scheme that called for the identification, training, and rehabilitation of safai karamcharis throughout the country.

According to the National Commission for Safai Karamcharis, the progress "has not been altogether satisfactory." As a result it has benefited only "a handful of safai karamcharis and their dependents. One of the reasons for unsatisfactory progress of the Scheme appears to be inadequate attention paid to it by the State Governments and concerned agencies." When confronted with the existence of manual scavenging and dry latrines within their jurisdiction, state governments often deny their existence altogether or claim that a lack of water supply prevents states from constructing flush latrines. This despite the fact that a sum of Rs. 4,640,000,000 (US$116 million) was allocated to the scheme under the government's Eighth Five Year Plan. Activists claim that the resources, including government funds, exist for construction and for the rehabilitation of scavengers; what is lacking is the political will to do so. Members of the National Commission for Safai Karamcharis consider it imperative that the commission be "vested with similar powers and facilities as are available to the National Commission for Scheduled Castes and Scheduled Tribes." Currently the commission only has advisory powers and no authority to summon or monitor cases.

## Dalit Women Face Structural Discrimination

Even as compared to dalit men, dalit women do not have equal access to employment opportunities or justice mechanisms. They must contend with threats to their personal security, including trafficking and sexual violence. "The dalit woman faces triple discrimination because she is an untouchable, of a poor class and is a woman," the report quotes the National Campaign on Dalit Human Rights (NACDOR) as saying.

## Untouchability is Very much Alive

Residential segregation of dalits is prevalent across the country, in violation of India's obligations under Article 3 of the ICERD.

Segregation is also seen in schools, in access to public services, and in access to services operated by the private sector. In his 1999 annual report, the UN special rapporteur on contemporary forms of racism, racial discrimination, xenophobia and related intolerance found "untouchability" to be "very much alive" in rural areas. A recently published survey investigating the extent of 'untouchability' in 565 villages in 11 Indian states found that the practice continues to profoundly affect the lives and psyches of millions of dalits. 'Untouchability' practices were documented in almost 80% of the villages surveyed.

Dalits are denied equal access to public places such as police stations, government ration shops, post offices, schools, water facilities and village council offices. More than 20% of dalits do not have access to safe drinking water. Only 10% of dalit households have access to sanitation (as compared to 27% for non-dalit households), and the vast majority of dalits depend on the 'goodwill' of upper-caste community members for access to water from public wells. Dalits are also excluded from, or receive discriminatory treatment at private businesses such as food stalls, barber shops and cinemas.

Strict prohibitions on marriage and other social interaction between dalits and non-dalits violate the rights of dalits to marry and choose their spouses. Inter-caste marriages are frequently extra-judicially punished by acts of public lynching, murder, rape, beatings and other sanctions against the couple and their relatives. In one of the worst examples of this, on August 6, 2001, in Uttar Pradesh, an upper-caste boy and a lower-caste girl were publicly hanged by members of their own families for refusing to end an inter-caste relationship.

Dalits are routinely and frequently denied entry into places of worship. Some dalits have responded to ill-treatment by upper-caste Hindus by converting *en masse* to Buddhism, Christianity and Islam. However, the loss of constitutional privileges upon conversion (to Christianity or Islam) is a serious impediment to dalits' freedom to choose their religion. In recent times, the introduction of anti-conversion legislation in several states has made religious conversion extremely difficult, if not impossible. Tragically, even conversion does not guarantee escape since 'untouchability' is practised across all faiths in India. Dalits are also systematically denied the right to own property. Landlessness -- encompassing lack of access to land, inability to own land, and forced evictions — constitutes a crucial element in the subordination of dalits, says the report. Land reform legislation is neither implemented nor properly enforced. When dalits do manage to acquire land, access to it is often denied. In 2004, the dalits of Kalapatti village, Tamil Nadu, were forced to flee after an attack in which upper-caste neighbours burned and destroyed over 100 dalit homes.

## Discrimination is Not Secured for Dalit Children

Dalit children face consistent hurdles in their access to education. Ninety-nine per cent of dalit students are enrolled in government schools that lack basic infrastructure, classrooms, teachers and teaching aids. They are made to sit in the back of the classroom and endure verbal and physical harassment by teachers and students. According to the UN special rapporteur on the right to education, teachers have been known to declare that dalit pupils "cannot learn unless they are beaten". The effect of such abuse is borne out by the low literacy and high dropout rates for dalits. Upper-caste hostility toward dalits' education is linked to the perception that dalits are either incapable of being educated, or, if educated, will pose a threat to village hierarchies and power relations, says the report.

## Claim their Rights Face Swift, Brutal Retribution

Attempts by members of the dalit community to demand their rights, or to lay claim to land that is legally theirs are consistently met with economic boycotts or retaliatory violence. For example, in Punjab, on January 5, 2006, dalit labourer and activist Bant Singh, seeking prosecution of the people who gang raped his daughter, was beaten so severely that both his arms and one leg had to be amputated.

In an incident that enraged dalits all over India and shocked people across the country after it belatedly made national headlines on September 26, 2006, in Khairlanji village, Maharashtra, a dalit family was killed by an upper-caste mob, after the mother and daughter were stripped, beaten and paraded through the village and the two brothers brutally beaten. They were attacked because they refused to let upper-caste farmers take away their land. After widespread protests at the police's failure to arrest the perpetrators, some of those accused in the killing were finally arrested and the policemen and medical officers who had failed to do their job were suspended from duty.

On February 1, 2007, the European Parliament found India's efforts to enforce laws protecting dalits to be "grossly inadequate," adding that "atrocities, untouchability, illiteracy, [and] inequality of opportunity continue to blight the lives of India's dalits".

"International scrutiny is growing and with it the condemnation of abuses resulting from the caste system and the government's failure to protect dalits," said Brad Adams, Asia director at Human Rights Watch. "India needs to mobilise the entire government and make good on its paper commitments to end caste abuses. Otherwise it risks pariah status for its home-grown brand of apartheid."

"International outrage over the treatment of dalits is matched by growing national discontent," says Professor Smita Narula, faculty director of CHRGJ at the New York University School of Law, and co-author of the report. "India can't ignore the voices of 165 million citizens."

Indeed, 'Hidden Apartheid's' scathing indictment echoes a statement made months earlier by India's prime minister. On December 27, 2006, Dr Manmohan Singh became the first serving Indian prime minister to openly acknowledge the parallel between the practice of 'untouchability' and the crime of apartheid.

CHAPTER 5

# Facing Despair Struggles and Challenges of Dalit Women

India has celebrated its 62th year of Independence. The country is now recording 2-digit economic growth every year and successfully takes quite an important and dominant position in international politics and in the economic arena. The success of India is built up with the international reputation of well-educated human resources, "democratic and stabled" political circumstances, and promises of land, benefits and other resources to the foreign and national investors-which are all based on exploitation of Dalit women. In reality India remains the world leader in maternal mortality, female infanticide and foeticide, deaths due to preventative disease, and other indicators of human development. Even in 2007, in Raitara village of Vanarasi in Uttar Pradesh, a five-year-old Dalit girl is facing imminent death from starvation as the family being slaved in a farm for free labour. Likewise, vulnerable villagers, namely, rural women, meanwhile, get a lot of impacts in the gap between two faces of the country. Those bad indicators are always appeared in Dalit women.

The Dalits and the marginalised are still colonised by the feudal lords the Elites without freedom from caste discrimination. Indians have driven out the colonizers but not the one who are discriminating Dalits. For Dalit women, they are also coerced to be victimised in the patriarchy. Dalit women are bearing the burden of double day caste and sexual division of labour. Dalit women are demeaned and degraded and their body is a free terrain of colonization by men from other community. Dalit women are a deprived section and at the lowest level of economic and educational structures. They are poor, illiterate, sexually harassed, faces state, caste violence and exploited. Doubly, triply or multiply discriminated, Dalit women face a lot of struggles in daily bases otherwise just being overwhelmed with those surges of discrimination up to them. Without being struggling, Dalit women would be just left in despair.

The struggles, however, spread out to wide area of Dalit women's life-too broad to cover just with a book. The book, therefore, tries to show a piece of dimensions of the struggle-which helps the readers to understand the overall background of the exclusion of Dalit women-anti-Dalit women's tendency in historical context as well as in cultural context. Secondly, it would be taken up the violation against Dalit women in the culture of globalisation with detailed analysis on their socio economic including rights to livelihood. The violation is now intensifying and internationalised. And lastly, the paper would suggest people's movement based methodology to tackle with multiple discrimination against Dalit women, which can alternated with the course which was set by the top or the others. Also, in throughout the paper, many cases would be presented including nation-wide known incidents as well as local problems of Dalit women.

## Dalit Women-their Pathway of Struggles

### Caste Discrimination against Dalit Women in Hinduism

Although it is now in modern world, caste discrimination, an age-old practice that dehumanizes and perpetuates a cruel form of discrimination continues to be practiced. India where the practice is rampant despite the existence of a legislation to stop this, 160 million Dalits of which 49.96% are women continue to suffer discrimination. The discrimination that Dalit women are subjected to is similar to racial discrimination, where the former is discriminated and treated as untouchable due to descent, for being born into a particular community, while, the latter face discrimination due to colour. The caste system declares Dalit women as 'impure' and therefore untouchable and hence socially excluded. This is a complete negation and violation of women's human rights.

Dalit women are thrice discriminated, treated as untouchables and as outcastes, due to their caste, face gender discrimination being women and finally economic impoverishment due to unequal wage disparity, with low or underpaid labour. According to the Hindu caste hierarchy, there are four castes namely the Brahmins (priestly caste), the Kshatriya (warriors), the Vaishyas (traders) and the Shudras (menial task workers). Below this four-tier caste ladder there is another rung of peoples, who are called the untouchables (Panchamas). Among the untouchables, the status of women is further eroded and closely linked to the concept of purity. This is what the rigid, fundamentalist Hindu promotes through continuation of caste system, imposing the Brahminical values to maintain the caste system.

The creation of a number of Hindu religious books including the *Manusmriti, Atharva Vedas, Vishnu smriti,* and many others like these and their strict compliance by the Brahmans (upper priestly Hindu caste), led to a society in which equality between men and women was far from existent (Agarwal: 1999). Dr. B.R. Ambedkar, an architect of the Indian constitution, also makes it very clear in his article titled "The rise and fall of Hindu woman" that the root cause of suffering for women in India are these so called Hindu religious books (Ibid.). Books like the Manusmriti divide people into a stratified caste system and promote inequality between men and women (Thind: 2000 and Agarwal). According to the *Manusmriti,* women have no right to education, independence, or wealth (Thind: n.pag). It not only justifies the treatment of Dalit women as a sex object and promotes child marriage, but also justifies a number of violent atrocities on women as can be seen in the following verses (Agarwal and *Manusmitri*):

A man, aged thirty years, shall marry a maiden of twelve who pleases him. Or a man of twenty-four a0girl of eight years of age. If (the performance of) his duties would otherwise be impeded, he must marry sooner. (*Manusmitri* IX.94)

By a girl, by a young woman, or even by an aged one, nothing must be done independently, even in her own house." (*Manusmriti* V.147)

Her father protects (her) in childhood, her husband protects (her) in youth, and her sons protect (her) in old age; a woman is never fit for independence. (*Manusmriti* IX.3) Even the killing of a Dalit woman is explicitly justified as a minor offence for the Brahmins: equal to the killing of an animal (*Manusmitri*). If the killing of an untouchable was justified as a minor offence, you can imagine the treatment they received throughout their lives. In a male dominated society, Dalit women suffered unimaginable oppression, not only through caste, but gender too, from which there was no escape. The laws in the *Manusmriti* and other Vedic scriptures close all economic, political, social, educational, and personal channels through which Dalit women could be uplifted (Thind n.pag). The horrendous Laws in the *Manusmriti* were incorporated into Hinduism because they were favourable only to the Upper castes, which form the majority of India. Even today, in modern times, we see the severe oppression and exploitation of Dalit women. The Laws of the *Manusmriti* have a devastating effect on the level of education reached by Dalit women.

The caste discrimination inherited by birth leaves Dalit women facing multiple oppressions that violate their economic, political, social and cultural rights. The most deprived section of the society comprises of Dalit women who are the poorest, illiterate and easy targets for sexual harassment. The women face not just caste violence inflicted on them by the dominant castes, but also state violence.

## Dalit Women's Struggle and Hindu Culture

Culture, meanwhile, regardless of its history-traditional culture or modern culture-reflects positionality of peoples collectively with rules, values and norms. Culture is dynamic changes never static with identities and shared experiences. Family, religion, and education system used to be the main elements of culture. Culture is influenced by media. Rituals are always carried out by people, which are reinforcing the meanings of life. The traditional culture which is locally interacting, reconstitutes against this the cultural imperialism which is institutionalized which is the identity of cultural power. Culture of the Oppressed is to resist the culture of the dominant to bring freedom. Traditional culture has continuity of people's lives and respects moral codes adopted by people. The stories of the oppressed revealed through symbols and practices. People's culture is a culture of multiplicity which is dominant over other culture. This involves a political structure which is decentralized sensitive to local culture. The alternative cultural politics leads to cultural and social change. India is, essentially, home for many cultures mutually enriching contact with each other. Indian culture has come from Dravidian culture. Indian culture is a living force. It has a significant role in moulding the culture of Asia.

The Hinduism History which has continued degrading Dalit women through dogmas and concept of purity, then, affects culture which can work as a catalyst for progress of Dalit women's living environment. With Sanskritization which is hinduization a dominant model, the ideals and beliefs of the Brahminic practices are imposed on Dalits to adopt a life style with untouchablility practices. Sanskritization is an alien faith to Dalits, the spirituality of Dalits is replaced by Sanskritic spirituality. The Dalit life is incontinuation, that is, of dead and living are the integral spirituality of Dalit culture.

Brahminical culture endangers Dalits' identity and integrity. It enhances and annihilates Dalit culture instead of enriching the culture. The culture is reflection of resistance from the past to the present and moves to shape a blueprint for the future life which becomes a flowing stream. There is continuity of collective life in Dalit culture. In addition, modernization introduced consumerism and market economy which has destroyed ethos, value system, celebration, and affirmation of the culture of the people, particularly the culture of Rural Dalits. Traditional culture is a way of living and producing for life, to sustain life. But through imperialistic modern culture, the mode of production is set only for consumption. It is called as neo-colonization of traditional culture which is not the people's culture.

Meanwhile, what would be the question of duties of a wife? Who is the head of the family? Wives are devoted to their husbands and afraid of even mentioning the name of their husband. Barren woman considered to be *"amangalam"*, bad omen and inferior to others, to be a curse to the society. Puberty is viewed as 'flowering' stage in a girl's life, as pleasurable. Fertility, women are referred to mud waiting to receive seed. Woman in marriage are framed to be obedient and submissive wives. Motherhood is expected to be nurturing, fearful, good wives and bearers of worthy sons. Sexuality of fertility is socially permissible and sexual acts such as homosexual, lesbian behaviours are considered to be deviant, perverse and abnormal. Society allows multiple forms of sexual behaviour to co exist practically but not socially. Erotic literature such as Kamasutra hints at the existence of homosexual desire and love.

Diverse sexualities are present and celebrated in Hindu temple sculpture. Pro-life existence of non-normative sexual culture is significant. They reveal the norms that a society lives by, to be constructed rather than given, clearly authorized by systems of patriarchal power. Madurai Meenakshi, Queen of the city, becomes bride given away every year in marriage. Marriage ceremony is the history of female domestication and husbandry authority.

Although it has been praised diverse of sexuality of the "human beings" at the one side of Hindu concept, Fundamentalist, Hinduism excludes plurality of the people even in sexuality. Particularly, lower caste, labouring women, who are Dalit women-are treated as the sexual "property" of the men of the all caste. The other caste women are treated as good and lower caste Dalit women as bad women because of Dalit women social status is low, subordinated that is why they are made to be sexually available to other caste. Dalit women are marked as natural and fit victims of violation, contrast to upper caste women who are considered to be pure and custodians of chastity. Chastity of upper caste women could be taken up as big issue in their "culture" because of being submissive wives who is called *pativiratas*. The lower caste women are considered not to be chaste. Sexual purity is anticipated caste purity which is honoured by the society.

Dalit women follow the Rituals more than the Dalit men. Dalit women associate with earth. They put the earth on the forehead, the mixture of water and mud strained that water is given to babies. They are related directly with the earth which is the life source. Worshiping the trees, decorating trees with *Kungumam,* turmeric that is worshiping old trees and rocks with the decoration. Cultural programme of festivals is only moment for the Dalit women who get into trance (or being "possessed" so to say). It is the only time they express their inner feelings and speak against other caste men, husbands, and demanding arak the local alcohol, chicken, good food, and behave like goddess. Before transplanting, the seeds are germinated in pots and Dalit women carry them by singing songs. Dalit women worship the nature for better and more food to be produced. Dalit women's dances are *Kummi,* and following to them they have *Kulavai*-wherever they work they sing. To show the closeness with the nature, they sing songs about their forefathers, mothers, the children and they abuse the landlords through their songs. After the hard work in the day during the night they sit together and chat with each other. They use lot of proverbs while talking and fighting. They tease each other and their blood related men from their kin who are about to be married with them. They relate with each other, and while calling the person they will not use the name but the relationship. They sing when a baby is born, when a girl attains puberty and also *Oppari* death. These practices we never find with women of other caste.

Dalit women are very strong and they give birth to more children. Dalit women work equally with the men, that is, why they oppose male domination and prove that they are stronger than the men. Dalit women work hard to survive. They are very open-minded, innocent, and not exploiting others but exploited by others. They have good characters. Dalit women, everyday, relate themselves with people in four ways. 1) With their family members, children, husband, 2) With the traders who buy their products, 3) The other caste landlords who give them work, and 4) Relate with distant relatives during marriages, deaths. Now beyond this the new effort is that Dalit women attend conferences, meetings, workshops and training programs which allowed them to meet with many Dalit women.

Dalit women are illiterates. They know only work related to land. They have not achieved even as one persent politically. They remain only us voters. They have no chance of learning about the country, the other ethnic groups and languages. Not all the Dalit women are member of the movement as well as in the political party. They are not involved in politics. Dalit women leadership is also controlled by the men. Dalit women have their own language. They preserve their language of their land. They have their own justice that is they do not have permanent enemies amongst themselves. For many years they follow the Rituals of the land. They are different from other caste women because they do not depend on their men like others. They work equally with men. When the men were taking the spade, Dalit women are ready with their basket to take mud. Every work it is both Dalit men and women work equally. Dalit women are workers, and they are not slaves to their husbands. Dalit women have very strong resistance power which has to be sustained.

Dalit culture was destroyed after the invasion of Aryans. Dalits lived through the dominant Brahminical culture. Sanskritization of Dalit culture, based on pure and impure concept was thrust on the oppressed, downtrodden communities especially on Dalit women. Dalit culture was silenced and destroyed. Dalits through a war, resistance gave life to the culture that faced the death by the dominant culture. Dalit culture is liberation, freedom, solidarity, equality, a culture of resistance towards freedom. Dalit culture is preserved through various forms of theatre which is revolutionary, disturbs and leads to action which is political action.

Dalit women perform dance which is devoted to Mathamma the Kulathaivam. The dancer is, however, almost exploited as being expected to dance in an erotic way. This is religious sanctioned prostitution. The month of June (*Anni Matham* in Tamil Calendar) is the temple festival for five days. The temple is built, festival conducted, the 'Car' is held in front all by the other caste. Out of five days the Mathammas, Dalit girl children are given to the goddess believing those children will be cured by the healing power of goddess. Once the child is cured, she is married to the goddess and named after her. She becomes a powerful replica of Mathamma. Later on she is mocked and treated as a public property. In public places she is teased and her children born are face lot of humiliation in the school by other children.

Mathammas socially and economically exploited by the community. She lives on her own without the support of families. A Dalit woman, becomes a dancer, then sexually exploited ends her life with nothing but left out with diseases.

The dominant brahminical culture from which the Devadasi system is extended to Dalit community is prevailing Dalit women. Tamil Nadu Dalit Women's Movement (TNDWM), meanwhile, faced harassment even from Dalit men in the community for exposing the issue of Mathamma. The Dalit movement with patriarchal norms started publicly attacking leaders from TNDWM "individually". They are accused, through wall posters, public meetings and black mailings. TNDWM faced harassment confronting the caste and patriarchal nature of the communities which is also influenced by Hindutva ideology. Hindutva Ideology perpetuates hatred towards other religion and maintains the culture, the exploitative dominant culture through caste.

## Contemporary Oppression against Dalit Women

### At Special Economic Zones (SEZs)

For Dalit women, "trickle-down effect" theory, in which people can expect "trickled" benefits dropped down from the country or big companies' economic growth, is just a mirage, not a reality at all. The alienation is creating widespread discontent amongst farmers and common people all over India. The state, meanwhile, behaves as an agent of the corporation. The state government, which is essentially responsible to the citizen not only becomes advocates of the corporations but also acts as corporations. The state government itself takes away the land, especially agricultural lands, coastal lands with the coastal regulation zones, salt pans, and forest lands for SEZs. The land taken for SEZs, meanwhile, only 35% is used for industry and the rest for non-industrial purposes: recreation centre-and housing. Although people are raising their voice, the oppression from the state government is intensified.

In Nandigram, West Bengal, 17 villagers were shot to death with the protest against government taking away lands for corporation; chemical hubs of Salim group. Out of 17 killed 12 are Dalits. The people of Nandigram have lived in daily fear of retaliation when the Citizen's Committee entered to the district. The mission found that women were extremely apprehensive, begging the mission to spend the night with them.

The state, however, is not restoring land rights and titles to landless Dalit women. Land given to SEZs promoters is more than 1000 hectors which obviously violates Land Reform Act. SEZs will not create employment for local Dalit women but it will push away Dalit women because SEZs employs skilled and educated workers. Communities, especially Dalit women in unorganised sectors, will not be employed in SEZs.

In Tuticorin, Tamil Nadu, for example, another Nandigram is about to be occurred. Even though there are vociferous protests against the Tata's titanium dioxide plant to be situated at Sathankulam of the district, there are a lot of oppressions from the ruling party to the pantchayat leaders to urge them to accept the project. Also, even before the pantchayat leaders accept the project, the state government made an agreement with the company for establishing the Rs 2,500-crore titanium dioxide project. Negligence of local people voices in the politics and economy in SEZs definitely erodes the livelihood of the most vulnerable groups in the region, the Dalit Women.

Besides of land conflict occurred by SEZs, the insecurity of women is intensified. Those who work as manual labourer in big factories are mostly poor women, such as Dalit women. When returning from the factory to their home late at night, women need to worry about their safety. In Ulundurpettai taluk of Villupuram district, there were 3 rapes – one was Dalit woman, and other women were from other community. All are workers in big factories, and attacked on the way to go home from their workplace.

SEZs are not only taking away the land, political rights, and dignity, but also depriving of Dalit women's opportunities for self-improvements, such as educations. In northern Tamil Nadu, where Society for Rural Education and Development (SRED) develops various community-based activities, it has been introduced between Chennai and Kancheepuram. From all over India and foreign countries-e.g. Reliance Group which runs many business all over India, Nokia, Hyundai, and Samsung-have invested to the zones and established huge factories along with the super highway which connects Chennai, Kancheepuram, and Bangalore. The establishment of SEZs firstly affects peasant landless Dalit women by displacing them from the lands without any compensation. They employ not only skilled workers, but also manual labourers from Dalit villages, mostly young women for manual works.

Buses with the company logo are waiting for Dalit young girls early in the morning in front of the Dalit villages. Dalit girls are encouraged to go for work with SEZs than continuing for higher education. Dalit girls cannot have opportunities to learn any skills, even as "on the job trainings", and would face the unemployment as "uneducated woman" when the economy goes bad. Very recently, the Swiss based international lingerie company-Triumph has decided to invest to the area in order to establish key factory for underwear business throughout of the Subcontinent. The key of the final decision of investment was the quality of traditional technology in Garment industry, which Rural Dalit Women have conserved for many years in order to sustain their rural life (The Indian Express). Meanwhile, they are planning to sell those women's underwear for 400-1000 Rupees which is almost impossible price for local Dalit women, whereas the provider of the skills would face of insecurity.

## At Dalit Women's Workplace

The studies conducted on the impact of floriculture on the health of Dalit women in Santana Gopalapuram were on half an acre of land there are 10 workers: both men and women. According to the villagers, floriculture has been around for last 20 years, but in the last 5 years, it has intensified and more farmers are moving to floriculture. Earlier they used to grow groundnut and rice. Women specifically mentioned that they have to get up early and finish household work before going to pluck flowers. They work from 6 am in the farm and they can eat only after 10 am at the earliest. Also, due to constantly bending and plucking of flowers for almost 6 hours for low wages, at a stretch, there is chest, back and leg pain. Pesticides are sprayed almost when they are on the field, and smell persists for 3 days or more. Women are suffering from excessive white discharge, rolling feeling in the stomach, hysterectomy, and even tumour in uterus.

Floriculture affects also the rights to education of Dalit girl children. Dalit girl children are employed in order to pluck the flower before going to school and after the school. Dalit girl children are not able to recheck what they have learnt in the school and this turns into potential factor of drop-out. Of course with the health problem with pesticide, Dalit girls are failed to access to the school as well. Even some of the family members fell down with diseases caused by the pesticide this affects children's rights to go to school. In Kollathur where the agricultural lands were taken away for aqua farm for exportation which is located by the Buckingham Canal, at the backwater area of east-coast of Kancheepuram District, Tamil Nadu, is a Dalit village. Dalits have worked for cultivation of cashew nuts, prawn and fish catching in the backwater. In 2004, a Chennai based entrepreneur, F. Bartholome has obtained the license from the Aquaculture Authority and opened an industrial prawn farm called Chinna Aqua Farm. The farm came up on agricultural land, right alongside backwaters. The farm discharges untreated effluences from the farm which salinated agricultural lands and the backwaters.

The Aqua farming in India was promoted by the government in 90's for one of the international business strategies of the country without thinking about the environmental impacts. Soon after, in 1996, the Indian Supreme Court has regulated the use of coastal area for environmental reason, including creeks and backwaters which polluted water bodies. Running the farm without registration and permission shall be a criminal offence, but in practice, Bartholome's farm, for example, successfully got the license although it violates the regulation which stated in the law due to the lack of seriousness in the implementation of the law and due to corruption.

Kollathur aqua farm is located on agricultural land whereas agricultural land should not be used for Aqua farming. Bartholome himself is also connected strongly with politicians. Ironically even after the inclusion of regulations, the production of prawns in the area for the exportation is increasing.

The land has been transformed from traditional agricultural lands for people's food to money making products for exportation. And now, with the toxic waste the Aqua farm cause loss of agricultural production which affects directly the daily food production of the Dalit villagers. Also, prawn catching and mussels collection by the Dalit women was totally affected with the pollution. This causes food insecurity as well as livelihood insecurity to Dalit women.

The toxic waste polluted not only plants and animals but also human beings, mostly Dalit women who work in the field and with the toxic polluted back waters directly. Women got itching, skin disease and dimming of eyesight. Ground water has been salinated, and Dalit women lost adequate water for agriculture as well as for drinking. Not only endangered the livelihood by losing their work, but also women had to suffer from the physical pain by the disease, and from no money for the medical cost for treatment. The Dalits of Kollathur village are suffering from impacts of the pollution directly and indirectly due to the false cases many villagers who struggled against the farm were beaten up and charged. Just in the last two years, more than 40 young men from this village of 4000 attend court cases four times in a month; need to pay a lot of cost for legal procedure; cost for advocates as well as transportation cost to the court.

The increasing vulnerability in rural traditional life encourages not only industrial transformation but also migration. At Thirumalpur of Vellore district of Tamil Nadu where women earn only Rs.12.50 as wage for half-a-day's labour for agriculture work forced them to migrate to neighbouring State to earn more than Rs.50 per day. The Dalit women leave their children with their elders. Both men and women migrate they are made to stay in big halls or in schools. The women migrant workers sleep in one corner and their husbands as well as other men in other side vice-a-versa. They have no privacy they rely on near by pump sheds, lakes and ponds to bathing and washing their clothes, which are very insecure places. Every time they migrate from their village for a maximum of 20 days. The contractor employs them with an assignment to carry out harvest in 20 acres of land. After taking his commission of 30%, the contractors pay the rest to the workers. Women lose freedom and dignity in bad working conditions when they migrate.

## Dalit Women's Struggles

### Challenge of Civil Society

Having faced the deprivation of human rights of Dalit Women, what kinds of actions have been taken by the civil society? In order to achieving "uplifting" or "development" of peoples in disadvantage class, Development NGOs as well as international institutions emphasize recently "rights based approach". The United Nations Development Programme has set so-called

Millennium Development Goals in order to "monitor" the implementation of the goal for human development. But those are neither our approach nor our goals. As it can be seen in Dalit women's situation, people are struggling for their livelihood, and the movement should reject those meaningless mercies from the top. The movement, in fact, pursues "struggle based approach" and "People's Goals". The "Right based approach" is a language of donors. This makes movements isolated in each cells. People's movements are compromising not confronting. We should rather keep up the "Struggle based approach", which leads movements to bring changes in people's lives. The peoples around so-called 'civil society', therefore, do not share the problem with Dalit women. The civil society is narrowing down by becoming fundamentalists under the name of "rights based approach". At the citizens' forum for celebrating $60^{th}$ years of independence, which was taken place at Bangalore, for example, there are a lot of oppositions to serve beef cutlet as a choice of the meal service. As the reality, however, there are people who have beef. Inclusiveness is important and not to exclude efforts of various initiatives. There is a need to join hands to stay with the people in multiple struggles against multiple discriminations and exploitations.

## Dalit Children

SRED, thus, extends the area of activities in various levels: from local to international level. For local level, if there are caste based oppression against Dalit women, immediately stay at the side of the people to protest against the oppression. In Rangapuram village, Dalit children are not allowed to go to school because the Non-Dalits blocked the way to go to school. SRED immediately sent fact finding mission of people's movement, such as Tamil Nadu Dalit Women's Movement, and made a petition to make a safe road to school-going children. When making a petition, police forces was sent from many place to the district educational office of Kancheepuram, and they immediately arrested unlawfully activists of Dalit women. This year, at last, the new road for children was successfully launched at the village.

In Anandapuram, village, without the bridge over the river, Dalit children are not able to cross the river in rainy season to go to the school. Dalit mothers, meanwhile, who work in the field, definitely need the place to send children whilst they are working. Since 2004, SRED launched Dalit day care centres, to provide space for children to play, to sing, to paint, to learn and to prepare for the formal school. Primarily the centres are used for day care centre, which enable Dalit women who have to go to the field to leave the children at safer place. After this day care centre, they will go to primary school.

The centres are, however, used for multi-purpose. Working children can get education after work in evening class. The centres are playing crucial role for school going children as the safer place after school for doing further learning. Some times the centres are used for meeting purposes. At Anandapuram, with the warm support from Nagano branch of Buraku Liberation League, successfully established a centre. But meanwhile, have limitation of the budget to launching the centre for many villages, therefore re-arrange meeting room to Day care centre. Actually Sred staff members are doing secretary work just by hearing children's voice, and also frequently have a discussion where there are a lot of paintings and learning materials for children. In the community based work, found out that the similar situation to other children, namely, Irulas, Tribal people as well as quarry workers. When families remain as bonded labourers, when parents have to take children to quarry work place because of lack of finance to prepare for their study, families migrate seeking for their work. Children's rights to education are denied. The centres and the programmes in the centres are particularly designed by paying attention with caste-free environment, and children are ensured to be away from any discriminated thoughts, practices, and behaviours.

Dalit communities, particularly girl children, face difficulty also in higher educations. Just only with falling to financial difficulty affected by Tsunami, Dalit girl students were sent back to their home without continuing the second year of the course whilst they managed for the first year of the course. Even getting the best scores at the twelfth grade, Bharati, a Dalit girl faced difficulties to find appropriate scholarship schemes and resulted to give up their education (nursing course). SRED collects supports for those Dalit girls and help them to continue their higher education.

## Dominant Culture

Supporting of Dalit women by providing services: children's day care centre, and urgent scholarship is of course one of our struggle against dominant culture of globalisation. Likewise, SRED and TNDWM also directly support the struggles for the victims of culture of casteism and patriarchy: such as Mathammas.

Our approach to Mathamma begins with their name and status. Mathammas refused to be called as Mathammas. The first change with in them is to have new names, and to remove the 'Sacred Pottu Thali'. The movement of Mathammas: Mathamma Liberation Movement was formed primarily to stop the practice of giving the Dalit girls to Mathammas. During the festivals, Mathammas from the movement were vigilant that no woman, no Mathamma dancing is taking place publicly. Now the temple festivals dress up men as women and the dance continues.

In Kaverirajapuram during temple festival the leaders stopped Mathamma dance with the help of police. But the movement found that it was the wrong strategy as it created incredible views from the villagers from other movements. The Mathamma movement is, now, visiting villages where Mathamma temples are, and conducting meetings, cultural programs, explaining the hurdles they went through by themselves. They keep persuading by saying that 'Stop the practice of Mathammas'.

Mathamma leaders from the movement contested in election with many threats and boycotts. They, however, claimed equal status, and went through all the procedure of the election which itself is an empowering process challenged the system, the community and the men in the villages. Devi, the leader of the movement who was contested, explains her experience in the election as follows;

*During the election campaign, those who are against me strongly said: "why do you nominate yourself for the election? You are Mathamma and who will vote for you?" But I didn't accept any words in the remarks. I did not win this time, but it was brilliant experience. There are a lot of problems that Mathammas are facing. If I become a ward member, I will give the rights for the mathammas and totally I would like to stop this practice. I will make employment, education and housing, and all basic needs-I will try to get them through government.*

They stopped dancing of exploitation but started to dance to liberate others because she is to be liberated. Now, some of them have leadership and empowerment training with the support of Yasuda literacy foundation of Buraku Liberation and Human Rights Research Institution. With the training, the women gains more force to struggle against the dominant culture.

Kollathur women are also challenging to the huge dominant entity by empowering themselves in the movement. They organised Kollathur Dalit Women's Sangam, and are fighting in the struggles in legal process as well as in their livelihoods. They keep embracing a slogan: "Close the Aqua Farm". Globalisation emphasises efficiency and competitive culture. Thus it appears that for the majority of Dalits and poor, globalisation has meant further deprivation. The struggles against globalised economy are also, for Dalit women, struggle against culture of dominant casteism and patriarchy.

## Invitation from Asian Rural Women's Conference

Apart from the community and grassroots based challenge for overcoming the difficulty surged up to Dalit women, the SRED and Tamil Nadu Dalit Women's Movement are trying to organising forums on rural women. Amongst Dalit women 81.45% lives in rural area. The globalisation, meanwhile, affects firstly the vulnerable sectors in rural area, where, obviously, Dalit women are working. But also, the rural women in other community, such as Irulas Tribes, Narikuravars, Dhobis, and fisherfolks are suffering in the similar situation. Not only in India, but also, there are many rural women who are struggling in current political economy of globalisation. The concerns on international trade, international agro-business, and patents to traditional seeds are all rural Dalit women's agenda as well as women from other community. Actually, Dalit women flew to Hong Kong to take an action at the 6 ministerial meeting of WTO to protest against promotion of pesticides and genetically modified foods. The forum, Asian Rural Women's Conference, which is taking place on 6-8th March, 2008 in Arakkonam/ Chennai, India, is putting together marginalised women in the region who are against imperialist oppression. By asserting dignity of rural women, which cannot be seen in any other rights-based documents, many marginalised women in the region create the power to struggle. The conference will develop a unity of analysis from the experiences of rural women and the situation of women in the context of a globalised world. Last July, some Indian women's organisations gathered at our office, and conducted National consultation on rural women, which of course include latest developments on rural Dalit women. On 31 July to 2 Aug, presenters from some Asian countries gathered in Manila, and have issued rural women's declaration. Of course caste based discrimination was clearly mentioned in the context of the struggle against patriarchal globalisation. Meanwhile, the Manila conference did not have any Japanese participants, particularly from Buraku community. It would be grateful for Dalit women to share the issue with Buraku women in March for "Rights, Empowerment and Liberation", which is the main slogan of the conference.

Asian Rural Women's Conference would also be the occasion for cultural expression of oppressed rural women. Dalit women are using *'Thappu'*, the drums, to show that drums can be beaten up by women not only by men. Drum beatings are to give life to the Dalit culture which was killed by the Brahminical culture. There are Dalit women's dances as well, such as *Kolatam, Oyilatam, Karagattam, Thappatam, Paraiyattam,* which all accompany with the drum music. The drums have languages that the Dalit women beat all rituals. *Parai* the drum is beaten by *Paraiyer* is the myth and the *parai* was treated like the Dalits as 'untouchable' by the dominant culture. The Dalit women revived the beating of *parai* and revolted against the dominant culture by giving new, revolving meaning to *Parai.*

Dalit women beat drum to oppose the domination which is systematic, structural and multiple. Beating drum is to destroy the ideology of domination. Beating drum is to beat up the monoculture and to bring inter-culture of the oppressed, downtrodden, the broken, people together towards liberating humanity, transformation to achieve Equality, Freedom, Justice for a 'Humane' society through cultural and social society. Dalit women in Tamil Nadu are ready to drum out the globalised patriarchal fundamentalism, which produces casteism and gender discrimination, with the solidarity of other minority women.

# CHAPTER 6 Violation of Human Rights of Dalit Women: Issues, Factors and Concerns

All human beings have the right to live as human beings. Human rights are not conferred or given. They already exist in society. The concept of human rights aims at protection of rights like right to life, liberty and property. These rights are attributed to human beings irrespective of class, caste, gender, colour and religion. The Universal Declaration of Human Rights was unanimously adopted by the UN General Assembly on December 10th, 1948. The preamble of Indian constitution adequately empowers the central and state government to eliminate human rights violation in the country.

Inspite of these international and national declarations and resolutions, human rights are violated in different countries all over the world. In Indian society, due to the social barriers such as castetism, untouchability, patriarchy, disparity, superstition, religious exploitation and class variations, specific groups are becoming weaker and marginalised. These groups are facing the problems of identity crisis, deprivation, discrimination and atrocities. These marginalised groups are also identified and recognised as dalits, SC (scheduled castes) ST (scheduled tribes), OBC (other backward castes) NT (nomadic tribes) DT (denotified tribes) religious and linguistic minorities.

Violence on human beings in any form results in violation of human rights. Human rights of dalits and women in general are normally violated by high castes and powerful communities to practice and exhibit patriarchy and castetism. But human rights of dalit women are violated extremely and in peculiar form. Dalit women are in worst position than dalits in general, in terms of sex ratio, wages, employment, occupation, assets, education, health, social mobility and political participation (Bandhu cited in Rao, 2003). Hence, it is important to discuss the status of dalit women and various problems they face even after 60 years of independence. Dalit women to suggest some alternatives to combat violation of their rights for social justice and equality. Explanation of relevant terms such as 'dalit', 'dalitism', and 'dalit women', is given below to broaden understanding about the issue.

## Dalit

Dalit ('oppressed' or 'broken') is not a new word. Apparently it was used in the 1930's as a Hindi and Marathi translation of 'depressed classes'. The British used this term for what are now called the scheduled caste. Dr. Ambedkar chose the term 'broken men', as English translation of 'Dalit', to refer to the original ancestors of the untouchables. Dalit Panthers, the youth activists from dalit community revived the term and in their 1973 manifesto expanded its reference to include the scheduled tribes, neo Buddhists, the working people, the landless and poor peasants, women and also those who are being exploited politically, economically in the name of religion.

### Dalitism

Dalitism essentially implies conditions of subjugation; economic, political, social and cultural. Dalitism also embodies different degrees of marginalisation. It includes not only marginalized status in the economic sphere but also in cultural, political, religious and social domains. That means Dalitism symbolizes marginalisation. It is a well known fact that marginalisation denies basic human rights and social justice.

### Dalit Women

Dalit women are one of the most marginalized segments in the society. The condition of dalit women is more vulnerable than non-dalit women. Dalit women are suffering from multi-disadvantages:

a) of being dalit i.e socio-economically and culturally marginalized section,

b) being women and sharing the gender based inequalities and subordination (Jogdand, 1995)

To explore these and other crucial issues concerning dalit women there is need to discuss some basic facts concerning the vulnerable situation of dalit women.

## Vulnerable Status of Dalit Women

It is easy for the historically dominating caste and gender to violate human rights of dalit women who are at the lowest rung of the hierarchical ladder. The type of violence inflicted on dalits is in the form of severest violation of human rights. Dalit and tribal women are raped as part of an effort by upper caste leaders, land lords and police to suppress movements to demand payment of minimum wages, to settle share cropping disputes or to reclaim lost lands. The recent incident of Khairlanji Massacare is not something new. A dalit family had refused to let upper caste villagers built a road through their fields. Hence on September, 29th, 2006, Bhaiyalal Bhotmange's family, – wife Surekha, daughter Prinyanka and two sons were killed by the villagers of Khairlangi in Bhandra district of Maharashtra. They were first attacked with huge iron chains and than abused by the other caste women of the village. Surekha and Priyanka were paraded naked and raped, and later, their bodies were mutilated and thrown into a pond. (Hindustan Times, 14th November, 2006)

This shows that dalit women are easy targets for any perpetrator Upper caste considers them to be sexually available. Hence they are largely unprotected by the state machinery. Further, there is prevalence of violence, making dalit women eat human excreta, parading them naked, gang-rape, murder, dacoity, robbery and burning of their huts or communities. These are the types of crime, which violate their human rights (Human Watch Report, 1998). According to SC/ST commission report between 1981 and 1986 about 4000 dalit women became victim of rape. In 1993 –94 this figure rose to 798 and 992 respectively. This means annually about 700 dalit women fall prey to sexual assault by high caste people. (Pal and Bhargav, 1999)

The main complaints of the poorer dalit women are that they have no good houses. In urban areas most of them stay in unhygienic slums and in rural areas their houses are away from main stream society (Pillai, cited in Michael 1999). Under conditions of grinding poverty and severe exploitation at work place, dalit women also suffer caste specific ban on water access from upper castes and may be beaten up in their own houses as well. A poem by a dalit poetess Teressama, a teacher from Guntur puts the situation in the following words:

*We go to work for we are poor But the same silken beds mock us, While we are ravished in broad daylight. Ill-starred our horoscopes are Even our tottering husbands Lying on the cots in the corner Hiss and shout for revenge If we cannot stand their touch* (Dietrich in Rao 2003)

At the outset, prevailing caste and secondary status of women in the society is largely responsible for violation of human rights of dalit women. To understand the root cause of the situation it is essential to examine basic factors responsible for their vulnerability.

## Socio-cultural and Religious Factors

First and foremost dalit women are victims of social, religious and cultural practices like Devdasis and Jogins. In the name of these practices, village girls are married to God by their helpless parents. These girls are then sexually exploited by the upper caste landlords and rich men and directed in to trafficking and prostitution. In his autobiography, Kale (1994) has described a ritual called 'chira'. The literal meaning of the word 'chira', is to cut or break. In this ritual when a girl from the lower caste community reaches the age of puberty, an elderly prestigious man from the higher caste breaks the hymen of the girl child by sexual act. This ritual is performed in a way to make the girl accept this fact as a routine practice. The 28$^{th}$ report of SC/ST commission reported that in February 1986 there were about ten thousand Jogins belonging to SC in Nizamabad district of Andhra Pradesh. The survey submitted by the district collector to Schedule Caste Finance Corporation revealed prevalence of 15,850 cases. Eighty percent of these Jogins belonged to SC (Pal and Bhargav,1999). This data is just an example of one district of the country. Practices such as Chira, Jogins, Devdasi which are prevalent even today are harmful and threaten the dignity of dalit women and violate their human rights (P. Sainath, not dated).

## Educational Status

Low level of education is a problem in itself and in turn gives rise to many other problems. (Thorat and Umakant, 2004). In 1991, literacy among the dalit women was indeed quite low. In rural areas only 19.46 percentage women were literate. A report published by Ministry of Welfare, Government of India in 1998 showed that there is much difference in the literacy rate of dalits and non-dalits in general, and gender specific. Literacy rate of non-dalits is 64.13 % and literacy rate of women is 39.29 %, where as dalit women's literacy rate is only 23.76 % (Paswan and Jaidev, 2002). There is a large disparity in the literacy rate due to wide spread prejudice based on castetism and patriarchy against dalits and women in general and dalit women in particular.

## Economic Deprivation and Unemployment

A careful look at the economic situation of dalit women reveals that their work force structure is such that they rarely own any land. A large majority of them are agricultural labourers. The rate of unemployment among them is also quite high. About 90% of women working in unorganized sector are mainly from lower castes (Jogdand 1999). In 1991, about 71% of dalit women workers in rural area were agricultural labourers. Only 19% of them owned land (Pal and Bhargav 1999).

A prominent researcher and sociologist while sharing her experience from a research on gender and land issue, informed that, when she enquired with dalit women about land owned by them in their names, they wondered about permissibility of owning land in their name. This indicates that neither do they own any land nor are they aware of their rights on land. When enquiries were made with Stri-mukti sanghatana and Prerana, Mumbai based organizations working on the issue of rag picking and prostitution respectively, to ascertain the proportion of dalit women in these occupations, it was learnt that NGOs usually do not keep record of caste (Tirmare, 2004). However, Human Rights Watch Report (1998) mentioned that a large number of dalit women are engaged in unclean, inferior occupation such as sweeping, scavenging and working in dumping grounds, rag picking and also in prostitution. These women have to face steep discrimination in the matters of social relation and employment due to their engagement in these occupations.

## Health and Nutrition Status

Dalit women's daily diet is the leftover of family meals, inadequate in quantity and quality. Health services are either not available in case of illness or unaffordable even if available. In addition to that, due to early marriage and too many pregnancies their health is always at risk. If birth control is practiced at all, 91% cases of tubetomy are performed on the women who have to carry the burden of family planning. In an overall situation where dalits are prone to ailments in general, women suffer from more serious and more varied kind of sickness. More than 80% of women in reproductive age group (15 to 45) are anemic. Poor health status of dalit women pushes her then into more vulnerable situation (Bandhu cited in Rao 2003)

## Political Status

Women constitute half of total population, but are unable to get equal share in active politics. Their socio-economic status directly depends on their participation in politics. Political parties in India speak much about equality of women but have totally ignored the dalit women (Jogdand, 1999). Traditionally, leadership in the village was confined to 'rural elites', who were aged and belonging to higher castes. In the year 1993, 73rd amendment in the constitution granted reservation to dalits, tribals and women in local government.

This amendment made it compulsory that one third of the seats reserved for dalits be filled by dalit women. In some states, there has been little or no acceptance of reservation for the lower castes and dalit women by the upper castes. This has resulted in atrocities against panchayat members including women. Dalits who stood for election were beaten, and dalit women were raped and ill-treated. The members of the higher castes, who are not prepared to relinquish power to the lower castes, grabbed their land. An easier method to retain power is to put-up proxy candidates but keep the control in the hands of the dominant castes, always men (Kumar, 2006).

The incapacity of women, particularly dalit women, to assert their rights is at the root of the problem. The reservation for dalits, particularly for women, is accepted in form but seldom in substance. Any change in the status quo is resisted. Dalit women's sitting on chairs is seen as threat to social hierarchy. So, the upper castes in the village vetoed chairs in the panchayat office (P. Sainath in Rao 2003) Dalit women also faced many problems in performing their duties due to illiteracy, lack of information and dependency on the male members of their families. An important obstacle is the no-confidence motion against dalit women as pradhan by the dominant sections. Rural elites are unable to accept the power, which has been given into the hands of the poorer and disadvantaged women (Manipal, 1998). Despite recognition and legal sanction for political rights, rigid caste system and patriarchy directly and indirectly has been suppressing dalit women and violating their political rights.

This proves that human rights of dalit women are violated right from her family to the society at large by one and all. All these factors are largely responsible for the precarious position of dalit women as far as their social, cultural, religious, economic, health and political status in the society is concerned. These factors force them to mutely allow violation of their civic and human rights. Thus they become victims of universal violence.

## Efforts to Protect Human Rights of Dalit Women

With the realization that violence is one of the potent threats to the peaceful existence of human beings, whole hearted and all round efforts are made at international, national and local level. The preamble to the Universal Declaration of Human Rights (UDHR) serves as a foundation and philosophy of Human rights. There are a host of international conventions including those for prevention and punishment of genocide and elimination of all forms of racial and gender based discrimination (chitnis 2005)

The World Conference Against Racism (WCAR) related to racial discrimination, xenophobia and intolerance held in Durban, South Africa in 2001, brought the issue of caste and untouchability based discrimination on the agenda of UN Conference in Durban. Among the several organisations, the National Campaign on Dalit

Human Rights (NCDHR) – a collective of dalit NGOs, other NGOs, academicians', activists and large number of supporters spearheaded the national campaign in India for inclusion of the issue of caste and untouchability based discrimination in the Durban Conference (Thorat and Umakant, 2004). The preamble of Indian constitution adequately empowers the central and state government to eliminate human right violation in the country (Pal and Bhargav, 1999) Article 17 of the constitution provides for removal of untouchability. Based on this article Protection of Civil Rights Act' (PCR), was passed in 1955. However, there was no conviction/ under this Act hence, Thirty-four years after the introduction of PCR Act, the Scheduled Caste and Schedule Tribes (Prevention of Atrocities) Act 1989 was enacted to bring various forms of atrocities to an end. In this Act the complainant is given more weightage. There are stringent provisions against the police for negligence (Pandit)

## Emerging Identity of Dalit Women and Formation of Dalit Women's Organisations

The focus on education of low caste women is one of the important factors responsible for the emerging identity of Dalit women. Reformist intervention by Savitribai and Mahatma Phule of opening school for untouchable girls way back in 1848 was a turning point for changing status of dalit women. (Chakrvarti in Rao 2003). Dr. Ambedkar's thought and action made important differences in the lives of dalit women. His movement and especially his organisations encouraged many dalit women to become educated to be active in public life and to gain leadership, self respect in the contemporary period encouraged women to participate in organisation for dalit women at regional, state and national level. [Zelliot in Rao 2003).

After independence in 1960's and 70's, the dalit movement and women's movement emerged to demand their rights against caste and gender respectively. However, specific problems of dalit women were not acknowledged by these movements. Hence in 1990's there were several special, independent and autonomous assertions of dalit women's identity; a case in point is the formation of National Federation for Dalit Women (NFDW) and All India Dalit Women's Forum (AIDWF) at the state level. The Maharashtra

Dalit Mahila Sanghatana (MDMS) was formed in 1995. A year earlier, the women's wing of Bhartiya Republican Party (BRP) and the Bahujan Mahila Sangha (BMS) was set up the Bahujan Mahila Parishad. In December 1996, at Chandrapur, a Vikas Vanchit Dalit Mahila Parishad (VVDMP) was organised and a proposal to commemorate 25th December (the day on which Ambedkar had set Manu smriti on fire) as Bhartiya Smriti Divas was advanced. The Christi Mahila Sanghatana, an organisation of Dalit Christian Women was established in 1997. These organisations have come together on several issues such as celebration of Bhartiya Stree Mukti Divas and on the issue of reservation for OBC women in parliament bodies. Indian Association of Women Studies (IAWS) network with dalit feminist across different regions had brought special issues on problems and identity of dalit women (Rege in Rao 2003)

Several efforts have been made since independence to secure human rights of women in general and dalit women in particular. Despite this, human rights of dalit women are seen to be violated in different forms. Such infringement of human rights echoes the need of evolving suitable mechanism to empower dalit women to assert for equal rights and justice in order to live a dignified life.

## Mechanism to Strengthen the Capacity of Dalit Women

To be human is to respond to human sufferings and pain with compassion and effective concern. It is not enough to feel with the dalit women in their pain, There is more need for effective action, otherwise it would be just sentimentalism' says Sequeira in his article 'Human Response to Dalit Women (Jogdand 1999) The needs and the problems of dalit women differ with city, village, area and caste. It is essential to keep in mind that dalit women are not mere individuals but belong to a sociological and dialectical system. Therefore to recognise the system and to prohibit violation, first and foremost proper perspectives about the issues has to be developed among all by considering following suggestions:

### Awareness for Assertion

Extensive reading of available literature can be done by young generation to understand the profile and problems of dalit women. Factual incidents & success stories of dalit women namely, 'We made History Too' by Meenakshi Moon & Urmila Pawar can be included in the educational texts.

**Access & Exposure Visits**

Special exposure visits to dalit localities can be organised for school and college students to assess basic amenities accessible to dalit women namely, water, electricity, health and hygiene. Similarly dalit women's visit to urban structured colonies can be arranged to impress upon the importance of standard of living of non-dalits. Such purposeful visits will broaden their horizons resulting in improved living of marginalised section.

**Academic Activities**

Academic institutions need to be encouraged to undertake studies to assess the problems of violence and atrocities against dalit women as also the reasons therefore and to work out ways to overcome them. Thought provoking sessions on harmful social religions practices namely, Chira, Devdasi, Jogin need to be held for basic understanding and effective interventional strategies.

**Campaigns and Sessions**

Campaigns for equal and rational distribution of natural resources among weaker sections can be organised to secure their rightful means of livelihood. Proper rehabilitation and shelter can be provided to those communities, which are out of the social periphery (NT/DT) to protect them from the risk of sexual abuse.

**Inclusion of Dalit Women in various system**

More dalit women in their population proportion (16.5% SC, 7.5% ST) should be given chance to enter in the system like police, judiciary, education, health and politics. Sessions can be organised for dalit activist and women activists to sensitize them about the magnitude of torture and oppression faced by the dalit women. Legal education dealing with protection of human rights of dalits and Prevention of Atrocities Act (1989) can be organised to prevent the problems of castism.

## Human Right Violations against India's Dalits

### Background

The main purpose of this article is not only to publicize the gross human rights violations against India's 250-300 million untouchables (now known as Dalits), but also to create international awareness and to seek international support for the plight of the Dalits in India. It is evident that the Afro-Americans suffered slavery for some centuries. The Jews suffered holocaust and martyrdom for some time, but Dalits have been suffering humiliation, loss of respect, dignity, culture and above all, unspeakable horror of the caste system for the last three thousand years of human history (Thind, *Our Indian* n.pag; Thind, *Tentacles* n.pag). The world communities must assume responsibility in bringing total justice to the Dalits who have been systematically deprived of their respect, dignity, culture and rights by the upper caste people of India. What is amazing that even after 55 years of India's independence, and as India is signatory to many international agreements such as the Universal Declaration of Human Rights and the International Convention on the "Elimination of All Forms of Racial Discrimination," and even though untouchablity was abolished by India's constitution in 1950, there is no difference in the lives of India's Dalits as their fundamental human rights are violated on a daily basis. India has been called the "world's largest democracy." It is merely "A democracy of the few for the few and by the few" and is probably the largest violators of human right acts in human history. What is worse to notice is that untouchables can not fetch a bucket of water from the village well or socialize in village tea stalls or cafes, as their touch pollutes every thing (Thind, *Our Indian*; Thind, *Tentacles*).

In fact, Dalits have been considered the most degraded, downtrodden, exploited and the least educated in Indian society. They are considered to be "*untouchable*" because their touch to high caste people is considered polluted and uncleaned. The caste hierarchy has excluded these people from the caste system and therefore, they are "*outcaste*." For decades and until today, they have been barred from sharing water, food and shelter and are forced to live in ghettos, and hence are referred as "*segregated*."

They have been socially, culturally, and politically subjugated and marginalized through three thousand years of India's history. What is still surprising is that the Dalits experience the agony of untouchability very deeply in all walks of life: social, economical and political.

Until today, India's caste system has compelled them to perform the most inhuman jobs, from the manual scavenging, skinning animals, disposal of the dead animals, cleaning streets, landless labour, bonded labour, child labour and performing the most inhuman tasks, such as cleaning the toilet and disposal of human waste (Thind, *Our Indian;* Thind, *Tentacles;* Narula).

## Caste System in India

India is a country with a lot of traditions, culture, and beauty. The most pathetic part of these traditions is an unwanted, ugly, and inhuman structure called the *Caste System.* One cannot but feel ashamed of the caste system as this system continue to discriminate the human persons and stratifies them into different groups. In Hindu society, caste is still the most powerful factor in determining a person's dignity. Socially, Dalits are placed outside the four-fold graded caste system of Indian Society. Hindu Scriptures divide the people on the basis of birth (descent-based discrimination). The social structure of India is stratified, with inbuilt inequalities and injustices, based on the caste system sanctified by *Brahmins (Hindus)* (Ambedkar, *Castes* n.pag; Viyogi n.pag). Although social stratification exists in almost all societies, the caste system is quite unique to Indian society. Sanctioned by the religio-philosophical system, the Dalits are socially placed outside the four-fold caste system and they are referred to as the fifth caste (outcaste).

India's caste system has existed for more than 3000 years and appears to be deliberately and intentionally developed by the Brahmins (priests) in order to maintain their superiority over the other castes. Typically, the caste system is divided into 4 distinct classes. This is referred as "Varnas". At the top the caste hierarchy are the Brahmins, the priestly class. According to the Hindu religious book called *Manusmruti,* the Brahmins came from the head of God. They are eligible for learning, teaching and perform religious ceremonies (Talukdar 1-16; Moon n.pag). The others cannot teach and perform sacrifice, hence they have 100% control on religion, education and Vedas. Next come the Kshatriyas. The people in this class are warrior, and according to *Manusmruti*, they originated from the shoulder of God. They are eligible for learning. Their work is to protect the people by waging war against the enemies (Talukdar 1-16; Moon n.pag). The Vaisyas are the trading class and came from the thigh of God. Their work is to trade and feed the above two classes. Finally stand the Sudras. This is the servants class and came from the feet of God. Their work is to do all menial work for the above three classes. They are not entitled to learn anything (Narula n.pag; Talukdar 1-16; Moon). In addition to the above four classes, there is a fifth class called "untouchables" or outcaste. They literally have no caste and means oppressed, downtrodden, broken and exploited social group (Narula; Moon).

Such a rigid caste system is not found anywhere in the world outside India. Once born in the caste, a person's status is predetermined and immutable. Birth decides any talent the person may develop, and one cannot alter one's status or wealth the person may accumulate. Similarly, the caste in which a person is born predetermines what profession or activities he will pursue. What is surprising is that even today most Hindus who are living abroad still practice the caste system in their country of residence (*India Abroad* 11).

## Human Rights Violations against Dalits in India

According to the Hindu religious belief, "All human beings are not born equal." This creates caste-based discrimination against Dalits, which is then open to various forms of violence against them, which include public humiliation, torture, rape, beating, and killing, etcetera.

The untouchability is the basis for atrocities and violence, denial of basic needs, land rights, legal discrimination, infringement of civil liberties, inferior or no people status, de-humanizing living and working conditions, impoverishment, mal-nourishment, bad health conditions, high levels of illiteracy and continuing social ostracism is continue to the reason for human rights violations against dalits.

Even today, in rural India, Dalits are prevented from most common social activities such as sharing water, food and drinks. They are barred from wearing shoes when meeting high caste Hindus. They are not allowed to cycle through village streets in which higher caste people live. They can be publicly dehumanized by small crimes such as shooing away a chicken, dogs, and other pets that belong to higher caste people. They are discriminated against, denied access to land, forced to work in the most degrading conditions, and are routinely abused by the hands of the police and higher caste Hindus who enjoy government protection. Most Dalits continue to live in precarious conditions and are not allowed to use the same well, visit the temples, drink from the same cups in tea stalls or even cannot claim the land that legally belongs to them. Most Dalits continue to live in extreme poverty, without land, and they lack opportunities for better employment and education (Narula; Ambedkar, *Annihilation*).

According to the National Commission of Human rights of India, more than 62,000 human rights violations are recorded annually. On average, two Dalits are assaulted every hour, three Dalit women and children are raped, two Dalits are murdered, and at least two Dalits are tortured or burned every day (Narula; *National Commission* n.pag). Due to space, it is not possible to describe an individual human rights abuse. Following are some of the most inhuman "Human Right Violations" that took place in recent time in India. For instance, recently, five Dalits in the Northern district of India, Haryana, were lynched by a mob of 4,000 Hindus on the allegation that they skinned the cow (according to Hinduism, the cow is considered holy), as these victims denied a bribe to police. In another incident, a four-month pregnant Dalit women from Tamilnadu district (Southern part of India), was beaten by upper caste Hindus from the same village. She was stripped naked and paraded in front of the village as well as her family members. Later, police beat her in jail, which resulted in her miscarriage (Ambedkar, *Annihilation*).

Less than 3.5% culprits are prosecuted for such crimes, and out of 10 cases of atrocities against Dalits, only one is prosecuted. The problem is not the law; implementation is a total failure because the less than 15% high caste Hindus who control 85% of the wealth, power, justice system, police and 100% of the media. Hence, the culprits go unpunished (*National Commission* n.pag).

Most importantly, these violations are not only performed against Dalits, but also on other minority communities in India. For the last few years, Hindu masses have been directly associated with the human rights violations against Muslims, Christians and Sikhs throughout India. For instance, Hindus killed more than 3,000 Muslims in a Mosque demolition in 1992. In 1994, more than 4,000 Sikhs in the Delhi area were killed in Communal riots. In recent years, more than 2,000 Muslims in Gujrat and hundreds of Christians have been killed (Varhade n.pag).

## Human Right Violations against Dalit Children

According to the national Commission for Scheduled Caste (SC) and Scheduled Tribes (ST), there are an estimated 115 millions children working in slavery, and amongst those, approximately 80-90% are Dalits who work as bonded labour in order to pay off debt (*National Commission;* Varhade). In slavery, children, often from poor families, are picked by a high caste restaurant or shop owner and are forced to work 16-18 hours a day at wages of not more than 2-3 dollars per year (Ambedkar *Annihilation;* Varhade). Their denial to the order of their owner or trying to escape can result in severe beating and no food and water for several days. According to government statistics, an estimated 800,000 Dalits are manual scavengers who are involve in clearing human feces from pubic and private latrines and disposing of dead animals (Ambedkar, *Annihilation*). A recent survey conducted by two teams of National Geographic stated that "in one toilet there can be more than 400 seats which all have to be manually cleaned. This is the lowest occupation in the wold, which is performed by the community occupying the lowest status in the caste system" (O'Neill 8-31). In addition to the above, there are approximately 50,000 Dalits girls who are forced to practice a Hindu religious practice of child prostitution, called *Devdasi*. Devadasis, literally meaning "female servant of god," and they usually belong to the Dalit community. Amazingly, this practice still exists in Indian states like Andhra Pradesh, Karnatka, Orissa and Maharashtra. Once dedicated, the girl is unable to marry, is forced to become a prostitute for upper-caste community members, and is eventually auctioned off to an urban brothel, where she may die due of many sexual diseases, including HIV/AIDS.

## Human Rights Violations Against Dalit Women

According to Arpita Anant, researcher on the behalf of South Asia Partnership of Canada, Dalit women in India face the triple burden: caste, class and gender (for details on Dalit women's issues, please refer to the chapter by Ms. Sonia Mahey) (Anant 1-8). As stated by another woman activists in India, "No one practices untouchability when it comes to sex." Rape is a common phenomenon in rural areas. Women are raped as part of caste custom or village tradition. According to Dalit activists, Dalit girls have been forced to have sex with the village landlord (Narula). In rural areas, "women are induced into prostitution (*Devadasi system*), which [is] forced on them in the name of religion." The prevalence of rape in villages contributes to the greater incidence of child marriage in those areas. Early marriage between the ages of ten years and sixteen years persists in large part because of Dalit girls' vulnerability to sexual assault by upper-caste men; once a girl is raped, she becomes unmarriageable. An early marriage also gives parents greater control over the caste into which their children are married. Moreover, Dalit women are also raped as a form of retaliation. Landlords and the police use sexual abuse and other forms of violence against women to inflict political "lessons" and crush dissent within the community.

One of the reasons that Dalit woman continue to be target of atrocities is that in rural areas, due to extreme poverty, lack of education, and as high caste Hindus own 80% land, Dalit women are forced to work on minimal wage. A slight denial to their orders or daring to ask for a raise in wages can result in humiliations, beating, torture, rape, killing and jail. More often, Dalit womens and children are held by as ransom to catch their spouses on minor charges (Ambedkar, *Annihilation*).

## Opportunities for Dalits in Education

The government has made reservations for Dalits, so that they can enter into jobs in the public sector, parliamentary State

Assemblies and Universities. This reservation, however, makes them even more vulnerable in the society. Most Dalits continue to live in extreme poverty, without land or opportunities for better employment or education, with the exception of a minority who have benefited from India's policy of quotas in education and government jobs. According to Constitution of India, reservation for Dalits in Government jobs is secured, but in reality, only a few are filled out as they have full control of recruitment. According to the National Commission for SC and ST and as per India's constitution, total job reservation for Dalits is 22.5% but only 2.1% in case of class-I (Dalits serving in pubic commission, civil services, chief executives in major companies) and 9.0% in the case of class-II (this includes Dalits serving as college lecturers, bank manager, in government, etcetera). To date, most Dalit students are prevented from entering in government as well as the public sectors as a part of the caste-based discrimination, hence there is a stiff increment in unemployment.

Many bright Dalit students are prevented from sitting in the front classroom row, sharing water or food, and mixing with high caste students. Teachers are often violent against them for showing greater aptitudes in classrooms. Often humiliated in front of class by the teacher and high caste students, most of those students return back to their family profession. For instance, most recently a Dalit girl student who accidentally joined a street dance performed by high caste performers was humiliated and was threatened with rape if she complained to the police. Turning to the police for a complaint only exaggerated the situation. She later committed suicide (Narula).

## The Role of International Non-Government Organizations (NGOs) in the Dalit Cause

Now the United Nations and the Human Right groups have exposed the sufferings of these voiceless peoples to the rest of the world. Many Non-Government Organizations (NGO) both in India and as well as abroad have been involved in raising the plight of India's 250 million untouchables.

Amongst many, one of the NGOs in North America is called "The Ambedkar Centre for Peace and Justice" (ACJP), named in honour of Dr. B. R. Ambedkar (1891-1956), who was India's foremost human right activist and an untouchable. He has been recognized as the Chief architect of India's Constitution. Dr. Ambedkar was an emancipator, scholar, extraordinaire, social reformer and a true champion of human rights. He was the first Dalits who received a Ph.D. and L.L.D. from Columbia University, USA, D.Sc. and Bar-at-Law from the London School of Economics, and D.Litt. from Osmania University, India. Moreover, he was the first law minister of Independent India (Keer).

The most immediate task of the ACJP is to bring the plight of the Dalits to the attention of the International community and to document and publicize human rights abuses. The mission of this organization is to foster recognition of the human rights of, and to develop support for, the indigenous peoples of India. The long-term objectives are to enfranchise Dalits as full citizens of their society. This will require broad-based financial and political support for the Dalits, as well as legal and educational changes in India, so that they may re-establish their dignity, culture and civilization.

As warned by the Vice President, Mr. Yogesh Varhade, since fundamentalist Hindu forces are pushing this caste system to the limits, this will result in civil war, instability in South Asia and Global Peace will be in danger. Millions of refugees could infiltrate North America and Europe, further resulting in a complete collapse of the economy, and could cost million of dollars (Varhade n.pag).

The Indian Government is only interested in developing trade with Canada, but does not reveals its "dirty secret" of human rights violations and caste-based atrocities on millions of Dalits. The Canadian government should show compassion to towards dissolving untouchability. For this, Canada should put pressure on the Indian government to recognize untouchabilty as "racial discrimination" and put policies in place to protect human rights and the dignity of million Dalits. Moreover, the Canadian as well as the world media should take an active role in publicizing the plight of Untouchables.

CHAPTER

# 7 Basic of Dalit Women's Prohibition and Discrimination

Despite the Government of India's exclusion of caste discrimination in its periodic report to the Committee, the Government has recognized it as an issue in its reports to other international treaty monitoring bodies. In 2000 the CEDAW Committee expressed its concern "with the continuing discrimination, including violence, suffered by women of the Dalit community, despite the passage of the Scheduled Castes and Scheduled Tribes (Prevention of Atrocities) Act of 1989." In response, the Government of India included the situation of Dalit women in its recent submission of its combined Second and Third periodic reports to the CEDAW Committee.

Nevertheless, the discussion of Dalit women in this report remains cursory, addressing the issue of violence against Dalit women by simply noting the passage of the Protection of Civil Rights Act, 1955, and the Prevention of Atrocities Act, 1989. While the Government details its efforts on other issues in greater detail—including education, segregation, manual scavenging, bonded labour, and lack of access to land —the extent to which these issues remain a problem in India is alarmingly minimized.

Caste discrimination in India has also been raised as an issue of serious concern by a number of other treaty bodies and special procedures. In 1997 the Human Rights Committee noted that scheduled castes in India "continue to endure severe social discrimination and to suffer disproportionately from many violations of their rights under the [ICCPR], *inter alia* inter-caste violence, bonded labour and discrimination of all kinds." And as recently as 2004 the Committee on the Rights of the Child was "deeply concerned at persistent and significant social discrimination against children belonging to Scheduled Castes and Tribes and other tribal groups." Additionally, the UN Special Rapporteurs on education, adequate housing, the right to food, violence against women, and torture have all included investigations on caste-based discrimination in their mandate and have cited India as a country of particular concern.

Because one's caste can be determinative of one's occupation, caste discrimination is also referred to as discrimination on the basis of "work and descent." The UN Sub-Commission on the Promotion and Protection of Human Rights passed a resolution in August 2000 reaffirming that discrimination based on work and descent is prohibited under international human rights law. In his 2001 report commissioned by that same resolution, Sub-Commission expert R.K.W. Goonesekere underscored that caste systems are inherently economic and social in their consequences and represent a deeply oppressive form of work and descent-based discrimination. In 2004 the Sub-Commission appointed two Rapporteurs to undertake "a comprehensive study on discrimination based on work and descent." The Rapporteurs were tasked with: determining the impact that the practices and policies of governments, local authorities, private sector entities, schools, religious institutions, and the media have had on discrimination based on work and descent; obtaining information on existing measures taken by governments, national human rights groups, the UN, and NGOs to combat discrimination based on work and descent; and drafting a set of principles or guidelines setting forth the measures necessary to effectively eliminate discrimination based on work and descent. The appointment of the Rapporteurs was approved by the CHR at its 61st Session in April 2005.

## States Parties' Obligation

*A Condemn caste discrimination and undertake to pursue by all appropriate means a policy of eliminating caste discrimination*

The Government of India has not refrained from committing and supporting discriminatory acts against Dalits, and has failed to implement measures to end caste discrimination. India has failed to encourage integrationist movements and has not provided for the development and protection of Dalits, who as a result remain an extremely marginalized social group.

## Refrain from Committing Discriminatory Acts

*Each State Party undertakes to engage in no act or practice of racial discrimination against persons, groups of persons or institutions and to ensure that all public authorities and public institutions, national and local, shall act in conformity with this obligation.*

India's failure to ensure that all public authorities and public institutions do not engage in caste-based discrimination is widespread. The discussion below focuses on two examples that exemplify this failure: treatment of Dalits by the police and discrimination in the provision of disaster relief. Further examples of this failure are dealt with throughout the remainder of the Report.

### a. *Dalits and Law Enforcement*

In 2004 the NHRC characterized the law enforcement machinery as the greatest violator of Dalits' human rights. This problem is not a recent one. In 1979 India constituted the National Police Commission to analyze problems in police performance. However, the Commission's recommendations, which include recommendations specific to police abuse of Dalits, have still not been adopted. Police continue to detain, torture, and extort money from Dalits without much fear of punishment. According to the NHRC, custodial torture and killing of Dalits, rape and sexual assault of Dalit women, and looting of Dalit property by the police "are condoned, or at best ignored..." Dalits who encounter the police are forced to listen to casteist name-calling, unfounded accusations on their character, and threats against their family and friends.

While under-reporting of police treatment (including torture) of Dalits means that the real magnitude is unknown, the national Preventing Torture project initiated by People's Watch, a Tamil Nadu-based NGO, asserts that Dalits suffer disproportionately at the hands of the police and are at high risk of being subjected to torture while in police custody. The Prevention of Atrocities Act,

1989, and the Supreme Court guidelines set out in the *D.K. Basu* case (1997) are available legal tools to prevent torture, illegal detention, or improper interrogation of Dalits. Jurists, human rights activists, and civil rights groups, however, claim that a lack of political will allows the problem of torture and other forms of custodial abuse to continue unchecked.

*Disproportionate Targeting of Dalits* : Dalits are disproportionately targeted by the police for a number of reasons. According to the NHRC, under a theory of collective punishment, the police will often subject entire Dalit communities to violent search and seizure operations in search of one individual. Dalit communities may also be perceived by the police as inherently criminal. Dalits and other poor minorities are disproportionately represented among those detained and tortured in police custody because most cannot afford to pay police bribes. Dalits are also likely victims of police misconduct because they are rarely informed of their rights, rarely have access to an attorney, and are not able to afford bail. Police officers' deeply embedded caste bias (most officers belong to the dominant castes) and a general lack of familiarity with legislative protections for Dalits further compound the problem.

State agencies have also colluded with private actors from dominant castes in committing human rights violations against Dalits. Through investigations conducted in 1997 in the state of Bihar, for example, Human Rights Watch found that government officials acted as agents of the Ranvir Sena (a private upper-caste militia) and turned a blind eye to their killings of Dalits. Soon after a massacre in Laxampur-Bathe village, Jehanabad district—in which the Ranvir Sena killed 61 Dalits, Naxalites (leftist guerrilla organizations advocating the use of violence to achieve land redistribution) retaliated by killing nine people suspected to be Ranvir Sena supporters. The police responded to the violence by harassing Dalit villagers who they accused of supporting the Naxalites. Rather than capturing Sena members, State security forces reportedly helped train militia members; in some cases, police accompanied the militias during their attacks on Dalit villages, disguising killings as "encounters." Upper-caste militia members, and the police who colluded with them, have rarely been prosecuted for their crimes.

*Improper use of Security Legislation against Dalits*: Dalits are particularly vulnerable to arrest under draconian security laws. For example, in at least two states, Jharkhand and Andhra Pradesh, the Prevention of Terrorism Act 2002 (POTA) was widely used against Dalits, who were targeted for their caste status rather than any involvement in criminal or terrorist activity.

Dalit activists are also accused of being "terrorists," "threats to national security," and "habitual offenders," and frequently charged under the National Security Act, 1980, the Indian Explosives Act, 1884, and even older counter insurgency laws such the Terrorist and Disruptive Activities (Prevention) Act 1987 (commonly known as TADA). Dalit activists are often subjected to specious prosecutions, falsified charges, and physical abuse and torture following arrest. Further, following bouts of violence in Bihar between the Ranvir Sena and Naxalites, Dalits were held in preventive detention under India's Criminal Procedure Code Section 107 in excess of the maximum detention period of 24 hours. Similarly, following periods of escalated violence between upper-caste community members and Dalits in Tamil Nadu between July 1995 and June 1996, many Dalit youths were arrested under preventive detention laws like the Tamil Nadu Goondas Act and the National Security Act, 1980. Additionally, police also engage in what are called "encounter deaths," whereby young activists who allegedly support any of the Naxalite or radical left movement organizations are picked up, tortured to extract confessions, and then killed under the pretense of self defense. Though upper-caste community members have also been picked up by the police in this manner, they are usually not subject to such harsh treatment as a result of pressure from influential people belonging to their caste.

*Custodial abuse and Torture of Dalits:* Dalits, including those arrested for minor offenses, are often held in custody for long periods of time, occasionally at distant and isolated locations to avoid publicity, where they are frequently deprived of food and water, subjected to verbal abuse and humiliation, severe beatings, sexual perversities, and demeaning acts. Often the injuries inflicted can prove fatal. To cover up custodial deaths, police often claim that the person was killed trying to escape or that he or she died of natural causes. Dalits who survive the torture often end up permanently disabled and suffer social ostracism, as well as psychological and emotional trauma.

*Police abuse of Dalit Women:* Dalit women are particularly vulnerable to sexual assault and rape by the police. As with sexual abuse of Dalit women by upper-caste men, the sexual abuse of Dalit women by the police is used as a tool to punish Dalit communities as a whole. Dalit women have also been arrested and raped in custody to punish their male relatives who are hiding from the police. Police also routinely sexually abuse Dalit women during police raids as a means of exerting pressure on their male family members to surrender, give false evidence, retract their complaints, or silence their protests regarding police mistreatment. Investigations in Bihar and Tamil Nadu conducted by Human Rights Watch also confirmed that women have been beaten, arrested, and sometimes tortured during violent search and raid operations on Dalit villages. Medical personnel often collude in these cases by issuing false certificates that deny sexual assault or by including statements in the medical examination report that cast doubts on the credibility of the victim's complaint.

The case of Ms. Lebra is illustrative of this widespread problem. Ms. Lebra, a mother of three, was accused of stealing her upper-caste neighbor's jewelry in retaliation for refusing to give him crops from her land. When she was called in by the police for questioning, the police officer began molesting her daughter. When she tried to stop him, he grabbed Ms. Lebra's hair, pushed her down onto the ground and raped her.

*Police Extortion and Looting:* The routine practice of police extortion and looting is well documented. Police targeting of Dalits comes about through:

- Illegal police raids on Dalit villages under the pretext of looking for suspects in the aftermath of caste conflicts. Human Rights Watch has documented a number of such instances.
- Specific targeting of Dalit villages that enjoyed relative economic prosperity. This practice has been documented by Human Rights Watch's investigation of raids conducted in Gundupatti, Tamil Nadu in February 1998, where the

police engaged in outright looting, stealing jewelry, clothes, cash, and consumables from the homes of Dalit villagers who enjoyed relative prosperity due to remittances from family members who were sent to work abroad. The looting served two purposes: to line the policemen's pockets; and to teach Dalits that they should not strive to increase their economic status.

- The pretense of conducting *kurki-japti* (legal attachment of movable property). Such seizures do not follow the legal procedures for seizures, such as the presentation of a court order and list of materials to be seized, or the requirement that two witnesses be present during the seizure.

Acts of extortion often lead to violence. For example, in 2002 in the Jhajjar district in Haryana, police allegedly killed five Dalits after failing to extort money from them. The Dalit boys, from families traditionally employed in the skinning of dead cows, apparently "refused to pay extortion money for being allowed to carry animal skins." In 2003 three constables and a sub-inspector in Lucknow were suspended and charged with instigating the suicide of a Dalit man. The man committed suicide while being detained by police who were holding him with the intention of extorting money from him. In addition to violence, extortion and looting may begin a cycle of borrowing by Dalits that ultimately leads to a state of bondage (see Section VIII(E)(1)(b)).

*Failure of Police to Properly Register Crimes against Dalits:* Police systematically fail to properly register crimes under the Prevention of Atrocities Act, 1989 and the Protection of Civil Rights Act, 1995. Improper and under-registration of Dalit cases is both a result of police officers' reluctance to entertain complaints by Dalits, as well as their lack of familiarity with provisions of the relevant legislation. For example, according to one study, out of 103 randomly selected atrocity cases against Dalits in the state of Andhra Pradesh from 1999 to 2003, First Information Reports (FIRs) were correctly registered in only 18 cases, while 29 were not registered at all. In 2002 India reported that in at least 15 states, between 0-2 cases had been registered under the Prevention of Atrocities Act, 1989. Similarly, the Government of India reported that in the same year that no cases were registered under the Protection of Civil Rights

Act in 24 states and union territories. The National Commission for Scheduled Castes and Scheduled Tribes has concluded that "a large number of cases of atrocities go unregistered, mainly because of reluctance on the part of police officers to register the cases." The NHRC has confirmed that the lack of registered cases does not represent an actual reduction in the practice of "untouchability."

In addition to non-registration of cases, police routinely engage in improper registration of cases. Dalit cases are often generally registered under the Indian Penal Code, instead of the Protection of Civil Rights Act, 1955 and the Prevention of Atrocities Act, 1989. Moreover, in a distorted interpretation of the Prevention of Atrocities Act, police officials require explicit mention of abuse by caste name for all atrocities.

Improper and under-registration of Dalit cases adversely affects case outcomes. Cases are less likely to be prosecuted and even when pursued, are more likely to result in acquittal when the police have failed to collect evidence. Perpetrators, if convicted, are punished with a lesser sentence, and/or are likely to be released on bail. Further, the appropriate relief may not be available when the proper sections of the law are not cited. More broadly, these problems have caused a loss of faith in law enforcement, which further diminishes the number of cases registered.

*b. Discrimination in the Provision of Disaster Relief*

According to separate investigations by the National Campaign on Dalit Human Rights and Human Rights Watch, India discriminated against Dalits in distribution of aid in the wake of two of India's largest natural disasters in recent years: the Gujarat earthquake in January 2001 and the Indian Ocean tsunami in December 2004.

Following the Gujarat earthquake in January 2001, while the government allocated equal amounts of compensation and food supplies to all communities, agencies did not ensure that the assistance went to Dalit communities. Dalit and Muslim populations also did not have the same access to adequate shelter, electricity, running water, and other supplies available to the upper-caste population, to whom the government had provided far superior shelter and basic amenities. Reconstruction projects were also segregated along caste and religion lines.

Following the tsunami in December 2004, the NCDHR and the Human Rights Forum for Dalit Liberation-Tamil Nadu reported that during the initial stages of the relief process, Dalits were not provided proper and adequate guidance on how to gain admission to relief camps, were not given a fair share of relief aid, and were sometimes abused when they demanded equal treatment. Dalits' political voicelessness prevented them from convincing authorities of their losses who maintained that only higher-caste fishing communities were affected by the tsunami.

2. *Refrain from supporting private actors committing discriminatory acts and prohibit and bring to an end caste-based discrimination by private actors*

The Committee has clarified the content of the States Parties' obligations with respect to private actors, stating that "to the extent that private institutions influence the exercise of rights or the availability of opportunities, the State Party must ensure that the result has neither the purpose nor the effect of creating or perpetuating racial discrimination." In its periodic report India cites to sections of the Indian Penal Code that make punishable acts and statements by private actors instigating or promoting caste (and other forms of) discrimination. A number of other legislative efforts to end caste-based discrimination also apply to private actors as well as State actors. However, in relation to private actors' treatment of Dalits, the State Party has, *inter alia*, failed to:

- ensure the security of Dalits, including through its failure to protect Dalits against retaliatory attacks (see Section VIII (B)(1)), its failure to properly register crimes against Dalits (see Section V(A)(1)(a)(vi)), and through its collusion with private actors and militias engaging in violence (see Section V(A)(1)(a)(i));
- address infringements on social, cultural, and economic rights by private actors, including through failing to deal with violations of the right to work by private employers, including discrimination in hiring and wage payments (see Section VIII(E)(1)(f)), social and economic boycotts against Dalits (see Section VIII(E)), prohibitions on inter-marriage (see Section VIII(D)(3)(a)), and infringements on

rights to equal participation in cultural activities (see Section VIII(E)(6));

- ensure the exercise of political rights such as the right to vote and stand for election and freedom of peaceful assembly and association, by failing to address practices such as booth-rigging and booth capturing, denial of access to polls, and intimidation and violence to discourage participation in local elections (see Section VIII(C));
- end the practice of segregation, including in housing arrangements and in privately run businesses (see Sections VI and VIII(F)); and
- eradicate propaganda inciting caste-based discrimination (see Section VII).

The nexus between political leaders and upper-caste community members account to some extent for these failures and for the disincentive to address violations by private actors. For example, social and economic legislation to further Dalits' rights adversely affects the interests of the classes and castes to which political leaders either belong or represent; political leaders are either landowners themselves or have close political and social links with land-owners, and those relying on cheap or bonded labour, including child labour.

## Reform State Policies

*Each State Party shall take effective measures to review governmental, national and local policies, and to amend, rescind or nullify any laws and regulations which have the effect of creating or perpetuating racial discrimination wherever it exists.*

While the 1950 Constitution abolished the practice of "untouchability" in all its forms, and while specific legislation has been adopted to address caste-based discrimination, the information detailed in this report demonstrates that caste-based discrimination by State and non-State actors persists throughout India and that the State Party has failed to undertake sufficient law and policy review of the under-implementation of these measures.

4. *Encourage integrationist movements and other means of eliminating barriers between castes, and discourage anything that strengthens caste division*

*Each State Party undertakes to encourage, where appropriate, integrationist multiracial organizations and movements and other means of eliminating barriers between races, and to discourage anything which tends to strengthen racial division.*

The Government of India has failed to encourage integrationist movements or eliminate barriers between castes. To the contrary, the government has turned a blind eye to segregation in schools (see Sections VIII(E)(5)(a) and VIII(F)(1)(c)), has encouraged segregation in housing (see Section VI(A)), including in relief camps following natural disasters (see Section V(A)(1)(b)), and has failed to faithfully implement constitutional and legislative abolitions of "untouchability" practices. Additionally, as Dalits increasingly organize to protest their discriminatory treatment and claim their democratic rights, the government has improperly used security legislation against Dalit activists (see Section V(A)(1)(a)(ii)), consistently failed to protect Dalits against retaliatory attacks by upper-caste groups, including rape of Dalit women (see Section VIII(B)), and failed to deal with social and economic boycotts against Dalits (see Section VIII(E)), thereby further discouraging integrationist movements.

*B. Ensure the development and protection of certain groups or individuals belonging to them*

*Article 2 (2): States Parties shall, when the circumstances so warrant, take, in the social, economic, cultural and other fields, special and concrete measures to ensure the adequate development and protection of certain racial groups or individuals belonging to them, for the purpose of guaranteeing them the full and equal enjoyment of human rights and fundamental freedoms. These measures shall in no case entail as a consequence the maintenance of unequal or separate rights for different racial groups after the objectives for which they were taken have been achieved.*

The extreme marginalization and persecution endured by Dalits in India necessitate efforts by the government to ensure their development and protection. In its periodic report, the Government of India cites to Article 16 of the Indian Constitution, which empowers the State to make provision for the reservation of posts in government jobs in favour of any backward class of citizens. Accordingly, under constitutional provisions and various laws, India grants Dalits a certain number of privileges, including "reservations" (quotas) in education, government jobs, and government bodies. Like many of the protective measures described in this report, the reservation policy has not been successfully implemented for Dalits. Additionally, there has been widespread public opposition to reservations for Dalits in local government bodies, often leading to violence (see Section VIII(C)(2)), and in government jobs that are highly coveted because of the economic security they are perceived as offering, as are seats in higher education. Finally, Dalits who convert to Christianity or Islam risk losing their "scheduled caste" status and the few benefits it affords (see Section VIII(D)(5)(a)).

## 1. Failure of Compensatory Discrimination Mechanisms and Discrimination in Public Employment

Caste-based occupational distribution is reinforced in reserved government employment. The NHRC reports that Dalits occupy over 65 percent of the total government posts for *safai karmacharis* (sweepers)and only 16.7 percent of non-sweeper posts. Dalits are also discriminated against when being considered for promotions. Recently, the government has moved to create quotas for promotions for scheduled castes and other backward castes. While the Supreme Court upheld the move, it required that governmental authorities prove that these groups were poorly represented in government positions, that quotas be capped at 50 percent, and that prosperous lower-caste employees be excluded from the plan.

Reservations in higher education continue to be met with a great deal of resistance leading to under-enforcement. In the country's 256 universities and about 11,000 colleges funded by the University Grants Commission (an apex body of the Government of India), Dalits and tribals comprise only 2 percent of the teaching positions; about 75,000 teaching positions reserved for these communities remain vacant.

## 2. Proposals to Extend Reservations to Other Sectors

In its 2004 report the NHRC recommended that the government identify institutions that had not accepted reservations—including judiciary and defense forces—and develop measures to ensure that Dalit candidates had the opportunity to compete for these positions. In 2002 the Supreme Court had one Dalit out of 26 judges, while the High Courts had 25 Dalits out of 625 positions (see also Section VIII(A)(3)(b)). The National Commission for Scheduled Castes and Scheduled Tribes has stated that the private sector, which continues to enjoy government patronage—through concessional land, financing, and excise and sales tax relief—should also be brought under the purview of the reservation policy.

According to government estimates in 2000, the unemployment rate for Dalits and tribals was double that of non-Dalits/tribals. Additionally, public sector divestment to private owners is estimated to have left 200,000 Dalit employees jobless. Dalits continue to be significantly underrepresented in most professional strata. Dalit representation in India's high industries, exports, imports, and electronic industries sectors is dismal. In response, civil society and government actors have supported the proposed extension of reservations in the private sector. However, there remains strong opposition to this proposal, both from private employers and certain political parties. Private employers have, for example, criticized the government for failing to provide Dalits adequate opportunities in education and instead imposing upon the private sector the obligation to employ individuals they deem unqualified.

### 3. Poor Implementation of Development Programs

The Government of India has also established several programs for the development of Dalits. According to the NHRC, however, the beneficial impact of these programs has been hindered by:

- inadequate investment of public resources;
- non-utilization or diversion of funds earmarked for Dalit development;
- lack of programs specifically targeted to Dalit development;
- poor preparation of such projects; and
- a lack of monitoring of development programs, leading to the failure of many such programs to reach their target groups.

The anti-Dalit bias of personnel in charge of implementing these programs has also hindered their effectiveness. Moreover,

Dalits rarely participate in the formulation and implementation of development projects. Many Dalits are also unaware of the existence of such programs, further restricting their participation.

## 4. Inadequate Development and Protection of Dalit Women

The obligation to ensure the development and protection of certain groups or individuals belonging to them is especially relevant for those individuals within the Dalit community who face multiple forms of discrimination. Dalit women face multiple axes of discrimination, with the NCDHR asserting:

> Dalit women are often described as the oppressed of the oppressed, the violence and oppression on them being more complex and manifold even compared to Dalit men. There is [an] inseparable relationship between caste status, occupation and discrimination. The Dalit woman faces triple discrimination because she is an untouchable, of a poor class and is a woman.

CERD has also noted that forms of racial discrimination have a "unique and specific impact on women." For more on the violence against Dalit women see Sections V(A)(1)(a)(iv) and VIII(B)(2).

### *a. Lack of gender equity*

Dalit women have unequal access to services, employment opportunities, and justice mechanisms as compared to Dalit men. In relation to employment opportunities, Dalit women are allotted some of the most menial and arduous tasks and experience greater discrimination in the payment of wages than Dalit men. The employment opportunities of professional Dalit women may also be limited by discriminatory practices that deprive facilities run by Dalit women of a customer or patient base or require accommodation of requests of upper-caste community members. In relation to services, Dalit women have less access to education and health facilities, ensuring that their literacy rate, and nutrition and health standards fall far below that of Dalit men and non-Dalit men and women. The number of Dalit women in decision-making positions is also very low, and in some central services, Dalit women are not represented at all. Benefits of various development programs for Dalits, such as distribution of land and other productive assets have essentially gone to Dalit males and have not improved the status of Dalit women. Investment in projects targeted to the development of Dalit women is also far lower as compared to those for men.

### *b. Forced Prostitution – Devadasi system*

The practice of *devadasi*, in which a girl, usually before reaching the age of puberty, is ceremoniously dedicated or married to a deity or to a temple, continues in several southern states including Andhra Pradesh and Karnataka. Literally meaning "female servant of god," *devadasis* usually belong to the Dalit community. Once dedicated, the girl is unable to marry, forced to become a prostitute for upper-caste community members, and eventually auctioned into an urban brothel. The age-old practice continues to legitimize the sexual violence and discrimination that have come to characterize the intersection between caste and gender.

While India has adopted measures to abolish the practice and "rehabilitate" *devadasis*, these efforts have been largely unsuccessful. Legislative initiatives are poorly implemented. The societal perception of *devadasis* as women who are sexually available to men makes it more difficult for *devadasis* to approach the police with complaints of sexual violence. Moreover, the police themselves have been known to exploit *devadasis*.

The Joint Women Programme for the National Commission of Women has found that *devadasi* rehabilitation programs neither address the whole range of problems faced by *devadasis*, nor target the population they were intended to assist. Further, *devadasis* find it difficult to earn a livelihood outside the system because the rehabilitation programs do not provide adequate means of livelihood and skill development, and because financial assistance is often in the form of a loan which must be repaid. Most *devadasis* also lack access to a residential house, health care, or educational facilities for their children.

CHAPTER 8

# Discrimination Against the Dalit Christians

For the Dalit Christians, the first aim must be to obtain from the Indian Government those basic rights that are owed to them under the Constitution. This is the first step to gaining that minimum of economic freedom necessary for survival and reasonable progress in terms of equality in society and in the church. Dalit Christians must be able to earn a decent living in society, and to live in dignity within the church.

One of the State Commissions has pointed out that the Dalit Christians are "twice discriminated against"- in society and in the church. This statement is true as far as it goes, but actually the Dalit Christians face discrimination from multiple sources:

- The Dalit Hindus;
- The Upper Caste Lay Christians;
- The Upper Caste Hindus;
- The Clerical Authorities in the Church.
- The State and Government;

The caste system has penetrated deep into the Indian psyche. There do exist some honest individuals who do not practise discrimination by caste but there is hardly a section of society that is totally free from this deplorable attitude.

While certain clerical authorities in the church have been remiss in this regard, certain other authorities in the church have from time to time seen their way to raise a voice of appeal and to condemn this denial of rights to Dalits. These appeals, however ,have not been pressed with enough vigour and constancy to produce tangible results. In many parts of the country, the Dalit faithful continue to be the victims of this baseless and irrational practice at the hands of their fellow Christians.

Even today Dalits are victims of being untouchable. It is the Indian expression of apartheid. Despite the Constitutional guarantee of abolishing untouchability, Dalits are victims of many violations. Bonded labour, child labour, prostitution and Devadasi (slave to god and men) come largely from Dalit communities. Dalits live in separate colonies, far away from the Caste Hindu localities. They do not have access to public wells to draw water or to public eating-places. Dalits have separate glasses for drinking tea or coffee at the village restaurants. They can not enter Hindu temples. Inter-caste marriages are forbidden both by religion and practice. Atrocities against Dalits, basically arise in the context of 'keeping Dalits' in their place within the social hierarchy, mediated by caste and untouchability.

The untouchability is the basis for atrocities and violence, denial of basic needs, land rights, legal discrimination, infringement of civil liberties, inferior or no people status, de-humanizing living and working conditions, impoverishment, malnourishment, bad health conditions, high levels of illiteracy and continuing social ostracism.

Dalits are poor, deprived and socially backward. Poor means that they do not have access to enough food, health care, housing and/or clothing (which means that their physiological and safety needs are not fulfilled). They also do not have access to education and employment. With deprived we would like to underline the injustice they face in every days life. Officially, everybody in India has the same rights and duties, but the practice is different. Social backwardness, lack of access to food, education and health care keeps them in bondage of the upper castes.

The oppression of Dalits has been going on for over 3000 years. They are segregated in all spheres of social life: places of worship, education, housing, land ownership, use of common wells, roads, busses, etc. They are the people who have to do the menial and degrading jobs. They are considered to be untouchable. In their daily life untouchability results in, among others, the following consequences (For more day to day examples also go through the press releases).

- The Dalits mainly live in separate communities, outside the actual village.
- In general, Dalits are not allowed to sit at the bus stop; they have to stand and wait till upper caste people have entered the bus. Dalits are also not allowed to sit on the seats, even though they are vacant.
- In a lot of the upper caste (rich) families the servants are Dalits. After the servant has cleaned the rooms, pots and pans, one of the family members will sprinkle 'holy' water to purify all that has been touched by the servant.
- Dalits are not allowed to wear shoes; if they wear them, Dalits will have to take off their shoes at times they meet a higher caste person.
- In the rural areas, Dalits are not allowed to cycle through the village streets in which the higher caste people live.
- Mira Saroj: Daughter of a toddy tapper in Uttar Pradesh, she is enrolled at Delhi University but jumps in with manual labour at home when she is free from studies. 'Sadly, an educated Dalit women is almost a contradiction in terms', says Mira. (Outlook Magazine, November 16, 1998)
- After half a century of Independence even the educated among the Dalits are not free to get a house for rent of their choice to live in.
- Most Hindus will avoid having a Dalit to prepare their food, because they fear becoming polluted.
- The government has made reservations for Dalits, so that they can enter into jobs in the public sector, parliamentary State Assemblies and universities. This reservation, however, makes them even more vulnerable in the society.
- 'We may touch a cat, we may touch a dog, we may touch any other animal, but the touch of these human beings is pollution.' (G.K. Gokhale, in Jesus the Dalit by M.R. Arulraja, 1996. Volunteer Centre, 7-1-30/6, Ameerpet, Hyderabad-16)

## Historic Evidences of Discrimination

The converts from Hinduism to Christianity brought with them their caste practices and symbols even after conversion.

The Bull of Pope Gregory XV, "Bulla Romanae Sedis Antistitis", dated 31 January 1623, accedes to the requests of the missionaries to accommodate themselves to certain caste practices and usages of the new converts. The Pope was granting this permission only as a provisional and conditional measure.

The Bull agreed to tolerate the continuance of certain traditional customs and usages. Taking into account the difficulties encountered by the Brahmin converts if they were obliged to abandon certain external signs (such as sacred thread, sandals, ablutions), and considering that these external rites could be interpreted as meaning signs of nobility and function (nobiliatis et officii) and to show some empathy for human sensibilities, the Bull agreed to tolerate those usages, provided all danger of superstition was avoided and the convert showed charity and respect towards people of obscure condition, this presumably being a reference to Dalits. This document shows the prevalence of the caste mentality among the convert Christians.

*Letter of the Propagation of Faith, 1779*

With regard to the distinctions of caste in the churches, the congregation for the Propagation of the Faith wrote in 1779 :-

"The separation in the church and at the entrance of the church, also the distinction of cemetries may actually be tolerated for fear of greater evil."

*The Synod of Pondicherry, 1844*

This Synod was convoked to foster harmony between the Dalit Christians and the Caste Christians, who wanted to have a partition in church to separate them from the Dalits.

1929-Christian Depressed classes of South India submitted a Memorandum to the Simon Commission.

1985-Court verdict upholding the 80 years old practice of separate graveyards for Dalit Christians of Trichy, Tamil Nadu.

There is an abundance of official church and police records

on cases like K.K. Puthur, Thatchoor, Pondicherry, Thondamanthurai. However, at no time of history did the Church in India officially affirm or promote the perpetuation of social discrimination inside the Church.

## Abuse of the Dalits in the Christian Media

Rev. John Duraisamy, an editor of Sarvaviyabi, a Tamil Weekly from the archdiocese of Pondicherry-Cuddalore published two cartoons consecutively on 4 & 11th July 1999. He published them deliberately to insult, to humiliate and to degrade the 240 million dalits or the untouchables of India. The editor wanted to take some revenge on the dalit population and therefore he abused his power and authority to degrade the dalits. The editor could be arrested under The Protection of Civil Rights Act, 1955, Sec. 3,4,5,6,7, The Scheduled Castes and Scheduled Tribes (Prevention of Atrocities) Act, 1989, Sec. 2. (1)(x), T he Scheduled Castes and Scheduled Tribes (Prevention of Atrocities) Rules, 1995, Sec. 3 (1)(x) for the use of derogatory language against dalits. Humiliating dalits in the form of language or act is an offence which is punishable by a term of six months to five years of imprisonment with a fine. The Government of India enacted the Protection of Civil Rights Act, 1955 (PCR Act) to enforce the abolition of "untouchability" under Article 17 of the Constitution. The PCR Act punishes offences that amount to the observance of "untouchability." Here are the two cartoons that provoked millions of dalits in India and abroad. Many were shocked to witness this kind of apartheid within the church and expressed their deep regrets to the editor and to the archbishop of Pondicherry.

The Archbishop belongs to the same caste of the editor. He remains very silent about this remark. He feels that his hands are tied tight. He has no comments when people approached him through letters and phone calls. One's silence in times of injustice is a sin because it encourages the other person to continue the evil things.

### Article 17, Abolition of Untouchability

'Untouchability' is abolished and its practice in any form is forbidden. The enforcement of any disability arising out of

'Untouchability' shall be an offence punishable in accordance with law.

CBCI Commission for SC/ST/BC has been inspiring, educating the people for the empowerment of Dalit/Tribals and Backward Classes. In spite of condemnation by CBCI and the repeated appeals by the individual Bishops, the Dalit Christians who form the majority of believers in India are discriminated against, humiliated, and even victimised. The message of CBCI General Body meeting held at Varanasi has declared that discrimination on the basis of caste is a sin against God and humanity and the caste system will be removed from the Christian community totally as part of our preparation for Yesu Krist Jayanti 2000. It has also proposed action plans to be implemented in all Dioceses.

The Catholic Bishops Conference of India has appealed several times to their own flock to end the discrimination within the church. The CBCI has repeated her teachings on several occasions. The CBCI Commission for the Scheduled Caste and Scheduled Tribes and the Backward Caste has strongly condemned all forms of caste discrimination. " The commission has made a powerful statement "The celebration of Jubilee 2000 may be 'postponed' until the true brotherhood and equality is practiced by all the faithful of a parish and religious communities."

## Reactions from Others

*Neethi, Pastoral Theologian, USA,*

Let me presently share with you a more recent case of blatant oppression on the Dalit community through the use of the print media. I wish to draw your attention to two cartoons that appeared in a catholic weekly on two successive issues on 4 and 11$^{th}$ July 99. It should be stressed here that the weekly in question (A Tamil Weekly named "Sarvaviyabi", meaning "The All Pervading One.") is the official publication of the Roman Catholic diocese of Pondicherry-Cuddalore, South India.

The intention of the editor in publishing these cartoons is not hard to understand. With a subtle manipulation of the ancient wisdom sayings, he has insulted the entire Dalit community by casting aspersions on the collective character of Dalits. The cartoons are meant to convey the message that decency and good character can not be expected from Dalits no matter what. The obvious implication is that the Dalits are always low and mean and will remain the scum of the society.

These cartoons have hurt the feelings of not only thousands of Dalit Christians in the diocese of Pondicherry but millions of Dalits all over the world. This is a clear case of psychological oppression of Dalits by the upper caste that has been carried on for centuries. Dalits have been subjected to both physical and psychological oppression for nearly 3500 years. Physical violence is open and direct and is easily discernible whereas psychological oppression is very subtle and indirect. It hides its ugly face behind the mask of culture and inflicts such deep wounds on the personality of dalit that he or she is totally dehumanized. It is this more sophisticated but deadly form of oppression that the editor of Sarvaviyabi employs in his periodical.

The editor, Rev. John Duraisamy, can argue that he has only borrowed these sayings from the rich literary cultural heritage that has been handed down to us. These golden words were born out of the wisdom and experiences of the sages and have stood the test of the time. That is exactly where the problem lies. Whose culture are we talking about? What did this culture do to the Dalit community over the years?

Dalit history reveals that the Dalit community had a rich culture of its own. Here, Dalits who are the children of the soil found ways of expressing their identity through folk arts and classic arts in oral and written forms. But these rich cultural treasures were stolen from them by the Brahmins and upper caste oppressors. Their cultural heritage was desecrated and destroyed and a foreign culture was imposed upon them. The Brahmins and the upper caste oppressors saw to it that the Dalits would never produce a culture of their own. Even while destroying the culture of the Dalits, the Aryans absorbed many Dalit art forms and codified and modified them to suit their evil purposes. Dalits, having been deprived of their glorious culture, which gave them meaning and strength, became a cultural people and consequently a powerless people, ie. No people. They were made to depend on the Aryans to supply them with the signifying system and value-system. The Aryans ingeniously used the art form and the various traits of their culture to oppress and dehumanize the Dalits.

Thus culture which is supposed to give a meaning system and value system to a society was made into an instrument of oppression and domination. This manipulation of culture to dehumanize the Dalits has continued down unabated through the centuries even till today. Just a casual look at those who are at the helm of communications media in India will prove that the manipulation of culture continues and the dominance of the Brahmins and the upper caste is here to stay. The Dalits have neither the money power nor the political clout to make their voices heard. It is the upper caste that determines what the Dalits should think and how he should act and how he should see his status in the society.

By the use of electronic media and the print media, the upper caste society has successfully preserved its dominance and has tried to convince the world that the so-called low caste people are indeed low people. What is even more outrageous is the attempt to make the Dalits themselves believe and accept that they are low and worthless only to be despised and cast out to become the outcastes.

As we analyze the situation in the secular society, the logical question that follows is what is the situation in the church?

The answer is unfortunately not very different. Cultural domination through the clever manipulation of mass media is one area where many a church institution continue to give counter witnesses to the gospel of Jesus. Rev. John Duraisamy is just one of the many upper caste ecclesiastical personnel who use their influence with church hierarchy and the access to the media to perpetuate the crime of oppression and dehumanization. The cartoons cited above may appear at first sight to refer to good and bad people in general. But taken in the context of Eraiyur incident and the aftermath of it about which we carried a written up over the web site, the unmistakable reference is to the Dalit community. If that is not the case, one wonders what then was the good news that the editor wanted to give to the readers of his catholic publications in the present context of the a confrontation between upper caste and the Dalit Christians in the above archdiocese of Pondicherry? Is not this message diametrically opposed to the spirit of Jesus who took a stance of resistance to all that is inhuman to all that violates human right and human dignity. Will Jesus tell his followers today that one's character is determined by the caste in which one is born?

Will Jesus who identified himself with the Dalits of his day (the Samaritans, Publicans, tax-collectors, sinners etc.,) and assured them places of honor in the kingdom have the heart to tell the Dalits of today that they will always remain low-people, despised and derided by one and all? The editor who is a priest for thirty years and who is called to serve and shepherd the poorest of the poor in the footsteps of Jesus, his master will do well to reflect on the above question.

Is there anything that the Dalits can do today in the face of such wide spread cultural domination and cultural imperialism that silences them and renders them powerless? The answer is yes. They not only can but must prepare themselves for a cultural revolution. It is only by creating songs, dances, proverbs, folk arts etc, that expose the lies that are perpetuated by the oppressive culture that they will slowly discover their own self-hood. It is the creation of a counter culture that will enable the Dalits to regain their lost dignity and their stolen identity.

Let me end these few reflections by inviting your comments on both the cartoons and my reflections on them. If you feel that the cartoons do in fact inflict a serious psychological wound on the dalit community, please free to write a note to the editor of the weekly condemning such an oppressive and dehumanizing act. Is it not a disgrace to humanity that such things happen even in the 21st century?

*Isaac*

This man takes us back to first century, in stead of taking forward. We are not living in stone age or copper age or industrial age, we are living in space age,,. age of communication, the world has become so small we all become members of one family. The communism, the Marxism has collapsed. The Berlin wall has collapsed, our pope challenged all communist countries and he gives the message 'fear not" are we are living in stone age? we have all passed all these ages now why do we quote a statement which was made someone several centuries ago we cannot use those old sayings which are outdate, they are pessimistic statement which do not give hope, love, which do not inspire us, which never help us to transcend or rise above these miserable condition.... Malice toward none and charity for all... we must transcend above these kind of low mentality in order to become better people, successful people. Jesus came to give us joy.. Jesus sets us free.... As a priest, are you setting us free or oppresses us... Jesus came to liberate... not to oppress... You are dragging us back to the stone age... Is this message help our young people to into third millennium? What is the function of God's word? to give freedom, we are called to greatness in serving people, following the model of Christ... It is insult to all people, mostly to the educated, Christian people...

It is not the church that commits the sins but it is the people, certain staff working in the institution commit sin... it is a social sin. There is a tremendous gap between what we communicate to our people and what we do. People are more willing to see your preaching than hearing your sermons (Pope Paul IV). What we do is more important than what we preach.

*Dominic, France*

This kind of statements reflect the true nature of a person. He reflects of what he is, his culture, his background Phil.4:8 As Paul said, we have to do " whether we preach or write, we have to till the minds of the belivers with things that are noble, true, honorable. good, deserves praise. Keep away from people who try belittle your ambition. Small people always do that. But the really great make you feel that you too can become great. Mark Twin. Power corrupts and absolute power corrupts absolutely. Lord Acton.

## How the Government Justifies the Denial of Rights to Dalit Christian

One can discern various arguments, explicit or implicit, used by the government to deny the Scheduled caste status to Dalit Christians:-

1. The Government argues or implies that Untouchability (or Dalit status) is essentially part of the Hindu religion and

that it plays no part in the non-Hindu religions. So a Dalit who adopts a non-Hindu religion like Christianity ceases to be a Dalit. In other words, it is not possible to be a Christian and an untouchable at the same time.

This is false. That is not how it came about. Untouchability was based on race and not on religion. An untouchable was made an untouchable, not because he was outside of the Hindu religion but he was outside the Hindu race. Even if he adopted the Hindu religion, he did not thereby cease to be an untouchable. This created the possibility of a group of people who were both Hindu in religion and untouchable in status. If such a person now becomes Christian or Sikh or Buddhist, this change away from the Hindu religion still leaves him an untouchable in status because of his race. The government has recognised this fact in the case of the Sikhs and Buddhists, recognising that some people are Sikh and Dalit, or Buddhist and Dalit, at the same time, but illogically it refuses to use the same principle to recognise the possiblity of a people who are Christians and untouchables at the same time, which is the same thing as refusing to include Dalit Christians into the list of the Scheduled castes, the list of Dalits.

There are many new converts to the Hindu religion in America and Europe, but the concept of caste and untouchability has not come to them with the new religion, for they are of the one white race. The same obtains with those who have become Buddhists in Japan, Korea and Taiwan.

Unfortunately, though dogmatically Christianity favors equal opportunity, caste discrimination did not die out at the time of conversion from Hinduism but still prevails in most parts of the country.

2. It may be argued that Sikh dalits or Buddhist dalits were given reservation because Sikhism and Buddhism are offshots of Hinduism.

   This is false. If it were true, they should have been recognised for reservation rights in 1936 and 1950. In fact they got reservation rights much later, in 1956 and 1990, and that by political pressure. The Constitution speaks of Scheduled castes only in articles 330, 332, 334, 335, 338 and 341. Nowhere in those in six articles is there any mention of religion.

3. It may be argued that if the Dalit Christians are included in reservation, it will do harm to the Hindu dalits by cutting into the limited resources available.

   This is false. Christian dalits form only a small percentage of the poplulation of India (1.4), and only 9.5 percent of the total dalit population. Similar inclusion was done for Sikh dalits in 1956 and for Buddhist dalits in 1990. At that time, no such economic objection was raised.

4. It may be argued that dalit Christians are already receiving help from Christian sources, and do not urgently need inclusion.

   This is false. Numerous State commissions have described the extreme poverty of the dalit Christians. In contrast to this, the Sikhs have the highest per capita income in the whole of India, but they have been included.

In 1993-94, of the total aid coming from abroad, 80 percent went to non-Christian entities and less than 20 percent to Christian ones. (The Week, 15 September 1996). Of these Christian resources, a great part went to non-Christian beneficiaries: for example, the Christian hospital at Vellore, Tamilnadu, has treated 50 crore (500 million) patients, of whom 81.53 percent were Hindus. There are 4,500 Christian high schools and 230 colleges serving the urban middle class, which is mainly Hindu. These fee-paying institutions are far beyond means of the Dalit Christians. Thus the Christians are subsidising the Hindus rather than their own poverty-stricken Dalits.

CHAPTER 9

# Attacks on Dalit Women: A Pattern of Impunity

Singularly positioned at the bottom of India's caste, class, and gender hierarchies, largely uneducated and consistently paid less than their male counterparts, Dalit women make up the majority of landless labourers and scavengers, as well as a significant percentage of the women forced into prostitution in rural areas or sold into urban brothels. As such, they come into greater contact with landlords and enforcement agencies than their upper-caste counterparts. Their subordinate position is exploited by those in power who carry out their attacks with impunity. Throughout this report, Human Rights Watch has documented the use of sexual abuse and other forms of violence against Dalit women as tools by landlords and the police to inflict political "lessons" and crush dissent and labour movements within Dalit communities. In Laxmanpur-Bathe, Bihar, women were raped and mutilated before being massacred by members of the Ranvir Sena in 1997; in Bihar and Tamil Nadu, women have been beaten, arrested, and sometimes tortured during violent search and raid operations on Dalit villages in recent years. Like other Indian women whose relatives are sought by the police, Dalit women have also been arrested and raped in custody as a means of punishing their male relatives who are hiding from the police. As very young women, they are forced into prostitution in temples under the devadasi system.

Cases documented by India's National Commission for Women, by local and national nongovernmental women's rights organizations, and by the press, reveal a pattern of impunity in attacks on women consistent with our findings. In all cases of attacks on women documented in this report, the accused state and private actors escaped punishment; in most cases, attacks were neither investigated nor prosecuted. Until recently, the plight of Dalit women has also been neglected by various political movements. As explained by Ruth Manorama, head of the newly constituted National Federation for Dalit Women:

Dalit women are at the bottom in our community. Within the women's movement, Dalit issues have not been taken seriously. Within the Dalit movement, women have been ignored. Caste, class, and gender need to be looked at together. Dalit women have contributed to this discourse... Women's labour is already undervalued; when she is a Dalit, it is nil... The atrocities are also much more vulgar. Other activists echo the notion that women are hit the hardest in everyday life and during caste clashes. One activist told Human Rights Watch, "Sexual violence is linked to debt bondage in rural areas." Another commented on the need to give priority to women's cases:

Making women eat human defecation, parading them naked, gang rapes, these are women-specific crimes. Gang rapes are mostly of Dalit women. These cases should be given top priority, requiring immediate action and immediate punishment.

## Women and the Law

### India's Constitution

Article 14 of India's constitution ensures equality by providing that: "The State shall not deny to any person equality before the law or the equal protection of the laws within the territory of India." Article 15(1) provides that the "State shall not discriminate against any citizen on grounds only of religion, race, caste, sex, place of birth or any of them," while articles 16(1) and 16(2) prohibit discrimination in general, and gender discrimination in matters of public employment. To promote equality, Article 15(3) provides that the state is free to make "any special provision for women and children."

Part IV of the constitution lists the Directive Principles of State Policy, including Article 39(b) of the constitution which provides that the state direct its policy toward ensuring equal pay for equal work for men and women. Section (a) of the same article provides that the state shall, in particular, direct its policy toward securing that citizens, men and women equally, have the right to an adequate means of livelihood.

Section (c) requires that the state secure the health of workers, men and women, and ensure that children are not abused, and citizens are not forced by economic necessity to enter vocations that are unsuited to their age and strength. Finally, Article 44 of the constitution, asks that the state strive to introduce a uniform civil code for citizens so that varying religious codes do not dictate the personal laws governing women's lives. These provisions cannot be enforced in the state through courts as they are a "directive principles" of state policy.

## Penal and Criminal Codes

In recognizing the history of police abuse against women, amendments to the Indian Penal Code and Criminal Procedure Code afford women a variety of legal protections in their dealings with state agents. For instance, when a woman is searched upon arrest, it must be done by a female officer with "strict regard to decency and modesty." A police officer has no power to compel a woman or a child below the age of fifteen to appear in a police station to obtain information from her, and must instead visit the place in which the informant resides.

When searching a place occupied by a person sought to be arrested, if the place is occupied by a female (not being the person to be arrested) the police must give notice to her before entering that she has the liberty to withdraw.

The Indian Penal Code also provides for stricter punishments when the crime of rape is committed in custody. Section 376 states that the crime of rape, when committed by a private actor, is punishable by a minimum of seven to ten years and a maximum of life imprisonment.

Under subsection (2), the rape is punishable by "rigorous imprisonment" for a term of ten years to life if it is committed by a police officer against a woman in his custody (or in the custody of a police officer subordinate to him), or on the premises of his police station or a station house.

### *Convention on the Elimination of All Forms of Discrimination against Women, 1979*

Under Article 2 of the International Convention on the Elimination of All Forms of Discrimination against Women, states parties are required to "establish legal protection of the rights of women on an equal basis with men and to ensure through competent national tribunals and other public institutions the effective protection of women against any act of discrimination." They must also "refrain from engaging in any act or practice of discrimination against women and to ensure that public authorities and institutions shall act in conformity with this obligation." Women are also entitled to equal remuneration and protection of health and safety in working conditions. With respect to the situation of rural women, the convention requires states parties to take into account the "significant roles which rural women play in the economic survival of their families, including their work in the non-monetized sectors of the economy," and to, "take all appropriate measures to ensure the application of the provisions of this Convention to women in rural areas."

## Failure to Prosecute Rape Cases

Beginning with the lodging of the First Information Report (FIR) at the local police station through to the judge's opinion, should a case reach that far, women in India are faced with daunting obstacles in prosecuting cases of rape. If a woman is poor, belongs to a lower caste, and lives in a rural area, it is even more difficult for her to gain access to the justice system. Those who are able to pursue cases of sexual assault have to battle entrenched biases at every stage of the process: with the police, the doctors, the judges, and even their own families. Even if the police agree to file the FIR, they often fail to efficiently and deliberately collect the necessary evidence. Witnesses, should they exist, rarely agree to come forward to testify or corroborate the victim's statement for fear of retribution from the perpetrators, who are often in positions of relative power in the community. If the case manages to get filed and investigated despite these obstacles, then new problems arise when the woman goes before a judge whose gender biases and caste affiliations can greatly influence the judgment in the case.

For the reasons outlined above, and because of low reporting, conviction in rape cases is uncommon. From 1989 to 1993, reported crimes against women in India increased by 25.2 percent. At the same time, the National Crime Records Bureau's 1994 report revealed that convictions for crimes against women were minimal.

Out of the total (rape) cases in which trials were completed, 41.5 percent ended in conviction during 1990, 34.2 percent in 1991 and 33.8 percent in 1992 and 30.3 percent in 1993. Thus the acquittal percentage is showing an upward trend over the years. The rate of disposal of cases in courts was 23.9 percent in 1992 and 16.8 percent in 1993. On an average, 80 percent of the cases remained pending for trial. This is a disquieting status.

The average conviction rate for rape has also been consistently lower than the less serious crimes of burglary and theft. In addition to compiling testimony on cases of rape by the police and during caste clashes, Human Rights Watch also interviewed several victims of rape on their experience with the legal system. Two illustrative cases are outlined below. Also included is the well-known case of Bhanwari Devi—whose rapists were acquitted on a judge's reasoning that "an upper-caste man could not have defiled himself by raping a lower-caste woman."—and other cases illustrating gender bias at the trial level.

## Story of Dalit Girl M. Meena

M. Meena is a twelve-year-old Dalit girl; her name has been changed to protect her identity. She was raped in September 1997 by a twenty-one-year-old Thevar man in a southern district of Tamil Nadu. Successful prosecution of her case was thwarted when the accused paid bribes to the police. Because of Meena's young age, Human Rights Watch obtained details of her rape and subsequent experience with the police largely from interviewing a social worker who had been active in her case; we then met with Meena to confirm the reports. The social worker described the incident:

On her way home from a local store, a Thevar boy named Karuppaswami called Meena over on the pretext that she would help him pick something up. She refused and kept going. He then showed her a bill hook and threatened her. He pulled her to a nearby tree, undressed her, and raped her. She was unconscious and could not walk. Some people took her home and called the Manur police station. The police said to come and file a report. So they took her there and gave a complaint. TheThevar people also went to the police station and gave Rs. 10,000 (US$250) to the police and threatened the girl's father not to divulge the facts or the family would face dire consequences.

As a result of pressure from the rapist's family, the police filed a case under Section 75 of the Madras City Police Act—instead of sections 375 and 376 of the Indian Penal Code for rape and punishment for rape. Section 75 of the Police Act refers to creating a nuisance in a public place and carries a fine as its punishment. With the help of the social worker, Meena's parents again approached the police to file a rape case.

The next day I went to the village and saw the girl. She was in bad condition. She had a fever, and she was unconscious. I talked to the parents and said, "Let's go to the police and government hospital." We took the girl to the superintendent of police's (SP) office. We only saw him at 5:00 p.m. Then the SP said that he will call the police to file a case and asked us to take the girl to a government hospital at High Ground Paliangotti. I was with them the whole time. The doctors refused to do a check-up without an FIR. We then took her in a van and came back to the police station. There was no inspector there. The police refused to register an FIR. At 11:00 p.m. the inspector came and registered an FIR. He then sent the police constable with us to the hospital. At 12:30 a.m. we reached the hospital. They did the check-up. At 10:00 a.m. the next morning we took her to court. The magistrate asked to admit her in the hospital. She was there for ten days. The police collected her panties. There were blood stains on it. She recovered and went back to school.

After much persistence, Meena's parents were finally able to register a case of rape under Section 376 of the Indian Penal Code. However, the police refused to simultaneously register the case under the Atrocities Act. The accused spent forty-five days in jail and was subsequently released on bail. In December 1997, soon after his release, he physically assaulted the husband of the social worker who had been helping Meena with her case. According to the social worker, "The rapist and his relatives blocked and damaged my husband's vehicle with their van and beat him. We went back and beat one of those boys, and they filed a case against us. But we also filed a case in a different police station." As of December 1998 no charges had been filed in the rape case, and the accused remained out on bail.

### Story of Dalit Girl R. Chitra

In 1996, twenty-six-year-old R. Chitra (also an alias) of Kammapatti village, Tirunelveli district, southern Tamil Nadu, was gang raped by Thevars from a neighboring village. After much public pressure from residents of her village, the police took up the case, but despite her positive identification of the rapists, and despite many eyewitnesses to the event, they ultimately dropped the investigation. Chitra told Human Rights Watch of her experience with the Thevars:

> It happened one and a half years ago. Another girl named Savariammal and I went to the forest for grass for our goats. There is a dilapidated building in the forest. Behind that building, four persons hid themselves... The four people came out and said "Where are you coming from?" I said I am from Kammapatti. They asked my village name, so they knew I was a Dalit. They left and went five steps ahead. When they passed, me and my friend started gathering our goats and prepared to leave. The men were holding bill hooks in their hands, and we knew it was not a safe place to be. All of a sudden, one man turned around and grabbed my hand. I tried to resist them for two hours. Among the four, one hid and the remaining three boys took turns. They had weapons, I only had a stick. They then took away my stick so I had no defense... Some other people from that village saw the struggle but did not come close, because the men had weapons. Three men raped me. It lasted for an hour. There was no bleeding, but there were bruises all over. When one committed penetration, the other two stood by and watched. In turn they all raped me. The fourth one was hiding and saw the whole thing. I had bruises all over, on mychest, my hip. My skin was torn and full of nail marks. I was hurt because I was trying to escape.

After a failed attempt to commit suicide by pouring kerosene on her body and setting herself on fire, Chitra was convinced by her family to go to the police. She did not know her rapists but recognized that they were Thevars from a neighboring village. She was also able to provide the police with details on their clothing, their appearance, and their age: "I gave an oral complain, and the constable reduced it to writing. That was the only time they were sympathetic." The day of her suicide attempt, Chitra visited the Tirunelveli government hospital, where four female doctors examined her and collected specimens. She also handed over to police the clothes she had been wearing when raped. Despite the strength of the evidence, the police told her brothers to persuade her not to register a complaint. But her brothers were persistent, and most of the residents of her Dalit-dominant village insisted that the police arrest the accused. They argued that if "anything was committed by Dalits, the police do not allow it, so why are they allowing this?" The day after the rape, the police arrested two persons and presented them for identification. The following day Chitra's brother complained to the deputy superintendent of police that the two remaining accused had not been arrested. After the police took the mothers of the two absconding men to the police station, they too surrendered.

So I identified all four. The sub-inspector recorded my statement. The police also talked to Savariammal, the girl who was with me. She said she saw it happen but did not know the identity of the people. But she must have known. She simply kept away from saying the truth. She was probably threatened. All surrounding villages belong to Thevars. The police arrested and remanded them to Koilpatti jail. I went for the line-up in front of the magistrate. They put eighteen persons in a row. They put the four among them. Even then I identified them.

After many promises of state compensation for Chitra, the money never came. Despite initial cooperation from the police, the case never went to trial. Chitra was not even informed if the culprits were arrested after she identified them: "I don't know how many days they were in jail. I haven't been contacted again by the police." She was denied access to her own medical records. "The doctors said they have to give them to police and they will send them to court." For social and monetary reasons, Chitra's family has been unwilling and unable to pursue the case. "My family is afraid to proceed because of their reputation," she explained. "The FIR should be there. I was never invited to court to depose, so I think the trial was not held. I didn't go again... We don't have money for an advocate, and we cannot travel frequently to court. Even if I decide to pursue I have to get permission from my mother and brothers."

*Caste and Gender Bias in the Courts*

The lack of law enforcement leaves many Dalit women unable to approach the legal system to seek redress. Women are often also unaware of the laws; their ignorance is exploited by their opponents, by the police, and, as illustrated by the cases below, by the judiciary. Even when cases are registered, the lack of appropriate investigation, or the judge's own caste and gender biases, can lead to acquittal, regardless of the availability of evidence or witnesses. The failure to successfully prosecute cases of rape also allows for crimes against women to continue unabated, and in the caste context, encourages the use of rape as a tool to punish and silence Dalit communities.

## Story of Dalit Girl Bhanwari Devi

Bhanwari Devi's case is a typical example of the influence of caste bias on the justice system and the inability of lower-caste women to obtain redress. It is also a striking example of rape as a weapon of retaliation used to punish and silence women's rights advocates. The nature of the district judge's opinion sounded many alarms, and the case itself was taken up by several women's rights organizations in north India.

Bhanwari Devi joined the Rajasthan Government's Women's Development Programme (WDP), called Sathin, in 1985 as a grassroots worker. In April 1992 she reported the child marriage of the one-year-old daughter of Ram Karan Gurjar to WDP authorities. The police came to the village and tried to stop the marriage, but the family proceeded with the ceremony in secret. On September 22, 1992, in the presence of her husband, Bhanwari was gang raped by members of the Gurjar family in retaliation for her intervention in the child marriage. Upon approaching the police, Bhanwari was told, however, that she was too old and unattractive to merit the attentions of young men.

The trial judge acquitted the accused on the reasoning that "rape is usually committed by teenagers, and since the accused are middle-aged and therefore respectable, they could not have committed the crime. An upper-caste man could not have defiled himself by raping a lower-caste woman." Those accused of raping Bhanwari also enjoyed political support. BJP leader Kanhaiya Lal Meena reportedly organized a rally in support of the accused. As of February 1999, Bhanwari was still in court appealing the acquittal.

Bhanwari's case, and in particular the manner in which it was handled by the police and the courts, is not an isolated incident. Cases at all levels have the potential to be influenced by the judge's personal perceptions of caste and gender that are brought to bear in determining the credibility of evidence or the likelihood of guilt. The case material that follows, though not specific to the report, is intended to illustrate the atmosphere of prejudice that Dalit women face—both as Dalits and as women. These biases are pervasive all the way to the top of the legal system. The few cases that manage to reach the Supreme Court still do not escape these deep-seated prejudices.

*Story of Dalit Women Shri Satish Mehra v. Delhi Administration and Another*

Gender bias that blames women for the actions of men also persists at the Supreme Court level. In *Shri Satish Mehra v. Delhi Administration and Another*, a July 1996 case of the rape of a three-year-old girl by her father, the Supreme Court concluded that there lacked sufficient evidence to proceed to trial and pointed to the "seemingly incredulous nature of the accusations against a father that molested his infant child." The court instead accused the mother of leveling false accusations to take revenge on her husband for an unhappy marriage.

The opinion added that the judge presiding over the case prior to the Supreme Court appeal ought not to have overlooked the peculiar circumstances of the case, including the fact that the accused's wife found their marital life to be "extremely painful and unhappy from the very inception" and that she had accused him of being an alcoholic and prone to inflicting severe physical violence. Based on these circumstances, the Supreme Court concluded that the wife's "attitude to the petitioner, even de hors the allegation involving the child, was vengeful." As in the Bhanwari Devi case, despite the legal basis it claimed for the decision, the court only briefly touched on evidentiary matters and seemed instead to be motivated by its professed disbelief that such crimes could actually take place.

*Story of Dalit Women Suman Rani (Prem Chand and Another v. State of Haryana)*

Dalit women are frequent victims of custodial rape. Section 376(2) of the Indian Penal Code mandates minimum sentences for state agents who rape women in their custody. Other loopholes in the law, however, allow the judiciary to sidestep mandatory sentencing. In the famous Suman Rani custodial rape case, the Supreme Court refused to apply the minimum ten-year sentence to the police officers charged because of the victim's "questionable character." The court's opinion quoted a medical officer who testified that the "victim girl [was] used to frequent intercourse and parturition and there was no mark of violence of sexual assault on any part of her body." The opinion further added:

[T]he victim Suman Rani was a woman of questionable character and easy virtue with lewd and lascivious behavior and that the very fact that this girl had not complained of the alleged rape said to have been committed at [the] police station by thesetwo appellants to anyone till [five days after the incident] shows that the present version is not worthy of acceptance. The court ultimately held that the peculiar facts of the case, coupled with the conduct of the victim, did not warrant the imposition of the minimum ten-year sentence. The court instead invoked the proviso to Section 376(2), which allows for the judge to use his discretion in reducing the minimum sentence, and cut the sentence in half.

## Violence and Crimes Against Indian Dalit Women

### Violence against Dalit

Violence against Dalits is commonplace. Hillary Mayell, (2003) sampled some mainstream Indian newspapers and found headlines such as: "Dalit boy beaten to death for plucking flowers"; "Dalit tortured by cops for three days"; "Dalit 'witch' paraded naked in Bihar"; "Dalit killed in lock-up at Kurnool"; "7 Dalits burnt alive in caste clash"; "5 Dalits lynched in Haryana"; "Dalit woman gang-raped, paraded naked"; "Police egged on mob to lynch Dalits" (as cited in Hillary Mayen, 2003). Fear of public humiliation, beatings, and rape keep India's Untouchables in their place. For Dalits, simple acts like drinking from a public well or walking through an upper-caste neighbourhood can evoke such violent reactions that these simple acts can in fact be a life-threatening offenses (Amnesty International, 2001, 2005, Hillary Mayell, 2003).

Statistics from India's National Crime Records Bureau indicate that in 2000 25,455 crimes were committed against Dalits (Hillary Mayell, 2003). Every hour two Dalits were assaulted; every day three Dalit women raped, two Dalits murdered, and two Dalit homes torched. Yet the actual reality of crimes against Dalits is much worse than these numbers suggest. Amnesty estimated that only about 5 percent of attacks are registered (Hillary Mayel, 2003, Amnesty International, 2005). Dalits are afraid of retaliation and intimidation. They are also often discouraged by the bribes demanded by police, who more often than not, do nothing about it.

## Violence against Untouchable Women

The plight of Dalit women is especially depressing. They suffer double discrimination, one based on caste, the other on gender. Many young Dalit girls for example, end up as prostitutes under the guise of the religious practice devadasis, meaning "female servant of god." They end up serving upper-caste members sexually. Many of them are eventually sold to an urban brothel. Other Dalit women are frequently raped, gang-raped, beaten, tortured or forced to walk through the streets naked as punishment for something she or her family has done (Amnesty International 2005).

Hillary Mayell (2003) mentions a 1999 case that illustrates the implacable mix of gender and caste.

To punish her for the fact that one of her sons had run off with the daughter of a higher-caste family, a 42-year-old Dalit woman was gang-raped and then burnt alive after she, her husband, and two of her sons had been confined and tortured for eight days by upper-caste relatives of the girl. While the local police knew that this was going on, they did not intervene because of the influence and status of the upper-caste family (Hillary Mayen, 2003).

Amnesty International (2005) reported on the following case.

Ram Chandra, a Dalit living in Munni Khera was married to Ramvathi. They owned a piece of land on which they had a house. Dalits are generally not allowed to own land, and upper caste villagers were trying to take the land from them. In September 1998, Ramvathi was gang-raped by five men. These men are believed to be higher caste villagers who raped her as a punishment for the couple's refusal to give up their land. For a while, the couple moved to Ramvathi's parent's village some distance away. They returned to the village on January 30, 1999 to repossess their property. They were met with violence. First Ram Chandra was severely beaten. He described what happened next as follows:

"They attacked my wife with stick, she fell down then and there. After that my wife came to me and laid over my body to save me, then they had beaten my wife with sticks and axes. She got deep injuries on the head and shoulder and her right hand and leg broken. [one of the attackers] put off all the clothes of my wife, raped her and inserted and pushed the stick in her private part".

Ramvathi died the next morning (taken from Amnesty International, 2005)

Amnesty International reported in 2001 on an "extremely high" number of sexual assaults on Dalit women. Landlords, upper-caste villagers, and police officers are primarily responsible for the assaults.

## In Closing

There are laws and regulations against caste-based discrimination, but they are not enforced or enacted. Many groups, including the police, continue to discriminate against Dalits. There is a culture of impunity when it comes to violating Dalits, and perpetrators are rarely brought to justice. Until India's "hidden apartheid" is abolished, as A K. R. Narayana said it so well in quoting Ambedkar, India's true Untouchable hero, the world's largest democracy is nothing but a palace built on a dung heap.

## Caste-related Violence in India

Caste-related violence and hate crimes in India have occurred despite the gradual reduction of casteism in the country.

According to a report by Human Rights Watch, "Dalits and indigenous peoples (known as Scheduled Tribes or adivasis) continue to face discrimination, exclusion, and acts of communal violence. Laws and policies adopted by the Indian government provide a strong basis for protection, but are not being faithfully implemented by local authorities."

### Phoolan Devi

Phoolan Devi (1963 – 2001) was an Indian dacoit (bandit), who later turned politician. Born in a lower-caste *Mallah* family, she was mistreated and abandoned by her husband. She was later kidnapped by a gang of dacoits. The upper-caste Thakur leader of the gang tried to rape her, but she was protected by the deputy leader Vikram, who belonged to her caste. Later, an upper-caste Thakur friend of Vikram killed him, abducted Phoolan, and locked her up in the Behmai village. Phoolan was raped in the village by Thakur men, until she managed to escape after three weeks.

Phoolan Devi then formed a gang of Mallahs, which carried out a series of violent robberies in north and central India, mainly targeting upper-caste people. Some say that Phoolan Devi targeted only the upper-caste people and shared the loot with the lower-caste people, but the Indian authorities insist this is a myth. Seventeen months after her escape from Behmai, Phoolan returned to the village, to take her revenge. On February 14, 1981, her gang massacred twenty-two Thakur men in the village, only two of which were involved in her kidnapping or rape. Phoolan Devi later surrendered and served eleven years in prison, after which she became a politician. During her election campaign, she was criticized by the women widowed in the Behmai massacre. Kshatriya Swabhimaan Andolan Samanvay Committee (KSASC), a Kshatriya organization, held a statewide campaign to protest against her. She was elected a Member of Parliament twice.

On July 25, 2001, Phoolan Devi was shot dead by unknown assassins. Later, a man called Sher Singh Rana confessed to the murder, saying he was avenging the deaths of 22 Kshatriyas at Behmai. Although the police were skeptical of his claims, he was arrested. Rana escaped from Tihar Jail in 2004. In 2006, KSASC decided to honor Rana for "upholding the dignity of the Kshatriya community" and "drying the tears of the widows of Behmai."

*Andhra Pradesh*

This state is considered to be one of the least caste-crime infested places of India which has not had many Dalit Massacres.

*Ranvir Sena*

Ranvir Sena is an caste-supremacist fringe paramilitary group based in Bihar. The group is based amongst the forward-caste landlord, and carries out actions against the outlawed naxals in rural areas. It has committed violent acts against Dalits and other members of the scheduled caste community in an effort to scuttle reform movements aimed at their emancipation.

*Tamil Nadu*

The state of Tamil Nadu has witnessed several caste-based incidents both against Dalits and Brahmins. In 2000, three young men belonging to the Dalit undercaste were killed in the Cuddalore district of Tamil Nadu. This fuelled some localized violence in the caste-sensitive region, which has seen numerous caste-related incidents in which the majority of the victims have been Dalits. Six of the killings have been registered as murders under the Indian Penal Code and others as "Deaths under suspicious circumstances". No arrests have been made in these cases.

However, several Dalits have been arrested as *goondas* (hoodlums). The Chief minister of Tamil-Nadu, M. Karunanidhi, has been accused of having an "anti-Dalit" bias by the radical organization "Dalit Panthers of India". Theories concerning these crimes against Dalits range from "alcohol bootleggers opposing prohibition movements among Dalits" to "inter-caste relations between an upper-caste Vanniya boy and a Dalit girl". Political parties sympathetic to the Dalits have protested against these incidents and have alleged systemic biases against Dalits in several parts of the country.

*Bant Singh case of Punjab*

On the evening of January 5, 2006 Bant Singh, a poor Sikh Dalit, was attacked by unknown assailants. His injuries necessitated medical amputation. He alleges that this was in retaliation for actively working to secure justice for his daughter, who was gang raped by upper caste members of his village in Punjab five years earlier.

A 55-year-old Dalit Sikh woman, Sawinder Kaur has been tortured, stripped and tied to a tree in Ram Duali village of Punjab because her nephew eloped with a girl from the same community. The police arrested four persons for allegedly committing the crime on 9 September 2007.

In January, 1999 four members of the village panchayat of Bhungar Khera village in Abohar paraded a handicapped Dalit woman naked through the village. No action was taken by the police, despite local Dalit protests. It was only on July 20 that the four pancha yat members were arrested, after the State Home Department was compelled to order an inquiry into the incident.

In Amritsar, a Sikh mother of four children, Gurmeet Kaur was allegedly paraded naked by a father and son duo at the bus station of Jhamaka village falling under Chabhal police station on Sunday.

A Dalit Sikh woman, Sukhwinder Kaur of Sumel Kheri village was molested and beaten up by an octroi contractor of Malaudh when she resisted his attempt to sexually exploit her.

*Kherlanji Massacre*

On September 29, 2006, four members of the Bhotmange family belonging to the Dalit underclass were slaughtered in Kherlanji, a small village in Bhandara district of Maharashtra. The women of the family, Surekha and Priyanka, were paraded naked in public, then allegedly gang-raped before being murdered. The criminal act was allegedly carried out by assailants from the Kunbi caste (classified as Other Backward Castes by Government of India) for "opposing" the requisition of their field to have a road built over it.

On November 23, 2006, several members of the Dalit community in the nearby district of Chandrapur staged a protest regarding this incident. The protesters allegedly turned violent and pelted stones. The police had to resort to baton charging to control the situation. Dalit leaders, however, denied that they had sparked the violence and that they were "protesting in peace".

*2006 Dalit protests in Maharashtra*

In November-December 2006, the desecration of a Ambedkar statue in Kanpur (Uttar Pradesh) triggered off violent protests by Dalits in Maharashtra. Several people remarked that the protests were fuleled by the Kherlanji Massacre. During the violent protests, the Dalit protestors set three trains on fire, damaged over 100 buses and clashed with police. At least four deaths and many more injuries were reported.

Later, the Kanpur Police arrested a Dalit youth Arun Kumar Balmiki for desecrating the Ambedkar statue. According to the police, the youth had "admitted to having damaged the statue in a drunken state along with two friends". Earlier in a similar case, a Dalit youth was held for desecrating an Ambedkar statue in Gulbarga, Karnataka.

In response to these protests, Raj Thackeray drew attention to another incident in Kherlanji, in which a Dalit allegedly raped a girl and killed her. Thackeray demanded action on those responsible for the rape and the subsequent death of the girl, and also remarked that nobody helped the girl's family.

*Rajasthan*

In the Indian province of Rajasthan, between the years 1999 and 2002, crimes against Dalits average at about 5024 a year, with 46 killings and 138 cases of rape. In January 2007, a Jat girl was thrown into a canal near the border with Haryana for marrying a Dalit boy, although she swam to shore and was rescued by strangers.

*Punjab*

On 25 May 2009, violence and rioting broke out when thousands of protesters took to the streets in almost all major towns and cities in the Indian state of Punjab after a Sikh guru impersonator, Sant Ramanand, was attacked by a rival group in a temple in Vienna, Austria. He was among 16 people injured, including another preacher Sant Nirajnan Dass, and later died in hospital. Both the preachers were from a low-caste Sikh sect which has a large following in parts of Punjab and had travelled to Vienna to conduct a special service. Several high-caste Sikh groups had apparently opposed his presence and threatened violence.

*Other Incidents*

On September 1, 2007 some Yadavs poured steaming dal on a Dalit woman and her infant daughter, and beat up several other Dalits, for allowing their children to play in the premises of a temple at Shivayalay Mushari, on the outskirts of Patna.

# CHAPTER 10 Violence Against Dalit Women During the Southern District Clashes

> Sexual oppression is intimately connected to land oppression. By keeping lower-caste women sexually subjugated, the upper castes control the men. — Father Manuel Alphonse, All India Catholic University Federation (AICUF)

As Dalit men migrate to cities in search of jobs, women are left to work as agricultural labourers in rural areas. Women "bear the brunt of attacks because they are stuck in these feudal arrangements." As a result of escalating caste clashes, attacks on Dalit women, by state and private actors, have also escalated.

## Violence by Private Actors

On January 25, 1998, the Dalit colony of Veludavur village in Villapuram district was attacked by members of seven caste Hindu villages. The attack was allegedly perpetrated by the Vanniya caste and instigated by the Naidars (both backward castes). Tensions began with a government auction of common properties in the village, such as ponds and tamarind trees; the Dalits were demanding their right to participate. The same evening, Vanniyas entered and destroyed 400 Dalit huts. Many of the young Dalit men were in Andhra Pradesh at the time, cultivating sugarcane. Only women, children and the elderly were left in the village, and the women were particularly targeted. A social worker in the village claimed that there were "sexual attempts on many women, but they don't want to talk about it. Many are unmarried or their husbands are away. They fear the consequences if these things are revealed." Over 700 families were displaced as a result of the attack. They took shelter in neighboring villages.

Burnad Fatima of the Tamil Nadu Women's Forum (TNWF) explained the number of cases TNWF had come across in which women were targets of caste clashes: Any time any caste riots take place, there is immediate action against women and immediate raping. During last year's riots, a forty-year-old woman was gang raped. A seventy-year-old was dragged out of her house and stripped. In Anchipet a handicapped girl was thrown from her wheelchair which was then damaged. Innocent women are butchered, raped, and killed even though they are not directly responsible for any of the riots.

TNWF and People's Watch members went on to describe another attack during the southern district clashes, and the lack of press attention to such cases: In Nammakal [district] a girl was gang raped, murdered, and then butchered. She belonged to the scavengers community. The men belonged to the weaving community. They cut off her hand and leg and shaved her head. They then cut her head and put a stick into her private parts and then hung her head with the stick. Why are they driven to this extent? Because for them Dalits are nothing. They give more respect to their animals... The papers are censored, they don't name the community, and they don't report the figures.

A representative of the Rural Centre for Women's Development in Tirunelveli district spoke to Human Rights Watch of instances of rape by landlords, other upper castes, and the police, "who always support the landlords... [W]omen never say anything because they are afraid and need employment. Also society would blame them. Even their husband would separate from them. I see it daily."

Punduthai, a forty-five-year-old widow and mother of two, told Human Rights Watch that she had to leave her village to protect herself and her daughter from sexual abuse by Thevar men during the clashes.

In the village, the Thevars entered the house and had sexual intercourse with the Dalit women. They used force and committed rape. My husband died, so if I had stayed then the same things would happen to me. My daughter is also a mature girl. She is twenty years old. I was also worried about my daughter. I can't arrange her marriage. I left all the lands. This is the regular lot of the dominated persons. If there are any riots then all of them jointly rape; they gang rape. I hid in the hills at the time of the riots. We were afraid of these things, so we left.

In November 1997 a twenty-two-year-old Dalit woman spoke up against the debt bondage of her husband and his family (Thevars are the dominant moneylenders and Dalits their primary borrowers). As a result she was brutally beaten and sexually abused by a Vanniya landlord: Her husband and father-in-law did not go to work for two days. The landlord came and asked why. He threatened and insulted her, and she said, "We are not living here under your mercy." The landlord went wild. He started beating her, he tore her blouse to pieces, touched her breast, hit her in the vagina and rolled her on the ground. There was no one to stop him.

Due to disinterest, ignorance of proper procedure, or their own caste biases, the police failed to register or properly investigate many cases of attacks against women during the clashes. Only with pressure from organized women's and human rights groups has the issue been placed before national commissions. The recommendations of these commissions, however, are not binding under statutory law.

## Police Torture of Women/custodial Violence

In addition to attacks by members of the upper castes, women are attacked by the police, security forces, and private militias or armies hired by Thevars. Human Rights Watch spoke to many government officials, activists, and villagers in the Tamil Nadu region about police torture and custodial violence against women. C. V. Shankar, director for the Adi Dravida Tribal Welfare Department, of the state government of Tamil Nadu, explained: We found that women are put in front in both communities and act as a buffer. This has resulted in police action against women. They are taken far away from their homes. Unless they were directly involved in violence, they should not be arrested. In some cases we felt that the arrests could have been avoided.

H. Hanumanthappa, then-chairman of the National

Commission for Scheduled Castes and Scheduled Tribes, added: Once the police start raiding, the menfolk run away. Then they [police] make women the victims. The procedure they adopt is to take the child or wife so that the men come back. They feel that they are the masters of the situation. It has resulted in mass rapes.

The police practice of taking family members as hostages in order to force their relatives to turn themselves in is a common occurrence in Tamil Nadu and other parts of the country. Specific incidents of hostage-taking and custodial violence against women are described below.

Guruswamy Guruammal, a twenty-six-year-old agricultural laborer, suffered a miscarriage as a result of brutal beatings during a police raid on December 2, 1997. She is a resident of Chilaumbotti village of the southern district of Theni andearns Rs. 20 a day (US$0.50). The raid had preceded a planned visited by Dr. Krishanaswamy; posters had been distributed to announce his arrival. On December 2, one such poster was burned by Thevars in the district which led to a Pallar protest and road block. Police raided the village in response to the protests and assaulted many Dalits with their lathis.

At 9:00 a.m. the police lathi-charged the villagers. Superintendent of Police Rajesh Das called me a pallachi, which is a caste name for prostitute. He then opened his pant zip. Sub-Inspector Arivanandam, who is from same community as me, was also there. Rajesh Das said, "Please stand, do not go," and other police scolded me. At 11:00 a.m. the sub-collector came. I told the collector that the superintendent of police had opened his zip and used a vulgar word. I also told him that they had broken my silver pot. The sub-collector said, "You go, I will deal with him." Das was angry that I had pointed him out.

The police, numbering in the hundreds, returned early the next morning and again lathi-charged the village.

They broke all the doors and arrested all the men in the village. Arivanandam and Rajesh Das said, "Where is Guruammal's house?" My husband hid under the cot. My mother was with me at the time. I was in my night clothes. The police started calling me a prostitute. I replied, "Your wife is a prostitute." They beat me. I was four months pregnant at the time. He pulled me naked on the road for one hundred feet. I got injuries on my legs. There were two elderly witnesses, a woman and my grandfather. The police also beat the woman when she asked them to stop dragging me. She is sixty years old; her hand was fractured. There were two men police and two lady police. They brought me to the police van and took me to the office of the Theni superintendent of police. Fifty-three men had been arrested. One of them took off his *lungi* [wrap-around cloth] and gave it to me to cover myself. He was only wearing shorts after that.

Guruammal begged the police at the station to help her. She explained that she was pregnant and in need of medical attention. In response, they called her names and mocked her for making such bold statements the day before. Eventually, Guruammal was transferred to the Trichi jail hospital, where she remained for twenty-five days. After ten days, she had a miscarriage. At the time of the interview, and as a result of being dragged and beaten by the police fists and guns, Guruammal was still visibly scarred on her neck, arms, legs, and abdomen.

She claimed that the police told her to testify that the raid on her village was in search of the illicit brewing of *arrack* (illicit liquor): They said if you accept the fact that the raid was for arrack, then you will be released. They said, "If you don't say arrack, we will file charges against you." So these are the cases that were filed against me and the fifty-three men.

Although Guruammal was attacked as punishment for speaking up against the police, many other women are punished for alleged crimes committed by their male relatives. Activists from People's Watch and the Tamil Nadu Women's Forum explained the tactics employed by the police: The police enter houses and attack the women even though they should never search when the women are alone. The police are arresting women if either the husband or son is absconding. They take them into custody and rape them. Three years ago, in a slum nearby, a forty-three-year-old woman lost her husband. Her son was involved in a murder case. She was arrested along with her daughter and daughter-in-law. They were taken to the police station where the police raped the mother in front of the other women. They then brought her home and burned her in her hut.

The activists also described a new tactic employed by the police of removing women's clothes and beating them from their knees to their shoulders, "because they know that women will not show others these parts."

At a Madras conference on women's rights, held on April 28 and 29, 1995, dozens of Dalit and tribal women publicly came forward to testify about their experiences of custodial rape at the hands of Tamil Nadu police. The conference was sponsored by the Tamil Nadu Women's Forum and Asia Pacific Forum for Women, Law and Development. In many of the statements, women claimed that the police were searching for their male relatives when they first came upon them. Pursuant to Section 160 of the Criminal Procedure Code, police conducting investigations are prohibited from questioning female witnesses at any place other than their residence. Women are often unaware of these laws, and their ignorance is exploited by the police. As she stated at the women's rights conference, Rangammal of Orathanadu village came into contact with the police when her husband was repeatedly arrested for selling arrack. One night, the police came to her house and forcibly took her to the police station.

They said I should not be going home at that time and dragged me into the room, and three of them raped me repeatedly. I lost consciousness. In the morning they allowed me to go with a warning that I should not reveal anything. Due to fear I remained silent.

Vijaya from Coimbatore was approached by the police late in the night: When I demanded to know where I was being taken, the police answered that I was providing food for [my brother] Vellaiyan... Since Vellaiyan was related to us the police caught hold [of] us like that... Later, one after another, five of them raped me repeatedly. I was unable to bear the pain since I was also a small girl... [T]he policemen said that I was pretending pain and I would even bear with another ten persons.

The police had also taken Vijaya's parents into custody. "The police said if I promised not to reveal anything to anyone, they would release my parents, and I agreed to it." Together with her aunt and mother, Vijaya arrived at the Anathapuram police station the next day.

The Sub-Inspector on duty was Krishnamoorthy. He said at least the Pondicherry police had raped and left [me] alive, if he telephoned the Dharmapuri police [they] would rape me and throw me [in] the canal... When we pleaded that we were uneducated and without any jobs, mostly engaged in manual works and needed justice, the Sub-Inspector threatened that he would have us beaten up if we further spoke. We had no other alternative but to return to the village.

With the help of civil liberties groups, Vijaya approached the police again. After some days, she added, "women police took me to a doctor. They explained to the doctor that I was of low character, a prostitute, that I was spreading rumours to prevent the arrest of my brothers, etc. They then advised the doctor not to take my case serious[ly]." Vijaya's family was soon approached by the police and offered Rs. 150,000 (US$3,750) to drop the case. She did not accept the money. The police charged Vijaya's father with theft and took him into custody for ten days. He claimed that he was tortured, while the police claimed that Vijaya was threatening the police with a false case of rape so that her father would be released. Because none of the villagers were willing to step forward as witnesses, Vijaya was unable to pursue her case.

In the village of Muthaandikuppam, South Arcot district, a husband filed a complaint against his wife, Vasantha, after a misunderstanding between the couple. On the night of March 21, 1994, Vasantha was forced to spend the night in the police station under the pretext that there were no women police available to escort her home. She was "gang raped by four constables and a sub-inspector of the same police station and [then] murdered. They attempted to dispose [of] the body but could not succeed. They spread a rumour that Vasantha committed suicide by hanging from the fan at the police rest room in the police station." Community members, civil liberties groups, and political parties demanded appropriate, severesanctions against the perpetrators. The Tamil Nadu government responded by temporarily suspending the constables involved.

On February 21, 1995, twenty-year-old Poonkothai witnessed the rape and murder of her forty-eight-year-old mother by police who were searching for her brother. The incident took place around

7:00 a.m. when police arrived at Poonkothai's house looking for her brother Murthy: "They blamed my mother [for] hiding the whereabouts of my brother, who is suspected in a murder of a person found dead_near his house." Despite her mother's repeated denials, the police took both of them, along with Poonkothai's one-and-a-half-year-old daughter, to the Vannarapettai police station.

> We were beaten up severely and were tortured with abusive words and brutal attacks... One of the senior personnel ordered the others to use the "Punjab method" to elicit facts from my mother. They stripped my mother in front of me and took her inside_ I repeatedly heard my mother groaning and pleading them not to torture her_ With tears she was telling me that four men gang raped her and tortured her by inserting the lathi in the vagina and beat[ing] her in her private parts.

The police later brought her mother home, stuffed a piece of cloth in her mouth, poured petrol over her, and set her on fire. They left the scene soon thereafter. A neighbor intervened and took the mother to the hospital, where she later died. When Poonkothai's husband approached the police station to file a case, the police registered the death as a suicide. After many NGO protests, the police filed a First Information Report (FIR). Poonkothai's two neighbors, whose sons were also police suspects, and her two sisters-in-law were also taken into custody for several days and similarly tortured. One sister-in-law had just delivered a child. A report produced by the women's conference stated: "The drama usually played by police is just this. They come in search of the offenders and finding them absconding, whisk away the womenfolk to the police station and outrage their modesty." The conference also concluded that atrocities committed on women by the police were increasing.

## Renewed Clashes

From October to December 1998, violent confrontations in the districts of Ramanathapuram, Pudukkottai, Perambalur, and Cuddalore signaled that caste clashes had not only continued but had spread to once-peaceful districts. In Ramanathapuram district, Thevars responded to a state-wide Dalit conference by organizing a rally on October 4, 1998. That afternoon, streams of lorries carrying Thevar youths were seen heading toward Ramanathapuram. On the way, several vehicles stopped at roadside villages and Thevars entered Dalit and Muslim hamlets throwing petrol bombs and ransacking houses. Two women were killed. Thevar youths claimed that they were provoked, allegedly by Dalits placing barriers on the road. As news of the attacks spread, Dalits retaliated. Despite all the violence, Koottamaippu—the Thevar coalition sponsoring the rally—was allowed to hold it. Among its demands: the repeal of the Scheduled Castes and Scheduled Tribes (Prevention of Atrocities) Act, 1989.

Dalits and journalists throughout the affected areas have blamed the police and district administration for their failure to effectively respond to increasing tensions in the district arising from publicity for the conference. According to *Frontline*, a bi-monthly news magazine, "The police presence was minimal and vehicles were not being checked for weapons. This was in contrast to the intensive searches carried out by the police when Puthiya Tamalingam [a Dalit organization] held its rally on September 11."

The situation remained volatile in the district for days afterwards. Police were given shoot-on-sight orders for arsonists, while a large contingent of the striking police force was rushed in. Both sides also alleged harassment and torture by the police conducting raids under the pretext of searching for criminals and weapons. According to People's Watch, the death toll on both sides reached fifteen.

On October 7, 1998, three days after the incident, state Governor Fathima Beevi called for an overhauling of the police system to prevent "police excess." The director general of the Bureau of Police Research and Development urged implementation of the National Police Commission recommendations, while the chairperson of the State Human Rights Commission recommended that police personnel should be made to undergo human rights awareness training every six months. None of these recommendations had been implemented as of February 1999.

Just over a month after the violence in Ramanathapuram, caste tensions erupted in Thirunallur village in nearby Pudukkottai district. On November 19, 1998, three Dalit youths were stripped, tied to a tree, and beaten through the night. According to a press report, their "heads were tonsured, and they were also made to roll around the village temple in the presence of a large gathering which included their kith and kin. The next morning they were asked to leave the village." The attack was part of a judgment handed down by twelve members of the all-caste Hindu local village council: the young men were being punished for marrying non-Dalit Hindu girls. Tensions remained high in the village for weeks following the beatings. Not until a month later were the culprits charged and the victims givenpart of their compensation, under the Scheduled Castes and Scheduled Tribes (Prevention of Atrocities) Act, 1989.

On December 1, 1998, in a massive operation reminiscent of the 1995 police raid on Kodiyankulum village, 300 armed policemen entered the Dalit colony at Ogalur village in Perambalur district. Under the pretext of rounding up "anti-social elements," police reportedly entered over 1,000 homes and, using lathis and iron rods, attacked the residents. After causing extensive damage to their homes and property, police arrested sixty-nine Dalits. Among them were thirty-four women, some with babies in their arms and a few who were pregnant. The reported background to the attack was a dispute between the Dalits and the caste Hindus over a piece of temple land and the attempted sexual assault of a Dalit woman by a caste Hindu man in the village; the man accompanied the police during their attack. As of January 1999, the Dalit labourers were still unable to work in the caste Hindu fields and their children were unable to go to school.

Another incident, reported by the news magazine *Frontline*, took place on December 16, 1998. In Puliyur village, Cuddalore district, a mob of caste Hindus (Vanniyas) numbering about 300 raided a Dalit settlement and attacked its residents with sticks and iron rods. Approximately 500 houses were ransacked and thirteen Dalits seriously injured. The day before the attack, a Dalit funeral procession was stopped as it passed a Vanniya house. "In the melee that followed, the caste-Hindu resident was reportedly assaulted by a Dalit, who, it is said, had been slapped a day earlier for smoking in the presence of the caste-Hindu resident." In this case, smoking was a luxury to which the Dalits were not entitled in the presence of a caste Hindu.

CHAPTER

# 11 Educational Status of Dalit Men and Women

A major concern of educational research has been to track educational progress of dalits and other disadvantaged groups in the country as a whole. The Commissioner of SC and ST which was set up as a watchdog institution by the State and more recently the Commission of SC/ST are assigned the responsibility of monitoring and reporting on their changing position. The issue of dalit educational status has attracted the attention of educational researchers from the outset. In the early decades after independence progress very slow. (Kamat, 1985; Nautiyal and Sharma, 1979) By the eighties dalit literacy rate had reached barely 40 per cent. We examine in this section the current educational status of dalit boys/ men and girls/women based on most recent available data. We examine the situation in the country as a whole and also bring out variations between the states and regions. The state-wise analysis is restricted to fifteen major states where dalits constitute a significant proportion in the population. They comprise 16 per cent of the Indian population. There are marked state and regional variations in terms of their proportion. Punjab has the highest proportion of dalit population at 28 per cent. U.P., Bihar, M.P, West Bengal have sizeable proportions of dalits. Among the larger states Gujarat has the smallest percentage at 7.41 per cent.

It should be stated at the outset that available statistical data varies in terms of quality and reliability and hence data from a number of sources need to be used in combination to arrive at some reasonably accurate picture. Micro studies and surveys provide supportive complementary insights. The primary concern is with educational achievements of dalits at school and college level. In the context of the continued failure to universalise elementary education, access continues to be an issue of central significance to the educational fortunes of dalits. Access is considered in a multidimensional way wherein enrolment, attendance, completion, and learning levels all have to be equitable. (Farrell, 1982)

## Unequal Outcomes: Learning Achievements of Dalits and Non-dalit Students

Assuming that talents and abilities are not the preserve of any group or community, and are evenly distributed across classes, genders and castes and other ethnic groups, disparities in scholastic achievement between dalits and non dalits can be held to be reflective of the influence of social background on learning abilities and processes. Considerable cross national evidence shows that differences in levels of achievements are systematically associated with differing social origins of children. Children who are poor, rural or female learners generally fare poorer than affluent, urban and male learners. The influence of gender operates substantially across cultures (Farrell, 1982). Unfortunately or perhaps intentionally data on performance was never made available by the Education Ministry in India. Research in this area has been sparse. Most of these studies take very limited and mechanical view of notion of scholastic achievement which are as good or bad as the official definitions and their operation in the examination systems. Studies are pitched at the level of the school where low socio-economic status is equated with government school. Large numbers of rural government schools cater to multi caste village populations but few studies probe into intra-school social correlates of achievement or systematically explore the relationship between home background and scholastic achievement. There are some older comparative studies, where two groups have been set up for comparison, such as dalit and Brahmin, dalit and caste Hindu, socially disadvantaged and socially advantaged or even 'high culture', and 'low culture'. (Sinha, 1982). Psychologists using standardised tests studies have studied achievement levels of primary, secondary and college going. It has been generally found that children drawn from the lower rungs have lower levels of scholastic achievement than their privileged counterparts. On this count, the former are deemed invariably 'inferior' in every area pertinent to learning: self-concept, cognition, motivation, personality and adjustment. Some of the studies explicitly define and measure background, while others simply assume a range of specific socio-economic, cultural and socio-psychological factors that intervene in the influence of social background on achievement. Some of the key factors identified as influencing both access and performance are: housing conditions and life style; high cultural value on education, parental motivation, encouragement and interest, in children's education; language development and usage; availability of books, magazine, reading habits; family size and relationships; and facets of the learning environment such as the amount and variety of sensory stimulation, verbal interaction and achievement motivation.

Little systematic evidence of gender-differences in academic performance exists. International Association for Evaluation of Educational Achievement (IEA) studies (not including India) which have looked at gender differences have found that boys scored higher than girls at all levels, with the gap increasing from ten year olds to fourteen year olds. There appears no reason to believe that things could be much different in India. However, in recent times it is reported that the performance of girls has begun to compare favourably or even surpasses with that of boys especially in urban areas. However, at the secondary stage there is a gender-socialised tendency among girls to choose the "softer", and so called 'feminine' options and withdraw from "meritocratic" competition. There have been no specific studies keeping dalit girls as the central focus.

Recently, studies are being produced by government organization or NGOs with claims and counter claims regarding quality of performance. (for e.g. the ASER report). It is important to point out however, that some of the studies are guided by short-term programme funding goals of pressing, pragmatic nature and do not meet criteria of theoretical or methodological rigour.

On the whole studies in the area have not been theoretically grounded nor specifically conceptualised to examine the impact of caste, class and gender interactions in relation to pupils' scholastic performance at school. They are largely empircist in nature and some are coloured by value biases of researchers. Achievement differences between children of different castes and communities within different kinds of schools are not systematically addressed. Studies have also not examined differences between dalit and non dalit students belonging to the same social class. In the American context, studies have found that within group comparison by social class shows a marked race difference. (Ogbu, 1978). In India it would be worth knowing whether middle class dalit children equal performance levels of upper caste middle class children? If not, why not? For the country as a whole, we have some indications from studies conducted by IEA in which India has occasionally participated. The studies have generally found that levels of reading and comprehension even in regional languages are poor for Indian children. Several NCERT studies over the years have revealed very low levels of learning in schools for the poor, both government and private (Kurrien, 1983; NCERT, 2006). The picture from detailed micro studies is largely negative in terms of satisfactory learning achievements of dalit children. (Jha & Jhingran, 2002) Since the reservation policy in higher education has been at the centre of many controversies there has been some research on academic performance at this level especially in professional education. Studies have noted gaps in academic performance in engineering and medicine between dalits and general category students. However, the gaps seem to be narrowing.

## Educational Disparities within Dalits

Caste, class and gender disparities exist within the dalit category. The processes of class formation have touched almost all caste communities though there are a few which live homogenously in socially oppressed conditions. Class divisions exist especially in numerically dominant castes and there is creation of a small priviledged class within individual castes. These differences get reflected in educational participation. Some Dalit castes register greater educational progress than others.on account of greater economic clout as well as greater political strength and political consciousness. Children from the subordinated groups (and poorer classes) are excluded from educational processes, drop out or fail.

In Maharashtra for example Mahar-Buddhists and Chambhars

are more advanced compared to the third numerically large caste of Mangs. Comparisons between the Malas and Madigas in Andhra Pradesh, the Pallars and Parayars in Tamil Nadu, and the Ad-Dharmis & Ramdasias and Mazhabis in Punjab also reveal similar differences. In Bihar the Musahars are in a state of acute educational backwardness.

The decade of the nineties seems to have registered concrete achievements in terms of increased access and attendance without getting rid of problems of survival especially of girls and completion of elementary levels. There is moreover the issue of the quality of education that dalits have succeeded in acquiring. The situation brings us to the role of the state as the main provider of public education and the quantity and quality of the provision it makes for dalits.

## State Schooling and the Dalits

As the main provider of mass education the state expresses special commitment to dalits and other weaker sections. How has education of dalits been constructed in policy and operationalised in programmes? The Indian state has been variously characterised as capitalist, elitist and dualist (Kaviraj, Mohanty, 1990; Byres, 1993; Chatterjee, 1994). In the domain of education, the Indian state's synthesis of meritocracy, equality of opportunity and compensatory justice was transalated into action through a strategy of gradual expansion of free education to dalits at all stages and a range of positive discrimination policies supportive of education such as provision of pre and post matric scholarships, (including special scholarships for children of those engaged in traditionally unclean occupations), hostels, book banks etc. The provision of basic schooling and colleges is the responsibility of the Ministry of Human Resource Development but funding of positive discrimination policies falls within the purview of the Ministry of Social Justice and Empowerment. Despite the rhetoric of equality and social justice, the first national educational policy of 1968 made no special financial, curricular or pedagogic commitment to the education of dalits. It was only in the context of alarming rise in illiterates noticed at the start of the eighties and an embarrassing failure to reach anywhere close to universalising even primary education, that policy makers gave attention to the educational situation of the SC, ST and women in the educational policy of 1986.

The historical neglect of equitable provision, especially in remote and dalit-concentrated areas has shown that even this limited responsibility was not adequately fulfilled. So much so, geographical location continues to be a significant predictor of whether a child particularly a dalit, tribal or girl child will attend school, how far she will continue in school, as also the type of school she will attend. The history of provision shows that very piecemeal increases have been made and expansion of mass education has been far less spectacular than it is made out to be. There has been massive unevenness and imbalance in the spatial and geographical provision of even primary educational facility and a general convergence in patterns of spatial and social disadvantage. This is apparent from data on schools in predominantly dalit habitations. The Fourth All-India Survey of Education found in 1978 that of the 69,000 dalit habitations that were identified-only 31 per cent of them had primary school/ sections within them, which served 62 per cent of the dalit population. Inadequacy of provision is exacerbated at the upper primary level. From the outset itself, upper primary schooling was not considered a priority for rural, especially dalit and tribal children. It was expected that children would walk 3 to 5 km to avail of it. The result was that in 1978 a miniscule 3.5 per cent of dalit habitations and only 12.92 per cent of dalit population were served with upper primary sections. Thus provision of schools within easy access has been relatively poor for dalit children as compared to children in general. The general policy of not providing an adequate number of girls schools has aggravated the situation for girls and adversely affected their enrolment. Table 14. below provides data on primary and upper primary school provision since the eighties till the year 2002. It shows that the situation has only gradually improved for the general population as well as dalits. In 1993, only 37 per cent of dalit habitations had a primary school within the habitation. Around 91 per cent population was covered within a kilometre and half. In 2002, 42 per cent of dalit habitations and 92 per cent of dalit population served within the habitation or within a km. as against 78 per cent of general habitations and 94 per cent of the general population.

The provision of upper primary schooling is as yet far from satisfactory with majority of general and dalit populations having a school only within 3 kms.

Under provision of basic educational facilities is directly linked to paucity of public funding for education. Studies in the political economy of educational provision have consistently pointed out the neglect of education in budgetary allocations and of elementary education within educational budgets. One need not labour the point that is well known and substantiated that the State has underspent on education. This has been so particularly with respect to basic educational needs of the poor, dalit and tribal households. They have to fend for themselves and end up spending large amounts of money on education in a supposedly "free" system of education. (Tilak, 1990; 1996). Trends in educational budgeting and expenditure have serious consequences for dalits who battle economic hardship and social stigma to avail of an education. In stead of lending a greater helping hand to them, the State has chosen to deploy its limited resources to liberally aid private secondary education and college education interests of the middle class and elites of society. The State commitment to redistribution of opportunity, reduction of imbalance and bring about greater equality of access was not pursued as a national goal. On the contrary, from the national to the local levels, educational policy making and implementation have reflected structures of patronage and power which have acted in favour of priviledged sections.

## Hierarchical System and Schools for the Dalits

The condition of dalits cannot be seen in isolation from these larger conditions, the broader policies which were framed to legitimise and further entrench the unequal colonial educational structure and the mechanisms of differentiation that it manifests. Most critically, post independence education policy ignored the Kothari commission's recommendation for common schooling and gave tacit approval to an imbalanced and hierarchically structured colonial system that corresponded to the caste-class and gender structure of society. Though government schooling numerically dominates the Indian schooling system and is by default if not design a common school system, it is characterised by processes cf exclusion through the non provision of schools as described above, differentiation (through selective upgradation of schools catering to priviledged castes/classes and privatisation) and open discrimination. Contemporarily private schooling is on the rise with state withdrawal and parent dissatisfaction It is the mismatch between state abdication and rising aspiration that has perforce led to the rise of private schools in rural and mofussil areas due to inadequacy of funds to finance public education system.The social power of nationally and locally dominant elites shapes the educational system both its government and private components and is a system that spells differential access. Contrary to professed ideology of equality, in principle we have a segregated but a hierarchical schooling system which follows the lines of caste-class gender hierarchy, and reproduces it. Schools for the poor too incorporate gradation in education in terms of resources, quality and social composition. The worst schools. i.e. having the worst provision in terms of infrastructure and teachers are where poorest and lowest castes tend to be clustered.. (Velaskar, 1992).

## Teaching Learning Conditions for Dalit and Other Poor

The following section describes the qualitative reality of educational provision made available to dalits. It is largely based on the recent Report of the Focus Group on SC/ST set up by National Curriculum Review and describes the teaching-learning conditions prevalent in schools accessed by SCs/STs, including private schools. Data from all over the country shows that physical / infrastructural facilities available in public schools are totally inadequate and particularly deplorable. The majority of dalit children are enrolled in regular government schools. Buildings are dilapidated or badly in need of repair. Basic furniture and teaching equipment is non-existent or of pathetic quality. Teaching–learning material, such as, blackboards, chalk, texts and other reading material, laboratory equipment, instructional aids are always in short supply, of poor quality or simply non-existent. There is also a high incidence of very poorly and irregularly functioning schools. We have reports from rural Punjab, Orissa, and Rajasthan's dalit and tribal dominated districts that reveal the shortage of basics, such as, classrooms, drinking water facilities, and teachers. Reports of neglect, indifference, and greater teacher absenteeism from dalit and tribal dominated schools have accumulated. Exceptions too have been noted, for example, studies of Garhwal, Himachal Pradesh, Gujarat, Maharashtra, and Kerala show that there are regions in which the provision of education to dalit and adivasis is fairly good. In certain areas of Maharashtra, for example, Zilla Parishad schools are fairly good (Berntsen, 1990). Rural schools are not necessarily worse than urban ones. Most rural schools have a mix of higher and lower castes/classes. Whereas in urban areas, where there are more schools and thus more choice, the municipal schools cater almost exclusively to the poor, the lower castes, and the tribes.

A highly inadequate teaching force has been a most adverse element in unequal provisioning as it affects classroom teaching – the heart of the educational process. Teacher-pupil ratios in schools frequented by dalits have been much higher than those in other schools meant for higher-caste villagers. Multi-grade teaching often amounts to very limited teaching or no teaching at all! This is almost a generalised pattern in dalit (and tribal) dominated schools. The quantity and quality of teaching is problematically low. The problem of insufficient number of teachers has been compounded by the problem of demotivated teachers, which is reflected in the phenomenon of teacher absenteeism and irregular attendance, especially teachers of non-dalit backgrounds. This is a common feature in schools located in remote areas. There are reports of non-functional schools existing on paper only that remain closed for years on end. It is common for teachers to mark the fictitious attendance of children (Jha and Jhingran, 2002; Leclerq, 2003). Dysfunctional and poorly-organized school environments, inadequate number of teachers, and the inadequate quantum of instruction exemplified in absence of teaching or adoption of most boring and uninspired teaching methods make for unsatisfactory teaching transaction. Teacher competence is questionable, training does not necessarily mean better knowledge and skill. These problems of low teacher quality afflict all states including Kerala. (Thomas, 2001) However to be fair to the teachers, harsh working conditions demotivate and demoralise even the most motivated of primary school teachers. Worse still, their teaching function is dislodged by obligation to perform all kinds of government work. State controls of teacher undermines the dignity and status of the primary school teacher. Despite several shortcomings and the halting and slow implementation by an apathetic bureaucracy, special schemes have played a key role in facilitating educational advance of dalits. However, the coverage of programmes continues to be inadequate and barely reaches a fragment. There is no commitment for improving achievement targets and enhancing financial outlays. Thus, actual benefits remain limited. Increasingly they accrue largely to the relatively better off SC/ST groups. (Kamat, 1985; GOI, 1990). There are also inadequacies in designing programmes. Every SC/ST student, subject to certain conditions, is eligible for a pre-matric scholarship. But at the higher secondary level the provision is narrower than the higher education stage and there is hardly any assistance at the elementary level. This has created a situation in which those people who have been able to cross the initial hurdles of obtaining primary and secondary level are able to move up with comparative ease but those who are unable to cross even the first hurdle are educationally doomed for life. There is also great delay in receipt of scholarships (Sharma, 1994; Wankhede and Velaskar, 1999). Schemes such as midday meals are of potential importance in educational retention of impoverished dalit children. A recent study conducted in Chattisgarh, Rajasthan, and Karnataka noted immense positive impact in terms of higher enrolment and attendance levels apparently signifying the end of classroom hunger. The study however did not specifically report on SC/ST children (Dreze and Goyal, 2003).

Interestingly, a study evaluating the scheme's recent performance in its state of birth Tamil Nadu, suggests that it may not currently be having a significant impact on educational attendance or enrolment. Moreover, it noted that implementation is poorer in schools where the social composition is predominantly dalit. (Swaminathan et al., 2004). There is a growing tendency for the special benefits to circulate within the SC/ST elites and effective access is limited and difficult for those who are left out of its purview.

Global economic forces and neo-liberal economic policies have spelt the demise of the welfare state and the decimation of any pretences of egalitarianism. Following the inherent logic of the New Economic Policy, the state is promoting markets and profits in education and has provided legitimacy and impetus for a number of educational reforms that pose a direct threat to dalits. The delegation of state responsibility to private agencies and non-governmental organisations (NGOs) has subjected dalits to a new dispensation which threatens to undermine both qualitative and quantitative opportunity. The rapid expansion of private-funded educational institutions at all levels, budget cuts on education and the slashing of teachers' salaries and teaching positions as economy measures, growing dependence on foreign funding are some of the changes that are negatively affecting the provision of public education. Education has become a component of the safety net; (Kumar et al, 2001; Velaskar, 2003).

Studies have noted that private schooling is playing a growing role in elementary education, a fact obscured by government reports and statistics (Kingdon, 1996). There is a proliferation of private schools for the poor in urban, mofussil, and rural areas. Unrecognised schools, which are not accounted for in official statistics, have mushroomed in cities, towns, and larger villages. An NCERT survey estimated that there are around 38,000 unrecognised primary schools in rural India (NCERT, 1999). Privatisation in education has allowed dalit children access private schools, a development which according to research has had some positive consequences in terms of enhancing access (Ramachandran, 2003). As much as 32 per cent of the increase in primary school enrolment among SC boys, between 1986 and 1993, was accounted for by private unaided (PUA) schools. In rural areas PUA schools accounted for a relatively smaller proportion of the increase in enrolments during this period, around 7 per cent for dalit boys and 4 per cent for dalit girls (Tilak and Sudarshan, 2000 cited in Nambissan and Sedwal, 2002). There is also evidence to show that the commercialisation and commodification of education that privatisation entails, results in a largelyinferior education for dalits. The cost is exorbitant and the sacrifices made are not eventually worthwhile.

The overwhelming majority of dalit children continue to avail of government schooling. According to the Sixth All-India Educational Survey (NCERT, 1998), 91.3 per cent or rural dalit children 64.6 per cent of urban children were in schools managed by the government and local bodies. At the middle school level, a relatively larger proportion of dalit children were enrolled in privately managed schools, though expectedly this is more in urban areas (49.6 per cent) as compared to rural areas (32.9 per cent). The state's response to the growing public demand for 'quality' education has been to launch innovative efforts on behalf of hitherto neglected segments, such as, Lok Jumbish in Rajasthan and Education Guarantee Scheme (EGS) in Madhya Pradesh, etc. These have had some visible positive impact. However critical evaluation of their functioning suggest that it is difficult to sustain successes.

## Schools as Sites of Caste and Gender Discrimination

Discrimination against dalits on the basis of caste is not a thing of the past. It is practised by upper castes in society as well as in schools. It is difficult to make quantitative assessments of the phenomenon or identify changing patterns since research is sparse and sporadic and quality is variant. Unlike racism, casteism as a concept in academic and non academic discourse is not rigorously defined.

We now have an appalling body of evidence that suggests that discrimination manifests itself in numerous ways in social relations in school and in the classroom. The teacher–pupil interaction which is central to teaching and learning processes is marked by teacher's preconceptions and bias. Teacher behaviour, subtle or overt, conscious or unconscious, discriminates against children of dalit background. The teachers' caste, religion, language background, affects interactions with students. Middle class higher-caste teachers are unhappy with the poor school environments within which they teach and are poorly motivated. Children of Dalits are "naturally" and derogatorily categorised as uneducable. Teachers are observed to have low expectations of dalit children and girls, and at times condescending and abusive attitudes. Teachers also hold stated or unstated assumptions of "deprived" and "deficient" cultural backgrounds, languages, and inherent intellectual deficiencies of dalit children. They follow pedagogic practices of labelling, classifying, and teaching styles and operate on the basis of "realistic" perceptions of low-caste childrens' limited cognitive capacities and life chances. For example, teachers' beliefs about Mushar children in Bihar are that they are just not interested in education and that they do not have any "tension" in life (Kumar, 2004). Such presumptions set effective, and in the teachers' view, legitimate limits to their teaching effort. Levels of hostility and indifference to dalit cultural traits and value systems are high. Teachers perceive dalit (and adivasi) children in a negative light, seeing them as unclean, dishonest, lazy, ill-mannered, etc. The children could be criticised for their clothes, the dialect they speak, the ignorance of their parents and even the colour of their skin! Teachers may abhor what they term as "uncouth" habits of dalit children such as meat eating and alcohol consumption. They are punished and shouted at in efforts to discipline and "civilize" them!

Several micro studies have borne out varied forms of direct and subtle discrimination in school. For instance, Artis, et al. (2003) find that in village schools of Gujarat, dalit children are forced to sit at the back, actively discouraged from participating in class, and are subject to food and water taboos. Similar experiences exist for village schools in Karnataka. In relation to dalits, teachers may refuse to correct their notebooks. Complaints to the headmaster result in teachers beating the children. Indeed teacher violence against dalit children is widely reported. (Balagopalan, 2003) Dalit children may not encounter practices related to untouchability in school (Jodhka, 2000, 2002; Shah, 2000). However old stigma continues in new forms.

A disturbing tendency noted by several studies and further substantiated by poignant personal narratives is the use of children as servants by high-caste teachers. Children are assigned a range of menial tasks—from cleaning and sweeping the school to fetching "paan" and cigarettes for the teacher. They assign menial jobs to dalit children and shift the onus of low learning on children and their families. Placing disadvantaged students in 'better quality' schools doesn't seem to solve the problem. Studies have suggested that feelings of isolation and alienation and experiences of discrimination neutralise the impact of better facilities. Like the children, dalit teachers also suffer humiliation and discrimination (Jha and Jhingran, 2002; Heredia, 1992; Samavesh, 2003; Jodhka, 2000, 2002). They are 'argely isolated or compelled to form their own separate social circles. They also find themselves succumbing to dominant religio-cultural practices in a bid to avoid conflict and gain acceptance (Teacher, Personal account). Schools are thus as a sites of visible and invisible discrimination where blatant discrimination exists. One can only imagine new subtle forms and new meanings that are generated and which could line the cultural discourse and ethos of a dominant class dominated school in the context of which dalit and non-dalit subjectivities get constituted.

# CHAPTER 12

# Untouchables and SCs of the Situation of Dalit Women

## Dalit Women in India

Dalit women in India constitute 80 million or 48 % of the total Dalit population, 16.3 % of the total female population in India. 81.5 % of Dalit women live in rural areas. They, along with their male counterparts, constitute a sizeable social group that continues to suffer work and descent based discrimination and untouchability arising out of the caste system.

Dalit women are particularly discriminated on the basis of their caste (which is lower than others – outcaste) poverty and gender. The Dalit women have to grapple with the discrimination due to the caste hierarchy and untouchability on the one hand and extreme economic deprivation and poverty on the other coupled with political, legal and religio-cultural discrimination. Dalit women continue to be illiterate, malnourished, in poor heath, overworked, oppressed and victimised by a number of factors, including their own family and community. They make up the substance of the body of research, knowledge and information in the country displaying the poorest social indicators, dismal social and economic achievement. They lack access to resources including the natural resources they work with every day, although their labour enriches their masters.

## Dalit Women as Victims

Descent based discrimination based on caste imposes social exclusion on persons belonging to Dalit castes, and their physical separation from the dominant castes in housing patterns, strict enforcement of the prohibition of inter dining at public places, seating arrangements in education institutions, particularly schools, and the forces the performance of degrading occupations like manual scavenging and carrying of night soil by Dalit women. Caste discrimination results in the violent appropriation and sexual control over Dalit women by men of the dominant castes, evident in the systematic rape of Dalit women and perpetuation of forced prostitution in the name of religion through the Devadasi system.

A recent case where four Dalits in Khairlanji village in Maharastra were killed in the broad day light on 29 September 2006. Four members of a Dalit family, specifically the mother and the daughter had been brutally murdered, raped and their bodies thrown into the canal by a crowd of non-Dalits as a off shoot of their resistance to the forceful grabbing the land from the family. Earlier the family appealed to the local police and various authorities to intervene in the case and the total silence led to this gruesome atrocity. Even in this incident, the police would not register the case immediately, only after a massive protest by the Dalit community the authorities moved into register the caste more than two months after it took place. In the name of maintaining law and order the state police arrested hundreds of Dalit demonstrators and charged them under various sections and put them in prison.

The insensitiveness and the continuous failure of the criminal justice administrative system, the impunity enjoyed by both dominant caste community and the state officials continues. This is clearly illustrated in a recent national study of violence against Dalit women based on 500 cases:

In 40, 4 % of the cases the women did not even attempt to obtain justice

In 26.6 % of the cases the victims were prevented to file cases

In 1.6 % of the cases the women were able to obtain informal justice

In 17.5 % of incidents the violence reached the notice of the police, but were thwarted

Only in 13.9 % of cases was appropriate police or judicial action taken.

Only 3.6 % of cases have ever reached the courts, only 3 of the cases – less than one per cent have ended in conviction.

Violence therefore forms the core result of gender based inequalities, caused, intensified and facilitated by caste discrimination, acting as crucial social mechanisms to maintain Dalit women's caste-gender subordinate position to men and particularly dominant caste men. Major causes of atrocities are related to the issues of wage payments, land and property rights, bonded or forced labour, access to water, indebtedness, issues related to human dignity, compelled to perform traditional and degrading jobs. Caste tensions are exacerbated by economic factors.

## Manual Scavengers

1, 5 million women are in manual scavenging and they are forced to earn their living this way. That is, as scavengers who clean out dry latrines by hand and who carry excreta in baskets on their heads. The women use metal pans to scoop up the night soil with short brooms in their hands, each household gives 5 rupees (less than one euro cent) per month, and one roti (a piece of bread) every day. In one count, a fifth of all women in a Dalit colony carry night soil in Gujarat. The practise kills their dignity. They would like to be rehabilitated by the state, but they they just don't believe it will get materialised.

## Devadasi System

In the name of religion, thousands of untouchable female children between 6 and 8 years are forced to become "maidens of God" (ritualised prostitution in temples). Once dedicated to the God, they are unable t get married, and are raped by temples priests and dominant caste men, and eventually auctioned off secretly to urban brothels. It is estimated that between 5000 and 15000 girls are auctioned every year.

All these forms of violence exists – known as atrocities-continues in India despite the fact that provisions of laws to prevent them have existed for many years. While India forges ahead on an emerging economic power, almost 200 million people live in a feudal lawlessness, where rape and murder are the order of the day.

## Discrimination, Oppression, Denial of Rights Contribute

### Dalit Women's Demand

In recognising the Dalit women as a distinct social group in the Indian population, and by studying the complex nature of the interfacing of caste, class and gender in Dalit women's lives for drawing policy frameworks, guidelines and evolve strategy formulations to deal with the concerns of Dalit women nationally and globally. We appeal to the European Parliament to undertake and support all possible measures to fight the widespread discrimination, violence and impunity committed against Dalit women. The European Union should make sure that caste discrimination is addressed whether it in matters of trade, developmental programmes or political dialogue with caste affected countries.

Dalit human rights are a global responsibility. Silence surrounding violence must end. I hope you will be our partners to stand up for freedom, inalienable rights to human dignity and equal status for all in the society.

## The Intersection of Caste and Women's Rights in India

Caste is a system of social stratification that is descent based and hereditary, determined by an individual's birth. Different to class, caste is something that an individual cannot easily transgress. Whilst referred to as an historical concept in India, the social classification of people by caste is still prevalent ? permeating housing, education, marriage, employment and social relations in general. There have historically been four predominant castes in India consisting of the Brahmins, the intellectual class, Kshatriyas, the warrior class, Vaishyas, the agricultural and trader class and Shudras, the service or manual worker class. The former 'Untouchables'-now known as 'Dalits' or 'scheduled castes' ? fall outside the traditional four-fold caste system and primarily continue to be considered by the upper castes as impure and polluting. As a result, this large portion of the Indian population has been relegated to "a lifetime of discrimination, exploitation and violence".

"Untouchability" is a concept related to the demeaning traditional work performed by Dalits such as sweeping and manual scavenging (the illegal-but-still-very-much-in-practice task of cleaning human excrement from India's roads and dry latrines). "Untouchability" was abolished in India's Constitution, meaning that the dominant castes can no longer legally force Dalits to perform any "polluting" occupation. Yet this type of work is "still the monopoly of the scheduled castes...Migration and the anonymity of the urban environment have in some cases resulted in upward occupational mobility among Dalits, but the majority continue to perform their traditional functions".

The Indian Government has implemented comprehensive Constitutional provisions and other legislation to combat discrimination based on race and caste, including quotas of reserved seats in Union and State legislatures and of posts in the public service. The Government has also established several institutions responsible for the implementation of anti-discrimination legislation and for the monitoring of discrimination and violence against members of scheduled castes and scheduled tribes, including the Ministry of Social Justice, the Ministry of Tribal Affairs, and the National Commissions on Scheduled Castes and on Scheduled Tribes. The Prime Minister himself has condemned the discriminatory treatment of Dalits and likened the practices of "untouchability" to that of apartheid in South Africa ? but at the same time has failed to demonstrate the political will to address it. Unfortunately caste discrimination against Dalits is "both a political reality and social fact".

## Reality of Caste Discrimination in India

In a recent shadow report to the United Nations (UN) Committee on the Elimination of Racial Discrimination (CERD) by Human Rights Watch (HRW) and the Centre for Human Rights and Global Justice, the current reality of discrimination against Dalits was exposed. The report is based on investigations by HRW and the findings of Indian Governmental and non-governmental organisations on caste-based abuses and suggests, for example, that the government's failure to address caste discrimination "has resulted in continued, and sometimes enhanced, brutalities against

Dalits". Excerpts from the report of some of the main issues facing Dalits follow:

* The police have systematically failed to protect Dalit homes and Dalit individuals from acts of looting, arson, sexual assault, torture, and other inhumane acts such as the tonsuring (shaving a person's head), stripping and parading of Dalit women, and forcing Dalits to drink urine and eat faeces.
* Strict prohibitions on marriage and other social interaction between Dalits and the upper caste routinely violate the rights of Dalits to marry and choose their spouse. Dalits who have married 'above' their caste have reportedly been forced to break all ties with their families.
* The denial of the right to work and free choice of employment lies at the very heart of the caste system. Dalits are forced to work in "polluting" and degrading occupations such as manual scavenging and are subject to exploitative labour arrangements such as bonded labour, migratory labour and forced prostitution.
* India's National Human Rights Commission (NHRC) has commented that the law enforcement machinery is the greatest violator Dalit's human rights... The police often target whole Dalit communities in search of one individual and subject the community to violent search and seizure operations. Dalit women are particularly vulnerable to sexual violence by the police, which is used as a tool to punish Dalit communities. Police also actively allow private actors to commit violence against Dalits with impunity.
* Residential segregation of Dalits is prevalent across the country, and is the rule rather than the exception. Segregation is also evident in schools, in access to public services, and in access to services operated by the private sector. A recently published survey documented "untouchability" practices in almost 80% of the villages surveyed.

## The Caste/gender Intersection

Dalit women are positioned at the bottom of the caste hierarchy, subject to multiple forms of discrimination on the basis of their caste, class and gender. According to a 2006 report, "Dalit women endure violence in both the general community and in the family, from state and non-state actors of different genders, castes and socio-economic groupings". Most of the violence that Dalit women face is perpetrated against them in public spaces and women find it almost impossible to obtain informal or formal justice. Dalit women are subject to a multitude of atrocities, including rape ? which is perpetrated with impunity with little or no redress in the courts-, sexual abuse and humiliation. As is typical in many situations, a woman's body is perceived as representing family and community honour, and to teach a family or community a lesson, women are generally the primary targets.

The practice of devadasi particularly illustrates the gender/ caste nexus with regard to the violation of women's human rights. This practice is where "a girl, usually before reaching puberty, is ceremoniously dedicated or married to a deity or temple... Once dedicated, the girl is unable to marry, forced to become a prostitute for the upper-caste community and eventually auctioned into an urban brothel". Devadasi's usually belong to the Dalit community.

In addition to the violence Dalit women routinely face from the upper castes, they are also found at the bottom of the Dalit hierarchy. This is directly related to their poorer social and economic status as women, and they are inevitably channelled into the most hazardous and degrading work for survival. Government estimates suggest that there are about one million manual scavengers in India, and 95% are women. Research indicates that despite manual scavenging being illegal, its practice is actually increasing. This type of work is demeaning, unsanitary and hazardous, and has a social stigma attached to it where even other Dalits won't associate with individuals who perform the work. Their stories are unfathomable, with one woman describing how she felt that she herself was human excrement.

The violation of Dalit women's rights is characteristic of the intersection of caste and gender, and is further legitimised by the subordination of women's rights in general. "India has failed to address the multiple axes of discrimination faced by Dalit women-including their unequal access to services, employment opportunities, and justice mechanisms as compared to Dalit men-and threats to their personal security, including through brutal acts of sexual violence".

**How can India Address Caste-based Discrimination?**

India is bound by its obligations under the UN Convention on the Elimination of all Forms of Racial Discrimination defines "racial discrimination" as "any distinction, exclusion, restriction or preference based on race, colour, descent, or national or ethnic origin which has the purpose or effect of nullifying or impairing the recognition, enjoyment or exercise, on an equal footing, of human rights and fundamental freedoms in the political, economic, social, cultural or any other field of public life".

In their fifteenth to nineteenth periodic reports, which were considered by CERD in February 2007, the Indian government claimed that discrimination based on caste falls outside the scope of Article 1 of the Convention. As a result, their reports did not outline any instances of caste discrimination nor any concrete measures undertaken by the government to address caste-based discrimination.

This is a clear indication of a lack of political will to fully acknowledge and address discrimination against Dalits in India. After consideration of India's position, CERD maintained and reaffirmed that discrimination based on the ground of caste is fully covered by Article 1 of the Convention-expressed in general recommendation No. 29 "that discrimination based on 'descent' includes discrimination against members of communities based on forms of social stratification such as caste and analogous systems of inherited status which nullify or impair their equal enjoyment of human rights." India will be required to report on caste-based discrimination in their next report to CERD, due in 2010.

The inroads taken in addressing this apartheid-style of discrimination-such as Constitutional amendment, specific legislation and monitoring bodies and reservations for Dalits in education and politics-are a positive step in the right direction, but are clearly not being effectively implemented. Further, there seems to be a need to focus on abolishing caste itself, not just the discrimination that is inherently built in to the system. An Indian academic asserts that "caste discrimination exists because people continue to believe in caste. Indian democracy is, paradoxically, a culprit. By encouraging the formation of democratic participation along the lines of identity, caste is, in fact, reinforced every time India goes to the polls. The recent electoral gains of the Bahujan Samaj Party in Uttar Pradesh must be seen in the context of this double-edged nature of caste."

Non-government organisations like the National Campaign on Dalit Human Rights, the National Federation of Dalit Women and other local organisations have been extremely active in campaigning and raising awareness of Dalits' human rights situation, as well as holding their government responsible for its inadequacies. In order for a complete cultural shift away from caste to take place in India, however, the Government urgently needs to back its rhetoric on India's 'apartheid' with real and quantifiable measures that address the litany of human rights abuses being perpetrated against Dalits, and in particular, Dalit women.

## Unheard Voices of Dalit Women

Dalit women are thrice discriminated against-treated as untouchables and outcastes due to their caste, face gender discrimination as women, and also economic impoverishment due to wage disparity.

According to the Hindu caste hierarchy, there are four castes: the Brahmins (priestly caste), the Kshatriya (warriors), the Vaishyas (traders) and the Shudras (menial task workers). Below this caste ladder is another rung of people who are called 'untouchables' (Panchamas). Among the untouchables, the status of women is further eroded and closely linked to the concept of purity.

The creation of a number of Hindu religious books, including the Manusmriti*, and the strict compliance to them by the Brahmins, led to a society in which equality between men and women was far from existent [Agarwal, S. (1999). Genocide of women in Hinduism. Sudrastan Books. Jabalpur, India]. Dr BR Ambedkar, an architect of the Indian Constitution, also makes it very clear in his article titled 'The rise and fall of Hindu woman' that the root cause of suffering for women in India are these so-called Hindu religious books (Agarwal, op.cit.). Books like the Manusmriti divide people into a stratified caste system and promote inequality between men and women (Agarwal, op. cit.). According to the Manusmriti, women have no right to education, independence, or wealth. It not only justifies the treatment of Dalit women as sex objects, and promotes child marriage, but also justifies a number of violent atrocities on women, as can be seen in the following verses (Agarwal, op.cit.; Manusmriti):

'A man, aged thirty years, shall marry a maiden of twelve who pleases him. Or a man of twenty-four a girl of eight years of age. If (the performance of) his duties would otherwise be impeded, he must marry sooner.' (Manusmriti IX.94)

'By a girl, by a young woman, or even by an aged one, nothing must be done independently, even in her own house.' (Manusmriti V.147)

'Her father protects (her) in childhood, her husband protects (her) in youth, and her sons protect (her) in old age; a woman is never fit for independence.' (Manusmriti IX.3)

'Women have no right to study the Vedas. That is why their Sanskaras are performed without Veda Mantras. Women have no knowledge of religion because they have no right to know the Vedas. The uttering of the Veda Mantras is useful for removing sin. As women cannot utter the Veda Mantras, they are as unclean as the untruth.' (Manusmriti IX.18)

'A Brahman, Kshatriya, or Vaishya Man can sexually exploit any shudra woman.' (Manusmriti IX.25)

Even the killing of a Dalit woman is explicitly justified as a minor offence for the Brahmins: equal to the killing of an animal (Manusmriti). If the killing of an untouchable was justified as a minor offence, you can imagine the treatment they received throughout their lives.

In a male-dominated society, Dalit women suffer unimaginable oppression, not only through caste, but gender too, from which there is no escape. The laws in the Manusmriti and other Vedic scriptures close all economic, political, social, educational, and personal channels through which Dalit women could be uplifted. The horrendous laws in the Manusmriti were incorporated into

Hinduism because they were favourable only to the upper castes, who form the majority of the Indian population.

Even today, in modern times, we see the severe oppression and exploitation of Dalit women. Dalit women face multiple oppression that violates their economic, political, social and cultural rights. The most deprived section of society comprises Dalit women who are poor, illiterate and easy targets for sexual harassment. They face not just caste violence inflicted on them by the dominant castes, but also state violence.

## Living Conditions and Livelihood

Dalit hamlets are usually located at the end of the main village or on the village outskirts. The Dalits live in small huts, and even the few who may have slightly better housing are devoid of basic amenities such as sanitation, light and safe and clean drinking water. The women have to walk miles to collect not just water but also fuel and fodder for their domestic chores.

The women work on construction sites, carrying heavy loads of construction materials. They also work in brick kilns for long hours, as casual labourers, to lay roads with hot tar in the burning sun, without sandals or any other protective gear. Manual scavenging continues as an occupation in India and most of the manual scavengers are Dalit women. The women are forced to do this humiliating and degrading work, which further results in discrimination and social exclusion. They have no protection or benefits that labour laws should provide, since the majority of the women are in the unorganised sector. They do not even get the minimum wages that the state/country has specified, since they are unable to organise and demand decent wages. Dalit women undertake manual, low-paying, tedious, and time-consuming work. They earn less than US$1 a day.

The process of globalisation has affected Dalit women considerably. With the introduction of new farming techniques, such as mechanisation for harvesting and transplanting, women have lost their traditional work in the agricultural sector. Food crops have been replaced by cash crops. Horticulture has been introduced by big agribusiness corporations for expoit purposes. This has deprived Dalit women of their land and the common resources in the village. Women used to collect greens, fish, and shells from fields for their food requirements for free. This is no longer available to them. Abject poverty has driven large numbers of Dalit women into the sex trade to earn for their families. The globalisation process has increased the feminisation of poverty and this has affected Dalit women in every sphere of their lives. There is also large-scale migration from rural areas to the urban centres in search of better livelihood options. Women are left behind to bear responsibility for the family. More and more female-headed households emerge and most of them are headed by Dalit women. Such situations push the women into further situations of impoverishment, making them more and more vulnerable to all forms of discrimination and violations.

## Political Power

Dalit women are excluded from decision-making. They are not in a position to exercise their power. Wherever Dalit women have contested, they have faced stiff opposition and even been brutally attacked. There are instances where Dalit women have been elected into local governance and, through the reservation policy, nominated as the president of the local governing unit (Panchayat). But when these women have endeavoured to exercise their role, it has met with resistance, even to the extent of physical violence. A Dalit woman president is not allowed to sit on a chair if the other caste members do not allow this. She is forced to be a mere figurehead, while the functioning of the Panchayat is taken over by upper-caste members.

There are several traditional practices and customs that violate human rights, including the practice of dedicating girl children to become Mathammas, which is practised by shoemakers (Arunthathiar). There is a strong belief that the goddess Mathamma has healing powers, so when a Dalit girl is sick, she is taken to the temple and left there till she is cured. Once cured, the child is named after Mathamma and married to the goddess. She becomes a dancer who belongs to the temple, and dances at festivals to earn her livelihood. She is not treated with respect and is publicly humiliated by men who harass her sexually. She cannot marry and lead a family life. Dalit women dedicated to Mathamma end up in the sex trade and become vulnerable to sexually transmitted diseases including HIV/AIDS. Superstition coupled with poverty and illiteracy is responsible for such practices. It is also using religion to sanction prostitution through the interpretation of mythology by the upper caste so that they can both economically and sexually exploit Dalit women.

Caste, class and gender discrimination prevent Dalit women from enjoying their basic human rights, particularly to dignity, equality and development. Atrocities and violence against Dalit women are both a means of sustaining systemic discrimination, as well as a reaction when particular untouchability practices and caste norms are challenged or not adhered to. Impunity for this discrimination and violence is then used as a means to preserve the existing caste and gender disparities. Before Dalit women can enjoy their human rights, and before the Millennium Development Goals can be achieved, discrimination, violence and impunity must stop.

## Health and Education

The health conditions of Dalit women are alarming, with a high incidence of maternal and infant mortality. Due to the denial of and sub-standard healthcare services, the life expectancy of Dalit women is as low as 50 years. Due to poverty, Dalit women are malnourished and anaemic. Working in agriculture, they often suffer acute back pain and develop skin irritations and allergies due to excessive use of pesticides. Due to a lack of awareness and medical care, many suffer from reproductive health complications, including sexually transmitted diseases and cervical cancer. Pregnant Dalit women receive discriminatory treatment in hospitals, and there are instances where doctors have refused to conduct the delivery of Dalit women's babies.

Dalit women comprise a large majority of the illiterate population, with 76.24% of Dalit women being illiterate. The girl drop-out rate among Dalit families is increasing, with girl children forced to work as child labourers. Dalit women are illiterate because they have less access to education, which is an inherent part of the caste system. Also, there is a lack of secure education and daycare facilities, so children join the adults to add to the income of the family. Dalit girl children are involved mostly in hazardous work like beedi making, working in match factories and in the fireworks industry.

## The Context of Caste Violence

The constitution has merely prescribed, but has not given any description of the ground reality. We can make a dent only if we recognise the fact that the caste system is a major source, indeed an obnoxious one, of human rights violations. — R. M. Pal, "The Caste System and Human Rights Violations"

With little land of their own to cultivate, Dalit men, women, and children numbering in the tens of millions work as agricultural labourers for a few kilograms of rice or Rs. 15 to Rs. 35 (US$0.38 to $0.88) a day. Most live on the brink of destitution, barely able to feed their families and unable to send their children to school or break away from cycles of debt bondage that are passed on from generation to generation. At the end of day they return to a hut in their Dalit colony with no electricity, kilometers away from the nearest water source, and segregated from all non-Dalits, known as caste Hindus. They are forbidden by caste Hindus to enter places of worship, to draw water from public wells, or to wear shoes in caste Hindu presence. They are made to dig the village graves, dispose of dead animals, clean human waste with their bare hands, and to wash and use separate tea tumblers at neighbourhood tea stalls, all because—due to their caste status—they are deemed polluting and therefore "untouchable." Any attempt to defy the social order is met with violence or economic retaliation.

As documented throughout this report, the perpetuation of human rights abuses against India's Dalit population is intimately connected to police abuse. Local police officials routinely refuse to register cases against caste Hindus or enforce relevant legislation that protects Dalits. Prejudiced by their own caste and gender biases, or under the thumb of influential landlords and upper-caste politicians, police not only allow caste Hindus to act with impunity but in many cases operate as agents of powerful upper-caste groups to detain Dalits who organize in protest against discrimination and violence, and to punish Dalit villagers because of their suspected support for militant groups.

Under constitutional provisions and various laws, the state grants Dalits a certain number of privileges, including reservations (quotas) in education, government jobs, and government bodies. The Scheduled Castes and Scheduled Tribes (Prevention of Atrocities) Act, 1989 was designed to prevent abuses againstmembers of scheduled castes and scheduled tribes and punish those responsible.

Its enactment represented an acknowledgment on the part of the government that abuses, in their most degrading and violent forms, were still perpetrated against Dalits decades after independence. The laws, however, have benefited very few and, due to a lack of political will, development programs and welfare projects designed to improve economic conditions for Dalits have generally had little effect. Dalits rarely break free from bondage or economic exploitation by upper-caste landowners.

Political parties have frequently fashioned their manifestos and campaign slogans around the need for "upliftment" of these marginalized sectors, while political leaders, mostly drawn from higher castes, offer the promise of equal status and equal rights. It would be difficult to convince the Dalits of Dholapur district, Rajasthan, that, fifty years after independence, the government had done anything to end the violence and discrimination that have ruled their lives.

In April 1998, a Dalit of the area was assaulted by an upper-caste family who forcibly pierced his nostril, drew a string through his nose, paraded him around the village, and tied him to a cattle post—all because he refused to sell *bidis* (hand-rolled cigarettes) on credit to the nephew of the upper-caste village chief. The message sent from the judiciary on caste discrimination is equally grim: in July 1998 in the state of Uttar Pradesh, an Allahabad High Court judge had his chambers "purified with Ganga *jal*" (water from the River Ganges), because it had earlier been occupied by a Dalit judge.

The remainder of this chapter describes the basic tenets of the caste system, the context for the abuses described in this report, the political movements they have helped fuel, and the legal framework of the government's response.

## "Untouchability" and Segregation

A 1997 report issued by the National Commission for Scheduled Castes and Scheduled Tribes underscored that "untouchability"—the imposition of social disabilities on persons by reason of their birth in certain castes—was still practiced in many forms throughout the country. The report described a number of social manifestations of caste-based discrimination in the 1990s: scheduled-caste bridegrooms were not permitted to ride a mare in villages, a marriage tradition; scheduled castes could not sit on their *charpoys* (rope beds) when persons of other castes passed by; scheduled castes were not permitted to draw water from common wells and hand-pumps; and in many tea-shops and *dhabas* (food stalls), separate crockery and cutlery were used for serving the scheduled castes.

The prevalence of "untouchability" practices was also noted by the United Nations Committee on the Elimination of Racial Discrimination in 1996, while reviewing India's tenth to fourteenth periodic reports under the Convention on the Elimination of All Forms of Racial Discrimination:

> Although constitutional provisions and legal texts exist to abolish untouchability and to protect the members of the scheduled castes and tribes, and social and educational policies have been adopted to improve the situation of members of the scheduled castes and tribes and to protect them from abuses, widespread discrimination against those people, and the relative impunity of those who abuse them, points to the limited effect of these measures. The Committee is particularly concerned at reports that people belonging to the scheduled castes and tribes are often prevented from using public wells or from entering cafes or restaurants and that their children are sometimes separated from other children in schools, in violation of article 5 (f) of the Convention.

Most Dalits in rural areas live in segregated colonies, away from the caste Hindus. According to an activist working with Dalit communities in 120 villages in Villapuram district, Tamil Nadu, all 120 villages have segregated Dalit colonies. Basic supplies such as water are also segregated, and medical facilities and the better, thatched-roof houses exist exclusively in the caste Hindu colony. "Untouchability" is further reinforced by s tate allocation of facilities; separate facilities are provided for separate colonies. Dalits often receive the poorer of the two, if they receive any at all.

As part of village custom, Dalits are made to render free services in times of death, marriage, or any village function. During the Marama village festival in Karnataka state, caste Hindus force Dalits to sacrifice buffalos and drink their blood. They then have to mix the blood with cooked rice and run into the village fields without their *chappals* (slippers). The cleaning of the whole village, the digging of graves, the carrying of firewood, and the disposal of dead animals are all tasks that Dalits are made to perform.

In villages where Dalits are a minority, the practice of "untouchability" is even more severely enforced. Individual attempts to defy the social order are frequently punished through social boycotts and acts of retaliatory violence further described below. Activists in Tamil Nadu explained that large-scale clashes between caste communities in the state's southern districts have often been triggered by Dalits' efforts to draw water from a "forbidden" well or by their refusal to perform a delegated task. Dalits have responded to ill-treatment by converting, en masse, to Buddhism, Christianity, and sometimes Islam. Once converted, however, many lose access to their scheduled-caste status and the few government privileges assigned to it. Many also find that they are ultimately unable to escape treatment as "untouchables."

## The Caste System

India's caste system is perhaps the world's longest surviving social hierarchy. A defining feature of Hinduism, caste encompasses a complex ordering of social groups on the basis of ritual purity. A person is considered a member of the caste into which he or she is born and remains within that caste until death, although the particular ranking of that caste may vary among regions and over time. Differences in status are traditionally justified by the religious doctrine of *karma,* a belief that one's place in life is determined by one's deeds in previous lifetimes. Traditionalscholarship has described this more than 2,000-year-old system within the context of the four principal *varnas,* or large caste categories. In order of precedence these are the Brahmins (priests and teachers), the

Ksyatriyas (rulers and soldiers), the Vaisyas (merchants and traders), and the Shudras (labourers and artisans). A fifth category falls outside the varna system and consists of those known as "untouchables" or Dalits; they are often assigned tasks too ritually polluting to merit inclusion within the traditional varna system.

Within the four principal castes, there are thousands of sub-castes, also called *jatis,* endogamous groups that are further divided along occupational, sectarian, regional and linguistic lines. Collectively all of these are sometimes referred to as "caste Hindus" or those falling within the caste system. The Dalits are described as *varna-sankara*: they are "outside the system"—so inferior to other castes that they are deemed polluting and therefore "untouchable." Even as outcasts, they themselves are divided into further sub-castes. Although "untouchability" was abolished under Article 17 of the Indian constitution, the practice continues to determine the socio-economic and religious standing of those at the bottom of the caste hierarchy. Whereas the first four varnas are free to choose and change their occupation, Dalits have generally been confined to the occupational structures into which they are born.

## The Relevance of Land

The caste system is an economic order. It prevents someone from owning land or receiving an education. It is a vicious cycle and an exploitative economic arrangement. Landowning patterns and being a high-caste member are co-terminous. Also there is a nexus between [being] lower-caste and landlessness... Caste is a tool to perpetuate exploitative economic arrangements. — R. Balakrishnan, chairman, Tamil Nadu Commission for Scheduled Castes and Scheduled Tribes

Most Dalit victims of abuse are landless agricultural labourers. According to the 1991 census, 77 percent of the Dalit workforce is in the primary (agricultural) sector of the economy. Those who own land often fall into the category of marginal landowners. Land is the prime asset in rural areas thatdetermines an individual's standard of living and social status. Lack of access to land makes Dalits economically vulnerable; their dependency is exploited by upper-and middle-caste landlords and allows for many abuses to go unpunished. India's policy of economic liberalization is also having an effect on Dalits and their livelihood. As the public sector shrinks due to privatization, the reservations model is affecting—and able to assist—fewer people, inasmuch as government-related jobs are being drastically reduced. Globalization has also led to coastal lands increasingly being acquired by multinationals (via the central government) for aquaculture projects. Dalits are the main labourers and tenants of coastal land areas and are increasingly being forced to leave these areas—to live as displaced people, for the most part—as foreign investment rises.

Land reform and increased wages for rural labourers are the central demands of most leftist guerrilla organizations active in West Bengal, Bihar, and Andhra Pradesh. Private landlord militias and state security forces have targeted civilians thought to be guerrilla sympathizers. The failure of most state governments to implement land reform legislation has only added to the sense of economic vulnerability that fuels militant movements. In Bihar in particular, guerrillas enjoy Dalit support, as most of the Dalit community lives on the edge of starvation. Laws and regulations that prohibit alienation of Dalit lands, set ceilings on a single landowner's holdings, or allocate surplus government lands to scheduled castes and scheduled tribes have been largely ignored, or worse, manipulated by upper castes with the help of district administrations.

In 1996 a nongovernmental organization undertook a door-to-door survey of 250 villages in the state of Gujarat and found that, in almost all villages, those who had title to land had no possession, and those who had possession had not had their land measured or faced illegal encroachments from upper castes. Many had no record of their holdings at all. Even those who had been offered land under agrarian reform legislation refused to accept it for fear of an upper-caste backlash. In the late 1980s in Chenaganambatti village in Madurai district, Tamil Nadu, 9.5 acres of idle land belonging to a temple under the Hindu Religious Endowment Act were auctioned and sold to villagers for cultivation. At the time, some 500,000 acres of such idle land existed in Tamil Nadu. Caste Hindus did not allow Dalits to take part in the auction. In 1989 Dalits began demanding participation and, in1992, finally succeeded in entering the auction. Caste Hindus protested and appealed to the commissioner of the Hindu Religious Endowment Act, a central government official. The commissioner decreed that the lands, once bought at auction, legally belonged to the Dalits. One month later, and in broad daylight, one hundred members of the Kallar community, an upper-caste group, invaded and destroyed nine acres of paddy (rice) fields belonging to Dalits. In subsequent attacks, the Kallars murdered two Dalit men and assaulted three Dalit women, who sustained head injuries. As the leader of the Dalit Panthers movement in Tamil Nadu recalled:

> They just cut their throat on the road. Even though the land belongs to Dalits, they [the Dalit owners] cannot plow it, even today. The accused were never punished. No trial took place.

## Social Boycotts and Retaliatory Violence

Whenever Dalits have tried to organise themselves or assert their rights, there has been a backlash from the feudal lords resulting in mass killings of Dalits, gang rapes, looting and arsoning, etc. of Harijan [Dalit] basties [villages]. — National Commission for Scheduled Castes and Scheduled Tribes

Whether caste clashes are social, economic, or political in nature, they are premised on the same basic principle: any attempt to alter village customs or to demand land, increased wages, or political rights leads to violence and economic retaliation on the part of those most threatened by changes in the status quo. Dalit communities as a whole are summarily punished for individual transgressions; Dalits are cut off from their land and employment during social boycotts, women bear the brunt of physical attacks, and the Atrocities Act is rarely enforced.

Describing one such boycott, a village resident and social worker in the Marathwada region of eastern Maharashtra recalled:

> The upper caste got together and said that we touched their god so we shouldn't live here. They put a social boycott on all the Dalits. We could not enter their land, we could not work for them, we could not get wood, we could not buy goods from their stores, and we could not grind grain in the flour mill. We were not even allowed to go near the wells in upper-caste territory to fetch water. We could use our government pumps, but that wasn't enough.

The social boycott is reinforced when the village council levies fines against caste Hindus who refuse to participate in it. In villages in Karnataka state, upper castes are generally fined Rs. 501 (US$12.53) for giving employment to Dalits during a social boycott.

## Violence Against Dalit Women

As Human Rights Watch was told by a government investigator in Tamil Nadu, "[n]o one practices untouchability when it comes to sex." Rape is a common phenomenon in rural areas. Women are raped as part of caste custom or village tradition. According to Dalit activists, Dalit girls have been forced to have sex with the village landlord. In rural areas, "women are induced into prostitution (Devadasi system)..., which [is] forced on them in the name of religion." The prevalence of rape in villages contributes to the greater incidence of child marriage in those areas. Early marriage between the ages of ten years and sixteen years persists in large part because of Dalit girls' vulnerability to sexual assault by upper-caste men; once a girl is raped, she becomes unmarriageable. An early marriage also gives parents greater control over the caste into which their children are married.

Dalit women are also raped as a form of retaliation. Women of scheduled castes and scheduled tribes are raped as part of an effort by upper-caste leaders to suppress movements to demand payment of minimum wages, to settle sharecropping disputes, or to reclaim lost land. They are raped by members of the upper caste, by landlords, and by the police in pursuit of their male relatives.

Despite overwhelming evidence to the contrary, upper-caste leaders deny the prevalence of sexual abuse against Dalit women. A prominent leader of the Thevar community in Tamil Nadu, who wished to remain anonymous, vehemently denounced the assertion that sexual relations between Dalit labourers and their landowning employers were nonconsensual. The very practice of "untouchability," he explained, was until recently looked upon favorably by Dalits. He added that in the present day, the practice has almost completely disappeared. In an interview with Human Rights Watch, he claimed:

In the past, twenty to thirty years ago, *harijans* [Dalits] enjoyed the practice of "untouchability." In the past, women enjoyed being oppressed by men. They weren't educated. They didn't know the world. Ladies would boast to others that my husband has more wives. Most of Dalit women enjoy relations with Thevar men. They enjoy Thevar community men having them as concubines. It is not done by force. Anything with Dalits is not done by force. That's why they don't react. They cannot afford to react, they are dependent on us for jobs and protection. Harijans formerly enjoyed their masters. "Untouchability" was there in various forms, but because of education, economic improvement, now in 95 percent of places, "untouchability" is not practiced. Thevars never say anything against them. Without Dalits we cannot live. We want workers in the fields. We are landholders. Without them we cannot cultivate or take care of our cattle. But Dalit women's relations with Thevar men are not out of economic dependency. She wants it from him. He permits it. If he has power, then she has more affection for the landlord.

Attacks on Dalit women during massacres, police raids, and caste clashes are discussed throughout this report. Dalit women are easy targets for any perpetrator because upper castes consider them to be "sexually available" and because they arelargely unprotected by the state machinery. The Bathani Tola massacre in Bihar in 1996 epitomizes this phenomenon.

The "landlords" wanted to reassert their feudal tyranny over the poor who have started becoming more vocal and by attacking the most vulnerable, women and children, they sent a clear message that they would not allow anyone to disturb the social structure... Women were raped and hacked. The huts and small houses in which the victims took shelter were burnt down. The shrill cries failed to draw the attention of the police posted a kilometre and a half away because their food came from the landlords' houses.

### Dalit Political Movements

In addition to a growing number of lower-caste-based political parties and human rights movements, Dalits have taken part in struggles against the state and their upper-caste counterparts since the 1960s to claim their rights; several of these movements have used arms and have advocated violence. While some Dalit leaders have argued that the fundamental rights of Dalits should be addressed within a constitutional framework, many non-urbanized Dalits have taken the position that their problems cannot be resolved without a militant struggle against those in power.

Mainstream political parties in India have generally adopted a top-down interventionist approach to Dalit problems, offering promises of loans, housing,and proper implementation of reservations (quotas allowing for increased representation in government jobs, education, and political bodies) as compensation for past mistreatment. Issues of "untouchability," temple entry, violence, and economic exploitation were largely left unaddressed by the state and political parties. As the traditional political parties abandoned or avoided efforts to mobilize support among Dalits at the grassroots level, they paved the way for an autonomous Dalit leadership to emerge in the early 1990s. This new leadership has been threatening for backward and upper castes.

## The Role of the Police

In 1979 the government of India constituted the National Police Commission to analyze the factors behind the dismal performance of the police throughout the country. The commission's eight-volume report, which includes recommendations to address the problem, is still considered by government officials and civil rights activists to be the most comprehensive and definitive document on the issue. Moreover, the problems of corruption, police brutality, and impunity documented in the report persist to this day. A *Times of India* editorial by a New Delhi-based human rights activist summarized the findings of the report as follows:

The sum of the report, in fact, detail and verify what common sense tells us. Subversion begins at recruitment which is rife with patronage. Promotions follow suit depending on the "reach" of lucky people. Transfers substitute for punishment as a bad egg is foisted on one community after another. At the police station, a normal young recruit enters such a strong atmosphere of routine violence that in a few years he has been molded into something quite unrecognisable. Low pay, bad housing, little insurance against the hazards of police work, absurdlylong hours, practically no forensic support to assist in crime detection, and punishing demands for results, all confirm the ordinary policeman's need for a "Godfather" to guide him through the thickets of survival. Favour for favour then ensures that the only agency legally allowed to use force against citizens gets transformed into a powerfully armed untamed assemblage that masquerades as the Law.

The National Police Commission's recommendations include a section on "police and the weaker sections," which detailed police abuses specific to scheduled castes. The section noted that "complaints against the police in their handling of cases arising from atrocities against Scheduled Castes often relate to refusal to register complaints, delayed arrival on the scene, half-hearted action while investigating specific cases, extreme brutality in dealing with accused persons belonging to weaker sections, soft treatment of accused persons belonging to influential sections, making arrests or failing to make them on malafide considerations, etc."

Two decades later, none of the commission's recommendations have been adopted, and police continue to detain, torture and extort money from Dalits without much fear of punishment. Frustration with the police has also helped to fuel armed and unarmed Dalit movements.

## Dalit Panthers of India

During the 1960s and 1970s, the Dalit Panthers, and several groups with a Marxist/Leninist or Maoist orientation, emerged outside the framework of recognized political parties and parliamentary politics to confront the established powers. The Dalit Panthers were formed in the state of Maharashtra in the 1970s, ideologically aligning themselves to the Black Panther movement in the United States. During the same period, Dalit literature, painting, and theater challenged the very premise and nature of established art forms and their depiction of society and religion. Many of these new Dalit artists formed the first generation of theDalit Panther movement that sought to wage an organized struggle against the varna system. Dalit Panthers visited "atrocity" sites, organized marches and rallies in villages, and raised slogans of direct militant action against their upper-caste aggressors.

The determined stance of the Dalit Panthers served to arouse and unite many Dalits, particularly Dalit youths and students. The defeat of ruling party candidates and the boycott of elections in some areas forced the government to take notice of the movement: Panther leaders were often harassed and removed from districts for speaking out against the government and Hindu religion. They also became frequent targets of police brutality and arbitrary detentions. Disagreements over the future of the movement and the inclusion of other caste groups ultimately led to a dispersal of Dalit Panther leadership. The former aggressiveness and militancy of the Dalit Panthers have for the most part dissipated, though small splinter groups or groups that have adopted the name still survive. In Tamil Nadu, for example, the Dalit Panthers of India have thrived since the 1980s as a nonviolent awareness-raising and organizing movement concentrating primarily on women's rights and land issues and claims. They are currently led by a man named Tirumavalavan. As documented in chapters V and VIII, their members are continually harassed and detained by the police.

## Naxalites

The origins of the Naxalite movement can be traced to a breakaway Maoist group in West Bengal, which in March 1967 split from the Communist Party of India (Marxist) (CPI(M)) over differences in ideology: while CPI(M) chose the parliamentary path to change, the Maoist group chose to engage in armed struggle. The group initiated a series of peasant uprisings beginning in a village in the state of West Bengal called Naxalbari, from which rebel leaders took the name "Naxalite." The peasant communities seized land, burned property records, and assassinated exploitative landlords and others identified as "class enemies." Although the uprising was brutally crushed within a few months, similar revolts broke out elsewhere in West Bengal and in other parts of India.

By 1970, Naxalite groups had expanded their efforts to large areas of the countryside stretching from West Bengal to the southern state of Kerala. They engaged in a campaign of land seizure and violence against the police and security forces, as well as against political figures, civil servants, landlords, and other civilians. In many instances, land seizures and other demonstrations of peasant resistance forced landlords to flee their lands. The Naxalites' abuses included targeted assassinations and kidnappings of political figures and police officials. Naxalite groups also carried out bombings and arson in areas where they were likely to cause civilian casualties and summarily executed, and in some cases tortured to death, suspected police informers. All such practices constitute gross violations of international law. Although the Naxalite insurgency was brought to an end in most parts of the country by a brutal police crackdown designed to eliminate the militants and their supporters, the movement continues to survive, albeit with some splits and regroupings, in the rural areas of West Bengal, Orissa, Andhra Pradesh, and Bihar.

From the outset of the Naxalbari uprising, the government has resorted to extra-legal measures to deal with the Naxalite threat, including extrajudicial executions, torture, and forced disappearances. Most of the victims of police abuse are peasants and labourers. Members and organizers of peasant unions are automatically labelled as Naxalites. Tribal and Dalit villagers are often singled out as Naxalite sympathizers, while attacks on rural activists and striking labourers are sanctioned as part of a campaign to fight "Naxalite terrorism." Senior police officers with a record of "killing Naxalites" even receive promotions, cash rewards, and favored postings.

### The Rise of the "Backward Castes"

For those within the four principal varnas, caste has not proved to be a completely rigid system. Just as the higher ritual status of Brahmins does not necessarily translate into economic or political supremacy, those lower in the ranks are able to move up in the local hierarchy through the capture of political power, the acquisition of land, and migration to other regions. A combination of these strategies and India's policy of quotas or reservations have particularly benefited the so-called backward castes, or Shudras. Referred to as "other backward classes" (OBCs) in administrative parlance, backward castes are defined as those whose ritual rank and occupational status are above "untouchables" but who themselves remain socially and economically depressed.

Contrary to the general presumption that the OBCs belong to the deprived sections of Hindu society, few groups in independent

India have made progress on a scale comparable to the OBCs. However, it must be noted that the term OBCs is a problematic categorization. One author writes that OBCs span such a wide cultural and structural arch as to be almost meaningless. There are at one extreme the dominant, landowning, peasant castes which wield power and authority over local Vaishyas and Brahmins, whereas at the other extreme are the poor, near-Untouchable groups living just above the pollution line. The category also includes many artisan and servicing castes.

Some academics have divided Shudras into two clearly identifiable subcategories: upper Shudras and lower Shudras. In north India the upper Shudras comprise such economically powerful and politically aggressive groups as the Jats and Yadavs. The Jats, though not officially included in the OBC list, still regard themselves as the leaders of the backward castes.

The inclusion of so many heterogeneous groups within the OBC category has both made for its enormous size and has enabled its leaders to advocate their claim for special status and land in post-independence India. The first wave of land reform in the 1950s aimed at conferring ownership rights on existing tenants of land. Land reform legislation was responsible for displacing the large class of *zamindars* (large landowners) and creating a substantial class of medium-sized owner-cultivators, many of whom were OBCs. After cornering the benefits of this first wave of legislation, these groups attempted to block all subsequent land reformmeasures designed to benefit marginal farmers and the landless, who usually belonged to castes and groups lower on the social hierarchy, most notably Dalits. Economic prosperity soon translated into political gains for OBCs, while the reservation system of quotas—successfully implemented—ensured them a presence in the state machinery.

In 1980 the National Police Commission noted a disturbing trend in caste conflicts between backward castes and scheduled castes:

In the recent years we have also seen a new factor emerging in the social struggle in rural areas in which the "backward classes" have been surging forward to take up positions of power and control in society, knocking down the upper castes who had held sway in such positions all along in the past. In this process of marching forward, the backward classes tend to push back the Scheduled Castes and others who occupy the lower rung in the social hierarchical ladder. There is greater tensionbetween structural neighbours in this hierarchy than between the top level and the bottom level.

The pattern has since solidified such that caste clashes are far more prevalent between scheduled castes and backward castes than they are between these groups and upper castes. The Home Ministry's Annual Report for 1995 reported that caste-related incidents in Tamil Nadu, Bihar, and Maharashtra increased by 25 to 30 percent from previous years. A majority of these incidents were taking place between scheduled castes and OBCs.

## Legal Context

The Constitution of India came into effect in 1950, the year that India became a republic and three years after India's independence from British rule. It embodies the principles of equality, freedom, justice, and human dignity and requires both state and central governments to provide special protection to scheduled-caste members, to raise their standard of living, and to ensure their equality with other citizens. To women, the constitution guarantees equal rights, liberty, justice and the right to live with dignity. Discrimination on the basis of religion and gender is prohibited, and compensation for past discrimination is promoted.

Building on constitutional provisions, the government of India has pursued a two-pronged approach to narrowing the gap between the socio-economic status of the scheduled-caste population and the national average. The first approach involves regulatory measures designed to ensure that relevant legal provisions are adequately implemented, enforced and monitored; the second focuses on increasing the self-sufficiency of the scheduled-caste population through financial assistance for self-employment activities and through development programs to increase education and skills.

The protective component of this two-pronged strategy includes the implementation of legal provisions contained in the Protection of Civil Rights Act, 1955 and the Scheduled Castes and

Scheduled Tribes (Prevention of Atrocities) Act, 1989; other state and central government laws; and reservations or quotas in the arenas of government employment and higher education. India's policy of reservations is an attempt by the central government to remedy past injustices related to low-caste status. To allow for proportional representation in certain state and federal institutions, the constitution reserves 22.5 percent of seats in federal government jobs, state legislatures, the lower house of parliament, and educational institutions for scheduled castes and scheduled tribes. These protective measures are monitored by the National Commission for Scheduled Castes and Scheduled Tribes. The development measures for the educational, social, and economic upliftment of scheduled castes are administered by the Ministry of Welfare through the state governments.

Like many of the protective measures described in this report, the reservation policy has not been successfully implemented for Dalits. In the highlights of its fourth report for the years 1996-97 and 1997-98, the National Commission for Scheduled Castes and Scheduled Tribes noted that reservations had only been provided in government services and stressed that reservations in defense forces and the judiciary should be enforced. It added that the private sector, which continues to enjoy government patronage in terms of concessional land, financing, and excise and sales tax relief, should also be brought under the purview of the reservation policy. Despite a large body of legislation and administrative agency mandates assigned exclusively to deal with the plight of scheduled castes, the persistence of caste-based prejudices and the denial of access to land, education, and political power have all contributed to an atmosphere of increasing intolerance. Violence against Dalits in their communities, which has steadily climbed since 1994, is only the most extreme form of that intolerance.

Between 1994 and 1996, a total of 98,349 cases were registered with the police nationwide as crimes and atrocities against scheduled castes. Of these, 38,483 were registered under the Atrocities Act. A further 1,660 were for murder,2,814 for rape, and 13,671 for hurt. Given that Dalits are both reluctant and unable (for lack of police cooperation) to report crimes against themselves, the actual number of abuses is presumably much higher. While there are not yet official figures available on killings and attacks in 1997 and 1998, the latest wave of attacks described in this and other reports confirms that the violence has continued.

## Case of India's 'Untouchables'

More than one-sixth of India's population, some 160 million people, live a precarious existence, shunned by much of society because of their rank as "untouchables" or Dalits-literally meaning "broken" people-at the bottom of India's caste system. Dalits are discriminated against, denied access to land, forced to work in degrading conditions, and routinely abused at the hands of the police and of higher-caste groups that enjoy the state's protection. In what has been called India's "hidden apartheid," entire villages in many Indian states remain completely segregated by caste. National legislation and constitutional protections serve only to mask the social realities of discrimination and violence faced by those living below the "pollution line."

For most of the world caste remains an ancient cultural artefact and untouchability a long eradicated practice. This paper attempts to shift the debate on caste and on broader issues pertaining to socially institutionalised discrimination. It begins with a brief description of the characteristics and mechanisms of caste discrimination and a summary overview of the Indian government's response. It then attempts to dismantle those misperceptions that have allowed the system to survive, and comments on the barriers that keep the international community from effectively intervening against a practice that relegates millions of people to a lifetime of segregation, discrimination, and violence.

India's caste system is perhaps the world's longest surviving social hierarchy. A defining feature of Hinduism, caste encompasses a complex ordering of social groups on the basis of ritual purity. A person is considered a member of the caste into which he or she is born and remains within that caste until death, although the particular ranking of that caste may vary among regions and over time. Differences in status are traditionally justified by the religious doctrine of karma, a belief that one's place in life is determined by one's deeds in previous lifetimes. Traditional scholarship has described this more than 2,000-year-old system within the context of the four principal varnas, or large caste categories. In order of precedence these are the Brahmins (priests and teachers), the Ksyatriyas (rulers and soldiers), the Vaishyas (merchants and traders), and the Shudras (labourers and artisans). A fifth category falls outside the varna system and consists of those known as "untouchables" or Dalits; they are often assigned tasks too ritually polluting to merit inclusion within the traditional varna system.

Within the four principal castes, there are thousands of sub-castes, also called jatis; endogamous groups that are further divided along occupational, sectarian, regional, and linguistic lines. Collectively all of these are sometimes referred to as "caste Hindus" or those falling within the caste system. The Dalits are described as varna-sankara: they are "outside the system"-so inferior to other castes that they are deemed polluting and therefore "untouchable." Even as outcasts, they themselves are divided into further sub-castes and practice untouchability against those ranked below; the discrimination is wholly internalised. Although "untouchability" was abolished under Article 17 of the Indian constitution, the practice continues to determine the socioeconomic and religious standing of those at the bottom of the caste hierarchy. Whereas the first four varnas are free to choose and change their occupation, Dalits have generally been confined to the occupational structures into which they are born.

With little land of their own to cultivate, Dalit men, women, and children numbering in the tens of millions work as agricultural labourers for a few kilograms of rice or less than US$1 a day. Most live on the brink of destitution, barely able to feed their families and unable to send their children to school or break away from cycles of debt bondage that are passed on from generation to generation. At the end of day they return to a hut in their Dalit colony with no electricity, kilometres away from the nearest water source, and segregated from all non-Dalits, known as caste Hindus. They are forbidden by caste Hindus to enter places of worship, to draw water from public wells, or to wear shoes in caste Hindu presence. They are made to dig the village graves, dispose of dead animals, clean human waste with their bare hands, and to wash and use separate tea tumblers at neighbourhood tea stalls, all because-due to their caste status-they are deemed polluting and therefore untouchable. In November 1999, after a cyclone slammed into the eastern state of Orissa, killing thousands and rendering millions homeless, the government brought in 200 Dalit manual scavengers from New Delhi, and planned to bring 500 more from other parts of Orissa, to load animal carcasses onto hand-drawn carts and take them away to be burned. Government officials had offered local upper-caste residents more than the daily minimum wage for each animal burned but they refused citing the decayed conditions of the carcasses and the fact that the task was beneath them: they had "some self-respect left." Even in times of natural disaster, the laws of purity and pollution prevail and the government moves quickly to accommodate the prejudice. At all levels, and under all circumstances, the discrimination is institutionalised.

Dalit women face the triple burden of caste, class, and gender. Dalit girls have been forced to become prostitutes for upper-caste patrons and village priests. Sexual abuse and other forms of violence against women are used by landlords and the police to inflict political "lessons" and crush dissent within the community. According to a Tamil Nadu state government official, the raping of Dalit women exposes the hypocrisy of the caste system as "no one practices untouchability when it comes to sex." Like other Indian women whose relatives are sought by the police, Dalit women have also been arrested and tortured in custody as a means of punishing their male relatives who are hiding from the authorities.

Any attempt to defy the social order is met with physical or economic retaliation. According to the most recent figures available, between 1994 and 1996 a total of 98,349 cases were registered with the police nationwide as crimes and atrocities against Dalits. Given that Dalits are both reluctant and unable (for lack of police cooperation) to report crimes against themselves, the actual number of abuses is presumably much higher. Whether the clashes are social, economic, or political in nature, they are premised on the same basic principle: any attempt to alter village customs or to demand land, increased wages, or political rights sets off a chain of events and leads to social boycotts and acts of retaliatory violence on the part of those most threatened by changes in the status quo.

Dalit communities as a whole are summarily punished for individual transgressions; Dalits are cut off from their land and employment, women endure physical attacks, and letter of the law is rarely enforced. Most of the conflicts take place within very narrow segments of the caste hierarchy, between the poor and the not so poor, the landless labourer and the marginal landowner. The differences lie in the considerable amount of leverage that the higher-caste Hindus or non-Dalits are able to wield over local police, district administrations, and even the state government. A theme that is almost universal in its application, it illustrates a crucial aspect of identity politics: one's identity as a person belonging to a certain caste is perceived not only by one's absolute rank but also by the relative treatment meted out to communities that are ranked below.

Building on constitutional provisions, the government of India has pursued a two-pronged approach to narrowing the gap between the socioeconomic status of the Dalit population and the national average. The first approach involves regulatory measures designed to ensure that relevant legal provisions are adequately implemented, enforced, and monitored; the second focuses on increasing the self-sufficiency of the Dalit population through financial assistance for self-employment activities and through development programs to increase education and skills.

The protective component of this two-pronged strategy includes the implementation of legal provisions contained in state and central government legislation, and reservations or quotas in the arenas of government employment and higher education. India's policy of reservations is an attempt by the central government to remedy past injustices related to low-caste status. To allow for proportional representation in certain state and federal institutions, the constitution reserves 22.5 percent of seats in federal government jobs, state legislatures, the Lower House of parliament, and educational institutions for scheduled castes and scheduled tribes. Though some have benefited the reservation policy has not been successfully implemented and has yet to achieve its desired effect. Moreover, most of the landless and illiterate Dalits in the country are not in a position to avail themselves of any of their constitutional privileges. Controversy over the reservations scheme has also allowed the debate to predictably stagnate around the distribution of privilege, taking the focus away from violations of basic rights. India's policy of economic liberalisation is also having an effect on Dalits and their livelihood.

As the public sector shrinks due to privatisation, the reservations model is affecting-and able to assist-fewer people, inasmuch as government-related jobs are being drastically reduced. Globalisation has also led to coastal lands increasingly being acquired by multinationals (via the central government) for aquaculture projects. Dalits are the main labourers and tenants of coastal land areas and are increasingly being forced to leave these areas-to live as displaced people, for the most part-as foreign investment rises.

The persistence of caste-based prejudices and the denial of access to land, education, and political power have all contributed to an atmosphere of increasing intolerance. Violence against Dalits, which has steadily climbed since 1994, is only the most extreme form of that intolerance. In 1989 the Scheduled Castes and Scheduled Tribes (Prevention of Atrocities) Act was enacted to prevent and punish caste-based abuses, to establish special courts for the trial of such offences, and to provide for victim relief and rehabilitation. Its enactment represented an acknowledgement on the part of the government that abuses, in their most degrading and violent forms, were still perpetrated against Dalits decades after independence.

A look at the offences made punishable by the act provides a glimpse into the retaliatory or customarily degrading treatment Dalits may receive. They include forcing members of a scheduled caste or scheduled tribe to drink or eat any inedible or obnoxious substance; dumping excreta, waste matter, carcasses or any other obnoxious substance in their premises or neighbourhood; forcibly removing clothes and parading them naked or with painted face or body; interfering with their rights to land; compelling a member of a scheduled caste or scheduled tribe into forms of forced or bonded labour; corrupting or fouling the water of any spring, reservoir or any other source ordinarily used by scheduled castes or scheduled tribes; denying right of passage to a place of public resort; and using a position of dominance to exploit a scheduled caste or scheduled tribe woman sexually. The potential of the law to bring about social change has been hampered by institutional prejudice and police corruption, with the result that many offences are not registered. Ignorance of procedures or a lack of knowledge of the act itself has also affected implementation. Even when cases are registered, the absence of special courts to try them can delay prosecutions for up to three to four years. Some state governments dominated by higher castes have even attempted to repeal the legislation altogether. Much like other "social welfare" legislation in India, the act remains a paper tiger with little actual effect.

The existence of constitutionally mandated quotas and a large body of legislation and administrative agency mandates assigned exclusively to deal with the plight of Dalits is held up by the government as a panacea to problems of discrimination. These so-called remedies have also shifted attention away from the institutional nature of caste prejudice. It would be difficult to convince the Dalits of Dholapur district, Rajasthan, that after over fifty years of independence, government intervention had made a difference. In April 1998, a Dalit of the area was assaulted by an upper-caste family who forcibly pierced his nostril, drew a string through his nose, paraded him around the village, and tied him to a cattle post-all because he refused to sell bidis (hand-rolled cigarettes) on credit to the nephew of the upper-caste village chief. The message sent from the judiciary on caste discrimination is equally grim: in July 1998 in the state of Uttar Pradesh, an Allahabad High Court judge had his chambers "purified with Ganga jal" (water from the River Ganges), because it had earlier been occupied by a Dalit judge.

India's distinction as the "world's largest democracy" also helps to mask the abuses. For Dalits throughout the country who suffer from de facto disenfranchisement, democracy has not been a self-fulfilling prophecy. During elections, those unpersuaded by typical electioneering are routinely threatened and beaten by political party strongmen in order to compel them to vote for certain candidates. Already under the thumb of local landlords and police officials, Dalit villagers who do not comply have been murdered, beaten, and harassed. Dalits who have contested political office in village councils and municipalities through seats that have been constitutionally "reserved" for them have been threatened with physical abuse and even death in order to get them to withdraw from the campaign. In Tamil Nadu in June 1997, a newly elected Dalit village council president was beheaded by caste Hindus displaced from their once secure elected positions. In 1999, a Dalit woman from Uttar Pradesh considered contesting elections. She was gang-raped and subsequently beaten and murdered as a lesson to other villagers not to disturb the status quo. As with most cases of violence against Dalits, the culprits have yet to be convicted.

Political mobilisation that has resulted in the emergence of powerful interest groups and political parties among middle-and low-caste groups throughout India since the mid-1980s has also largely bypassed Dalits. Dalits are courted by all political parties but generally forgotten once elections are over. The expanding power base of low-caste political parties, the election of low-caste chief ministers to state governments, and even the appointment of a Dalit as president of India in July 1997 all signal the increasing prominence of Dalits in the political landscape but cumulatively have yet to yield any significant benefit for the majority of Dalits. Laws on land reform and protection for Dalits remain unimplemented in most of India's twenty-five states.

Political parties have frequently fashioned their manifestos and campaign slogans around the need for "upliftment" of these marginalised sectors, while political leaders, mostly drawn from higher castes, offer the promise of equal status and equal rights. However, the laws have benefited very few and, due to a lack of political will, development programs and welfare projects designed to improve economic conditions for Dalits have generally had little effect. Dalits rarely break free from bondage or economic exploitation by upper-caste landowners.

Equally insidious, though not as apparent, is the fact that Dalits are denied their place in the public consciousness. The plight of India's "untouchables" elicits only sporadic attention within the country. Public outrage over large-scale incidents of violence or particularly egregious examples of discrimination fades quickly, and the state is under little pressure to undertake more meaningful reforms. Despite ambitious calls for action by central and state governments in the aftermath publicity of massacres and police raids, the Indian authorities have shown little commitment to resolving the root causes of caste conflicts. Society as a whole has turned a blind eye to the institutional character of caste-based abuse and discrimination. Laws are openly flouted, police allegiance is routinely up for sale, and society continues to sanction what the legislature defines as crimes. In the eastern state of Bihar, for example, the first person to be convicted under a decadesold law combating child labour was in 1998. A loss of faith in the state machinery and increasing intolerance of their abusive treatment has led many Dalit communities into organised movements to claim their rights.

In response, state and private actors have engaged in a pattern of repression to preserve the status quo. Unable to find sustainable alliances within, and in an effort to counter their invisibility at home, Dalit movements have from time to time turned outward to look for parallels in struggles abroad. During the 1970s, for example, the Dalit Panthers emerged outside the framework of recognised political parties and aligned themselves ideologically to the Black Panther movement in the United States. During the same period, Dalit literature, painting, and theatre challenged the very premise and nature of established art forms and their depiction of society and religion. Many of these new Dalit artists formed the first generation of the Dalit Panther movement that sought to wage an organised struggle against the varna system. Dalit Panthers visited atrocity sites, organised marches and rallies in villages, and raised slogans of direct militant action against their upper-caste aggressors.

The determined stance of the Dalit Panthers served to arouse and unite many Dalits, particularly Dalit youth and students. The defeat of ruling party candidates and the boycott of elections in some areas forced the government to take notice of the movement: Panther leaders were often harassed and removed from districts for speaking out against the government and Hindu religion. They also became frequent targets of police brutality and arbitrary detentions. Disagreements over the future of the movement and inclusion of other caste groups ultimately led to a dispersal of Dalit Panther leadership. The former aggressiveness and militancy of the Dalit Panthers has for the most part dissipated, though small splinter groups or groups that have adopted the name still survive.

In the 1960s, leftist guerrilla organisations with Marxist, Leninist, and Maoist orientations began advocating the use of violence to achieve land redistribution. By 1970, these so-called Naxalites had initiated a series of peasant uprisings to seize land, burn property records, and assassinate exploitative landlords and others identified as "class enemies" in large areas of the countryside stretching from West Bengal to the southern state of Kerala. Although the Naxalite insurgency was brought to an end in most parts of the country by a brutal police crackdown designed to eliminate the militants and their supporters, the movement continues to survive, albeit with some splits and regroupings, in the rural areas of West Bengal, Orissa, Andhra Pradesh, and Bihar. Higher-caste landlords in Bihar have organised private militias to counter the Naxalite threat. These militias, or senas, also target Dalit villagers believed to be sympathetic to Naxalites. Senas are believed responsible for the murders of many hundreds of Dalits in Bihar since 1987.

Though offshoots of militant movements still thrive in many parts of the country, the strategy for the actualisation of rights has in the past fifteen years undergone a major shift. Beginning in the 1980s, a handful of Dalit organisations began turning to the United Nations as a possible forum for the mobilisation of international support and condemnation of caste-based abuses. However, the difficulty of slotting caste-based abuses into standard categories of human rights violations, and the prevalence of constitutional and legislative protections at the national level, has allowed these abuses to escape international scrutiny. The government of India has consistently asserted that the caste issue does not fall within the mandate of various "race"-based UNHCHR bodies. The government has also refused to allow relevant working groups and special rapporteurs to gain access to the country.

In turn, the response of the international community has been superficial at best. Dalit activists now find themselves struggling to overcome their invisibility abroad. Though caste identity is used as a justification for segregation and exploitation, the discrimination is so entrenched that the victims' shared membership in lower-caste communities is often ignored by upper-caste families and international bodies alike. While the world was united in its condemnation of increasing attacks on India's Christian community this past year, for example, it ignored a significant underlying cause: a majority of Christians in India are Dalits and tribals for whom conversion offers a partial escape from untouchability and exploitation. Conversions are therefore threatening to the social and economic status quo.

Like evaluating the symptoms without diagnosing the disease, most international interventions have also overlooked the fact that Dalits, numbering in the tens of millions, comprise the majority of those driven to bonded labour, manual scavenging, and forced prostitution, under conditions that violate national law and their basic human rights. Despite their mandate of reaching the "poorest of the poor," international development institutions have yet to understand that for those at the bottom of its hierarchy, caste is a determinative factor for the attainment of social, political, civil, and economic rights.

Which strategies then are likely to be effective in reforming socially institutionalised discrimination? Part of the answer lies in supporting the work of grassroots Dalit and human rights activists throughout the country who for many years have assumed many state-like functions and have stepped in where the administration has failed. The second part is to involve the international community in forcing the government to remedy its failures.

In 1998, the National Campaign for Dalit Human Rights was born out of an initiative of grassroots Dalit activists in eight Indian states. Many of these activists were involved in the drafting of over forty recommendations to the government of India and the international community that are contained in a Human Rights Watch report on caste violence released earlier this year. The campaign, which has since expanded to include fourteen states and eleven countries, seeks to mobilise a national coalition that operates at the grassroots level while eliciting the participation of the international community in its struggle. Still, there are other prejudices to be overcome before such participation can be ensured. Internationally, the cyclone in India received little attention in comparison to other recent tragedies of similar or lesser magnitude. Like disparities in responding to crises in Europe and Africa, the "otherness" of those most vividly affected by violence, disaster, or day-to-day deprivation, eases the decision not to respond. When the victims of attacks, even massacres, are non-Christian Dalits, the news barely breaks into international headlines.

Interventions on caste discrimination, if any, have been limited to inquiries regarding the mechanisms of protection offered by the state, without asking for evidence of their effective implementation (which, generally speaking, is a recurring problem in the nature of international intervention on race and ethnicity matters). The Indian government needs to place a priority on strengthening institutional mechanisms aimed at addressing issues of violence and discrimination. But it also needs the active support of-and pressure from-the United Nations, multilateral financial institutions, trading partners, and national and international non-governmental organisations to eradicate the pervasive problem of caste-based abuse. Will the international community respond or even apply the necessary pressure to stimulate domestic political will? Or will it continue to deny Dalits and others their place in the public consciousness? Entrenched forms of discrimination stemming from the world's longest surviving system of social hierarchy may offer some lessons as we prepare for a global forum on modern day "racism." The first and most obvious is to look beyond race as the only arbiter of rights. The second is to look beyond democracy, affirmative action, and the existence of domestic legislation as sufficient guarantors of basic freedoms. The third is to recognise the resilience and adaptability of ancient custom to contemporary global trends: The fourth is to scrutinise the discrimination inherent in the international community's decision to act, and more importantly, in its failure to respond

# CHAPTER 13 The Battle Against Fear and Discrimination of Indian Dalit Women

## Introduction

Amnesty International has expressed concern for many years about the torture and ill-treatment of women in custody in India. In 1992 the organization's campaign against torture in India highlighted the problem of rape in custody. In January this year, as part of its third international Campaign against Torture which focuses on three major areas: preventing torture, confronting discrimination and overcoming impunity, Amnesty International published a series of detailed recommendations for the prevention of torture in India focussing on custodial situations including the particular problems of women in custody and their vulnerability to torture and ill-treatment including rape. In that report Amnesty International commented on its concern at a widespread tolerance and social acceptance of forms of torture and ill-treatment in India. It pointed out that publicised cases of torture and ill-treatment of domestic employees, the routine use of violence by political groups against one another's cadres, the beating and stripping of*dalits* and other vulnerable groups as a method of community punishment, as well as the widespread use of violence against women in the home and community underline the urgent need for steps to be taken to end torture and ill-treatment prevalent throughout society.

The organization's concerns led it to carry out research into the area of violence against women in the community and the state's response to such violence. Under international standards states clearly have an obligation to act with due diligence to prevent, investigate and punish abuses of human rights even if not carried out directly by agents of the state. Amnesty International considers that acts of violence against women constitute torture for which the state is accountable when they are of the nature and severity envisaged in the definition of torture in international standards and the state has failed to fulfil its obligation to provide effective protection.

This report provides background information on the context of violence against marginalised groups of women in Uttar Pradesh and Rajasthan, demonstrating the vulnerability of certain groups of women to violence in the context of gender as well as caste and other forms of social and racial discrimination. It then looks in some detail at the problems these groups have in obtaining access to justice and sets the theory of safeguards and judicial process against practices of non-implementation, inaction and discrimination that are a reality for many victims. Presenting evidence of connivance by public servants in covering up crimes of violence against women and ensuring that perpetrators are not prosecuted as well as evidence of discrimination within organs of the criminal justice system, it argues that the state has failed to act with due diligence to prevent, investigate and punish many acts of violence against women which occur in the community. It recommends a series of actions which Amnesty International believes are necessary in order for India to fulfil its international human rights obligations towards women.

By raising its concerns about this aspect of torture within its Campaign against Torture, Amnesty International is seeking to broaden the debate about torture in India and the specific conditions— social, economic, legal and cultural — which allow the torture of women to occur and persist in India in many different contexts. By focussing on the situation of *dalits*, "backward caste", *adivasis* and women otherwise marginalised by their economic position, the report also seeks to highlight the role of discrimination within society and the state — also highlighted in its earlier recommendations — in not only increasing the vulnerability of women to torture but reducing their chances of obtaining justice.

While recognizing that violence against women in India takes many serious forms including trafficking and sexual exploitation,

Amnesty International delegates limited their research to crimes of rape and other violent acts, such as assault (including stripping) which occur in the community. Amnesty International delegates also looked at the issue of violence against women in the home and the state's response. Amnesty International's intention is to address concerns arising from its findings on this issue in a separate submission to the Government of India at a later date.

In December 2000, Amnesty International delegates visited Uttar Pradesh and Rajasthan to conduct research into the torture and ill-treatment of women. A request had also been made to visit the state of Bihar. However, by the time delegates arrived in India the Bihar government had not yet responded to the Union Government concerning its willingness to cooperate with the visit so with regret this part of the visit was cancelled. The research carried out in Uttar Pradesh and Rajasthan focussed on the particular vulnerability of socially and economically disadvantaged women to torture and ill-treatment and problems of accessing justice that they face. An emphasis was placed on the situation of scheduled caste and scheduled tribe women, given the large populations of these communitiesin those two states and the existence of specific legislation designed to protect them; it is widely held that this legislation is not being fully implemented. Meetings were held with human rights organizations and victims of torture and ill-treatment, as well as lawyers and others involved in processing cases through the criminal justice system. Meetings were also held with officials in the Home and Women and Child Departments of the two state governments, as well as police officials in those states. Meetings were also held in Rajasthan with the State Commission for Women and the State Human Rights Commission. Amnesty International delegates were grateful to the Rajasthan government for open and frank discussions held with officials and for detailed information on crimes against women provided by the government. Unfortunately, despite requests prior to, during, and following meetings with officials in the Home department of the government of Uttar Pradesh, for details concerning government policy and figures in relation to violence against women and in relation to violence against members of the scheduled caste and scheduled tribe communities, it is regretted that no such information has been made available to Amnesty

International to date. Prior to leaving the country, Amnesty International delegates met with officials in the Union Department of Women and Child Development in New Delhi to convey a preliminary impression of their findings and to hear of central government policies concerning violence against women.

Amnesty International does not claim that the situation in Uttar Pradesh and Rajasthan is representative of the whole of the country. Both have particularly feudal and patriarchal societies where caste divisions are strong and where landowning classes continue to wield significant power in many areas. However, the organization believes that many of the problems identified and the recommendations made will be applicable across the country and hopes that they will be fed into discussions concerning women's empowerment which are currently taking place at the government level in India and that they will support the numerous initiatives of the women's movement in the country.

## International Standards and the Government of India's Responsibilities and Commitments

The responsibility of states for acts which impair the rights of women is sometimes mistakenly perceived as applying only when state agents or officials are the actual perpetrators of acts which violate human rights. The protection afforded by human rights law is far greater. There is a clear responsibility on states under international law which extends beyond violations by those acting on behalf of the state and its organs. Human rights treaties spell out the obligations of the State, including: to promote those rights; to secure those rights for all and translate them into policies and strategies; to prevent violations of the rights under the Conventions and to provide remedies to the victims should their rights be violated. The Declaration on the Elimination of Violence against Women, adopted by the UN General Assembly in 1993, affirms that states must "exercise due diligence to prevent, investigate and, in accordance with national legislation, punish acts of violence against women, whether those acts are perpetrated by the State or by private persons".

Applying international human rights law without understanding the responsibility of the state for abuses of women's rights by private actors — including employers, partners, husbands, family members or neighbours — simply robs women of protection and of remedies for the majority of abuses against them. Human rights law is not silent on these abuses. It clearly points to a positive responsibility on the part of the state.

As a party to the Convention on the Elimination of All Forms of Racial Discrimination since 1968 and the International Covenant on Civil and Political Rights since 1979, India has been committed for many years to ensuring civil and political rights to all its citizens without discrimination of any kind. This commitment was reinforced with its ratification of the Convention of the Elimination of All Forms of Discrimination against Women (Women's Convention) in July 1993. India's Constitution sets out fundamental rights made available to all its citizens which it explicitly states are to be realised without discrimination. The Constitution upholds the right to equality before the law (Article 14) and prohibits discrimination on the grounds of religion, race, caste, sex or place of birth. Various laws reinforce safeguards against discrimination and provide for positive discrimination for certain groups identified as vulnerable within society. These include scheduled castes and scheduled tribes and women.

As a vast democracy with many regional variations and a "developing" economy, India has an enormous amount to achieve and an enormous amount of commitments to fulfil to all its citizens, including women. Recognizing its international commitments towards the rights of women and urged on by a dynamic women's movement, successive governments have unveiled policies of empowerment for women which have sought to address the full range of women's human rights. As a result, there are many positive aspects of women's empowerment which have taken place in recent years in India. This includes political representation of women at the lowest levels of government, increases in life expectancy amongst women and education. There have been several government initiatives to empower women economically and politically, many of which are operational in Uttar Pradesh and Rajasthan. In Uttar Pradesh the government-backed *Mahila Samakya*development scheme has contributed to the increased empowerment of thousands of marginalised women through education and other programs. Amnesty International delegates were told by officials of the Government of Uttar Pradesh of schemes which provide financial support to widows who often find themselves ostracised socially and economically, pension schemes and self-help schemes running in 20% of the districts of the state for women to mobilise savings and run rural banks. In Rajasthan, the state-sponsored women's development programme posed a challenge to feudal patriarchal values by empowering women at the local level to question and oppose feudal practices such as child marriage. Amnesty International delegates were told of the establishment of self-help groups in rural areas in Rajasthan encouraging economic empowerment through thrift groups and how training programs presented opportunities for women to have their complaints heard by local officials.

Political representation of women has increased at the local level. The 73rd Constitutional Amendment Act, 1992 (Panchayati Raj), included a provision for statutory minimum reservation of 33% seats for women in Panchayati Raj Institutions (this Amendment came into force on 24 April 1993). This has allowed a number of women to participate in community decision-making processes, including those from marginalised communities given that there are also reservations for scheduled caste, scheduled tribe and backward caste categories. The involvement of women in *Panchayats*[village councils] was noted by Amnesty International delegates in both Uttar Pradesh and Rajasthan — there are reported to be around 3,000 women *Sarpanches*[village heads] and 33,000 elected women representatives on *Panchayats*in Rajasthan — although there are continuing problems associated with womens' participation. Political reservation for women at the central level has however proved more problematic and successive parliamentary sessions have failed to reach a consensus on the Constitutional (85th Amendment) Bill 1999 which would provide 33% reservation for women in the national parliament and state legislatures.

Following the Fourth UN World Conference on Women in Beijing in 1995, the Government of India promised several measures to ensure the advancement of women's rights in India. The Department of Women and Child Development began work on a National Policy on Women which would seek to bridge the gap between the equal de-jure status and unequal de-facto position of women in the country. In January 2000, while hearing India's first periodic report, the Committee on the Elimination of Discrimination Against Women (CEDAW) recommended that a national plan of action be developed to address in a holistic manner the issue of gender-based violence, in line with the Committee's general recommendation 19. In January 2001 the Prime Minister of India announced that 2001 would be the year of Women's Empowerment and that a National Policy on Women's Empowerment would soon be unveiled. The policy (Amnesty International has so far been unable to obtain a copy) reportedly included a plan to ensure that all laws deemed discriminatory to women be reviewed and suitably amended by 2003. It also included plans to establish an effective machinery to monitor the delivery of justice to women in a context of rising crimes against women and suggested requesting State Governments to set up District Committees to monitor and expedite disposal of cases of atrocities against women. On 22 March 2001 it was announced that the Cabinet had cleared the policy.

Amnesty International delegates were interested to see the Rajasthan government's Women's Policy which was launched in March 2000 and to obtain a copy of the Uttar Pradesh government's draft Women's Policy. Both refer in part to measures to ensure justice to women victims of violence although the majority of these policies relate to economic empowerment of women.

Amnesty International welcomes these indications that the Government of India and state governments wish to address continuing problems of violence against women throughout the country. However, it is concerned that these policies should be more than just further rhetoric and should firmly address ongoing problems of non-implementation and/or discriminatory implementation of safeguards and impunity for perpetrators of violence against women. By highlighting some of the problems it identified in the course of its research in two states in India and by suggesting remedies, Amnesty International hopes to contribute to discussions about how to change this situation.

The reality of the situation on the ground for women and

members of vulnerable groups continues to be extremely harsh despite the Constitutional, legislative and administrative framework in place in India. The failure to implement protective provisions and continuing gender, caste and class biases within society ensures that Constitutional and legal safeguards are rendered meaningless to many. In January 2000, CEDAW, hearing India's first periodic report made a series of recommendations on the basis of a broad range of concerns about implementation of the Women's Convention. These included the establishment of a comprehensive and compulsory system of registration of births and marriages and implementation of laws. The Committee expressed concern at the failure of the Government of India to provide adequate information relating to the general issue of violence against women.

Amnesty International acknowledges that at the highest levels of government the directives are clear that the fundamental rights set out in the Constitution should be granted without discrimination. It also acknowledges that numerous policies for the empowerment of women are in place around the country. However, Amnesty International is concerned that its research in Uttar Pradesh and Rajasthan indicates that despite this, at the level of implementation there is sufficient discrimination and inaction in bestowing rights to argue that the Government of India is failing to exercise due diligence in preventing abuses.

Amnesty International is well aware of the Government of India's argument that changing discriminatory attitudes and practices which are so deeply ingrained within society is something which cannot be done overnight, and that they are making progress in particular in bestowing economic and political rights on women throughout the country regardless of caste, religion or other identity. The organization recognizes the challenges presented to the state given the size and complexity of the country, and the continuing need for women to be provided with state help to access the most basic amenities such as food and water. Amnesty International is publishing this report to highlight the continuing problems of violence against marginalised women in Uttar Pradesh and Rajasthan which occur in the context of many other abuses of women's rights — many of them social and economic — because it believes that women cannot enjoy the full range of rights while being repressed through violence and while sections of the administration and the criminal justice system reflect and perpetuate discriminatory practices prevalent in society. Violence against women does not only have a physical impact but also an impact on their ability to enjoy the full range of rights including social, economic and political: the right of women to enjoy the full range of rights is indivisible.

## The Context of Violence against Women in India

Despite the many positive developments in securing womens human rights, patriarchy continues to be embedded in the social system in many parts of India including Uttar Pradesh and Rajasthan, denying the majority of women the choice to decide how they live. The over-riding importance of "community" in a patriarchal sense ensures that women rarely have an independent say in community issues. The way in which the concept of "honour" is used is also a severe barrier to the realisation of women's rights. Practices persist which led one member of the UN Human Rights Committee to observe in 1997 that "women are expendable in India". Female foeticide continues to be common. Impoverished families have little interest in educating girl-children and will often engage them in marriage as children as a means of ensuring that they are provided for economically from an early age.

As in many parts of India, levels of violent crime against women in Uttar Pradesh and Rajasthan are extremely high (alarm at these high levels have led to recent calls for the imposition of the death penalty for crimes of rape). According to National Crime Records Bureau (NCRB) figures for 1998 issued by the Ministry of Home Affairs, Uttar Pradesh ranked first and Rajasthan ranked fourth in the ratings of recorded crimes against women. These include rape, kidnapping, dowry death, mental and physical "torture", molestation, sexual harassment and trafficking. According to Rajasthan government statistics, crimes against women in the year 1999 reported an increase of 6.7% over the year 1998. In particular "torture" (which they categorise as crimes under section 498A of the Indian Penal Code (IPC)) registered an increase of 9.66% and "molestation" (crimes of sexual violence not amounting to rape) an increase of 6.91% although rape registered a decrease of 5.37%. The draft Policy on Women of the Uttar Pradesh government claims that every year more that 1,500 cases of rape, nearly 2,500 cases of indecent behaviour and nearly 200 kidnappings are recorded in the state.

Violence within the home is also widespread in both Uttar Pradesh and Rajasthan and affects women throughout society — in wealthy urban households as much as the poorest rural households, across all religious, class and caste boundaries. It includes beating, slapping, kicking and rape. Methods of killing women in the home include soaking them with kerosene and setting light to them and poisoning, either claiming that the death was accidental or that the woman committed suicide. Violence within marriage in India is often associated with the practice of "dowry" although it is by no means the only cause of violence. The practice of dowry has been prohibited in law since 1961 when it was recognised that it was contributing to high levels of violence against women as husbands and their families harassed wives for increased dowry. However, the practice continues. According to the Annual Report for 1999 of the Rajasthan Police, dowry deaths over the period 1997-1999 increased by 24.43%.

Women activists in India have played a crucial role in highlighting the problems faced by women. Amnesty International delegates saw clear evidence of this in Rajasthan and Uttar Pradesh where alliances of women's organizations come together regularly in protest against incidents of violence and put pressure on the authorities to take action against the perpetrators. Without such pressure, many victims would be left alone and without any means of obtaining justice. Many of the positive initiatives of the state have been taken as a result of the forceful arguments of the women's movement in the country. However, for women in Uttar Pradesh and Rajasthan as in many other parts of India, the challenge in defending human rights is compounded by gender discrimination inherent within traditional societies as well as within state structures. Women are often condemned by their own families as well as their community for speaking out against discrimination and abuse. When they seek help from the state to enable them to carry out their legitimate activities they are often confronted with further discrimination from the criminal justice system and from the state machinery which pushes them to conform to a gender stereotype which decrees that women should not question the *status quo*and thereby undermine family and community.

## Violence and Discrimination of dalit, adivasi and other Marginalized Groups of Women

Women in India are subject to discrimination not just on the basis of gender but on numerous other factors such as caste, community, religion etc. This report looks at the particular problems faced by *dalit*and other marginalised women who face this complex web of discrimination.

Amnesty International saw evidence of the intersection of gender inequality and other forms of discrimination throughout its visit to areas of Uttar Pradesh and Rajasthan. The concept of gender equality continues to be alien to many communities and many state institutions particularly at the local level. In the areas of Uttar Pradesh and Rajasthan visited, caste and land rights are crucial factors which impact on political, social and economic relationships. In Uttar Pradesh political parties representing *dalit*and lower-caste communities have played a role in recent years in empowering some of these groups in certain areas. While it is difficult to generalise about a situation in which caste groups and relationships between them are extremely complex, groups such as *dalits, adivasis*" backward castes" and others continue to be most socially and economically vulnerable as a result of lack of access to land ownership, meaningful political participation and free employment. Estimates suggest that at least two thirds of the bonded labourers in India are *dalits* and that over half the *dalit* workforce are landless agricultural labourers. Sixty-six per cent of all women agricultural labourers are *dalits* earning between Rs.8-25 [$0.17-0.54] per day. *Dalit* women, and often children, dominate certain spheres of work, such as civic sanitation, scavenging and leatherwork.

Many of those who belong to *dalit* castes are expected to stay in the profession which they are born into. In Lucknow, Uttar Pradesh, Amnesty International delegates learnt of the situation of members of the *Balmiki* "sweeper" caste of whom there are around 10,000 in that city. The majority work as sweepers, often cleaning latrines and live in slum areas close to sewers and gutters as those are the only areas that they are able to obtain for habitation. *Dalit* activists from the Balmiki caste told of how they had struggled to set up an office in the city and how their neighbours while eventually accepting them socially, continue to refuse to eat or drink anything from the office. *Dalits* are also expected to marry within their own caste and relationships between *dalits* and other castes often result in punitive acts. In July 1999 it was reported that a *dalit* woman was gang-raped and burnt alive in front of villagers in Bhavanipur village in Kanpur district of Uttar Pradesh. 17-year-old Usha Yadav [a caste Hindu] had eloped with the woman's son, a *dalit* boy, in June. The girl's father detained the boy's mother and brother-in-law in his house where the mother is reported to have been gang raped and tortured. She was then burnt alive. Three policemen were suspended for negligence.

## Discrimination on the Basis of "Descent"

India's caste system involves a social hierarchy and is a feature of Hinduism. Individuals are born into a particular caste and remain in that caste throughout their lives. Broad caste categories (varnas) separate caste groups according to occupation (although mobility between occupations seen in more recent times does not lead to changes in caste identity). Outside these caste categories are the "untouchables", now commonly known as dalits whose occupations — sweepers, tanners etc — were viewed as "polluting". Untouchability of dalits continues to be practised in India in many forms, reinforcing an iniquitous social hierarchy and allowing for the continuing disempowerment and humiliation of millions of people. Localities housing dalits are often segregated from those housing non-dalits, a segregation which often extends to the provision of separate wells, eating places and temples and restrictions on the use of land to defecate. These conditions of segregation were described by many of the victims of violence with whom Amnesty International delegates spoke in Uttar Pradesh and Rajasthan in December 2000.

Adivasis are also subjected to forms of untouchability in some areas of India including Uttar Pradesh and Rajasthan where the economic and social differences between adivasis and dalits are often indistinguishable making them vulnerable to similar abuses and exploitation. In its 1996 examination of India's 10th to 14th periodic reports, the Committee on the Elimination of Racial Discrimination stated clearly that discrimination to which both communities are subjected falls within the scope of the Convention under its definition of racial discrimination set out in Article 1 which includes the notion of "descent". There are also castes in India not designated as scheduled castes but as "backward castes". While not "polluting" and therefore subject to untouchability, they are recognised as continuing to suffer from severe social and economic discrimination.

Article 17 of the Constitution of India states that the practice of untouchability is abolished and its practice in any form forbidden. It further prescribes that the enforcement of any disability arising out of "untouchability" shall be an offence punishable in accordance with law. Nonetheless, dalits and adivasis regularly suffer verbal and physical abuse at the hands of higher castes. Uttar Pradesh accounted for 25.4% of the total crimes committed against dalits in India during 1998 and Rajasthan 21.8%, both far higher than the next highest: Madhya Pradesh with 15.8%. Rajasthan accounted for 26.5% of the total crimes committed against adivasis in India during 1998, Uttar Pradesh accounting for 2.6% (its population of adivasis is significantly smaller). According to the 1999 Annual Report of the Rajasthan Police there was a significant increase in crimes recorded under the Scheduled Castes and Scheduled Tribes (Prevention of Atrocities) Act between 1997 and 1999. There were 808 cases registered in 1997 and 1,041 in 1999.

Overall, members of *dalit* and *adivasi* communities are less well educated than their non-*dalit* counterparts. Within *dalit* communities in Uttar Pradesh and Rajasthan, literacy levels amongst *dalit* women are amongst the lowest in the country. In Rajasthan an average of 8.3% (dropping to 4.73% in rural areas) of scheduled caste women are literate as opposed to 42.38% of the scheduled caste male population. In Uttar Pradesh an average of 10.96% of scheduled caste women are literate as opposed to 40.79% of the scheduled caste male population. The national average for female and male scheduled caste literacy is 27% and 49.91% respectively. The national average for non-scheduled caste literacy is reported by the UN Development Program to be 38% and 66% respectively.

While poverty is not directly responsible for violence — when Amnesty International delegates asked victims whether they felt they had been targets of violence because they were a *dalit*, they often felt that it was impossible to distinguish between their caste and their economic position of poverty, i.e. that exploitation was the root cause — the dependency of these groups on more powerful groups in the community encourages exploitation which is often accompanied by violent acts. While this situation affects both men and women from these groups, given that women embody the concept of honour, violence against women becomes a symbolic gesture of exploitation and discrimination within communities. During the hearing of India's initial report under the Women's Convention in January 2000, the Government of India representatives acknowledged that women bore the brunt of caste-based atrocities.

*Dalits* living in Munni Khera village in Hassanganj, an area in Unnao district of Uttar Pradesh, live in an area separated from the rest of the village. Thirty-five per cent of the village are upper castes, 25% are "backward castes", 12% are Muslim and the rest are *dalit*. Ram Chandra, a *dalit* from the village was married to Ramvathi and they owned a piece of land on which they had a house. Upper caste villagers were trying to take the land from them and Ram Chandra and Ramvathi had objected to this.

In September 1998, Ramvathi was gang-raped by five men. Higher caste villagers are believed to have raped her as a means of isolating her and her husband within the village and the *dalit* community because of the stigma attached to rape and to punish them for refusing to give up their land.

After the rape, Ram Chandra went to Hassanganj police station to lodge a complaint. However, police refused to lodge a First Information Report (FIR). There are allegations that police took money from one of the accused. The couple were constantly threatened by influential people in the village and their house was attacked. Ram Chandra finally made an application to the

Superintendent of Police of Unnao district concerning the rape and the failure of the police to lodge an FIR. However, despite the Superintendent of Police ordering that the incident should be investigated (no action was taken against police for refusing to lodge an FIR) local police again managed to ensure that the incident was not investigated. Finally under severe pressure, the couple moved to Ramvathi's parent's village some distance away.

They returned to the village on 30 January 1999, reportedly determined to reclaim their property. They were met by three men armed with sticks and axes who were soon joined by others. Ram Chandra sent his wife to the house, fearing violence. He was then beaten by around 17 men with sticks. His left leg and left hand were broken. When he started screaming, Ramvathi and several other women came to find out what was happening. Ram Chandra described what happened next:

*"They attacked my wife with stick, she fell down then and there. After that my wife came to me and laid over my body to save me, then they had beaten my wife with sticks and axes. She got deep injuries on the head and shoulder and her right hand and leg broken. [one of the attackers] put off all the clothes of my wife, raped her and inserted and pushed the stick in her private part".*

The attackers left Ramvathi for dead and ran away. Ram Chandra and his wife were taken to the district hospital where Ramvathi died the next morning.

When the next day activists approached the Superintendent of Police about the incident which had been reported in the media, he reportedly denied that the incident had occurred and said that the media had exaggerated the facts. Activists went to the village to investigate but villagers were too scared to speak about it. They found Ramvathi's husband in the district hospital. He could only move his neck because he had been beaten so badly. He had not even been told that his wife had died.

After a series of demonstrations by activists, an FIR was filed against the accused under section 302 [murder] of the Indian Penal Code (IPC). They were arrested after some time. The court to which the case was sent is as of March 2001 hearing evidence although no evidence has yet been placed before it. Amnesty International delegates were told that the post mortem on Ram

Vathi had not recorded all her injuries that there were fears that due to this and the reluctance of witnesses to come forward, there would not be sufficient evidence to convict the accused.

Eight months later activists heard that Ramvathi's husband had been prevented from entering the village as the accused and their relatives were continuing to threaten him. Activists tried to pursue the case with the National Human Rights Commission and the National Commission for Women but they reportedly took no further action.

As of December 2000, Ram Chandra was staying with his wife's parents in their home away from Hassanganj, continuing to fear for his life, and reluctant to pursue the case. He has received no compensation.

Placed within the context of both gender and caste discrimination, more often than not inhabiting rural areas of severe impoverishment, *dalit* women become an easy target for exploitation and violence. Male members of *dalit* families often leave to go to cities to find work leaving *dalit* women heading households. Sexual harassment by landowners, moneylenders and their hired thugs is common.

In June 1999 Amnesty International delegates interviewed Kali Bai [name changed for security], a Kol tribal (a community designated as scheduled caste in Uttar Pradesh — the same community is designated as scheduled tribe in neighbouring Madhya Pradesh) working for a contractor in Banda district of Uttar Pradesh. The area is largely inhabited by Kol tribals where many of them work as bonded labourers in stone quarries breaking large stones into chippings for construction work. Kali Bai and her husband had been working for ten years and were earning Rs.300 [$6] for every trolley of small stones filled — several days work. They were bonded to the contractor from whom they had borrowed Rs.3,500 [$75].

In August 1998 Kali Bai and her husband heard that another contractor in another village was offering Rs.600 [$13] for every trolley filled so they went to the contractor they were working for and asked him what they owed as they didn't want to work for him any more. The contractor along with three other men started beating them. He took Rs.9,000 [$193] from Kali Bai's husband and started pulling at her hair and clothes. Her whole sari was removed and she was left in a blouse and petticoat and her bangles were broken. She was dragged around the outside of her house. She ran away, embarrassed at her nakedness. She ran to her sister-in-law's house and borrowed a sari and went to the nearby town of Shankergah. She tried to file a complaint with police but they refused saying that her quarrel was with the contractor and not with them. A few days later the police came to Kali Bai's village in connection with another case. The Station House Officer reportedly advised her to leave the village.

An activist working against bonded labour also attempted to file an application to release Kali Bai and her husband from bondage. An application was filed with the Sub-Divisional Magistrate but no action was taken. When interviewed, Kali Bai expressed her helplessness: "they've stripped me. They can only now kill me". As a result of losing the Rs.9,000, she and her family were living a bare existence and continued working for upper castes who kept half of their earnings. Kali Bai has two children. A third child died of cholera when he was one-and-a-half years old. Kali Bai had approached the contractor who employs her for a loan to pay for medicines when he got sick but he had refused and the child had died.

Of serious crimes against scheduled castes including murder, rape, kidnapping and abduction, *dacoity* [banditry], robbery and arson, rape was the highest in the period 1996-1998 according to NCRB figures. The same was true of serious crimes against scheduled tribe women. While 516 cases of murder of scheduled castes were recorded in 1998, 923 cases of rape were recorded in the same year. Rajasthan officially recorded 136 cases of rape of scheduled caste women during 1999. This is certainly a severe underestimate. Well-known journalist P. Sainath, after researching the situation of *dalits* in Rajasthan, reported that on average a *dalit* woman is raped every sixty hours and that one *dalit* is murdered every nine days.

*Dalit* women also suffer violence within their own communities. Cases were documented by Amnesty International delegates of *dalit* women being raped by *dalit* men of the community. Despite the fact that they are forced by economic circumstance to leave their homes in order to work and thereby enjoy greater mobility and economic independence than many middle-class women, it is also clear that *dalit* women suffer domestic violence.

While it is undoubtedly the case that some economic development has benefited women, the pervasiveness of corruption and exploitation and disregard by economic actors of the livelihood of under-privileged groups has meant that women have often borne the brunt of economic "development" or economic empowerment of powerful groups. The fight against policies of economic development and corrupt economic practices which are perceived as benefiting only a privileged few such as the illegal liquor trade have often been led by women from marginalised communities who are adversely affected by these policies and practices through the break-up of the family or community unit, exploitation, the loss of income etc. In addition, economic empowerment of women has not been matched by equality of property rights. While many women in poor families are forced to contribute to the family income out of economic necessity, they do not have rights over property either in relation to their parents or within marriage so that in the event of the break-up of a marriage they are left destitute. In Rajasthan Amnesty International delegates heard of the widespread practice of *Natha* in which women are married several times. While a small percentage of these second or third marriages are reported to be through choice, the majority occur when women are pressurised into remarriage through desertion by their husbands and are forced by their families into a further marriage. In many of these cases women are literally sold by one man to another with her parents, former husband or relatives often acting as intermediary. In those circumstances where women do have rights over property — usually after becoming widows — they often become the target of violence by family or community members wishing to take the property from them. Property is thereby not only a context for violence but a reason for women being unable to escape violence.

Violence against women within the community is often characterised by attacks on the honour of women and by association their communities by one group against another. The stripping and parading of women who are seen to have broken the community's rules including the position of certain castes or to have called into question the community's honour in some way, is common in many states throughout India. It can also be accompanied by social ostracization. In some areas this extends to the killing of women as witches or *dayans*. Amnesty International delegates were unable to document this practice which is reported to be common in Bihar although it has also been reported in Rajasthan. It is widely believed that most women killed as *dayans* are in fact targeted as a result of property disputes – the majority are widows.

Atrocities on dalit women are an increasing trend. They are victims of landlord oppression, police excesses and goondaism. In all instances of caste tensions dalit women are victimised. Many of the women who have stood against the local landlords or supported inter-caste marriage are punished by being paraded naked. It was reported that on an average three dalit women get raped every day. [Report of discussions during a session on Dalit Women at the Sixth National Conference of Women's Movements held in Ranchi, Bihar, December 28-30 1997].

In May 1999 it was reported that a young widow named Chunni was tied to a tree and brutally beaten on the orders of the *panchayat* (which included seven women) for failing to prevent the deaths of livestock in Amara village of Banda district in Uttar Pradesh. She was reportedly hung upside down, her genitals stuffed with chilli powder and thrashed with lathis. She died of her injuries. Villagers told police she had committed suicide. All 13 *panchayat* members were arrested and charged with murder.

It also has to be recognised that the process of empowerment of women can lead itself to violence as male members of a family or community react in anger to challenges to the patriarchal social structure which benefits them. Of grave concern to Amnesty International in this context is the apparent punitive nature of much violence against *dalit* and other marginalised groups of women by other members of society including men from their own community, in response to attempts to assert their rights or fight against discrimination. This can be in relation to assertion of their economic rights regarding labour conditions, including attempting to extract themselves from situations of bonded labour as well as their political rights. While the advent of reservation for the participation of a certain number of women in the *panchayats* has had some positive impact, there have also been backlashes against women, particularly *dalit* women, who are elected to the *panchayat* and who attempt to assert their rights within that forum, especially when they challenge corrupt and illegal practices.

A study of the experiences of women *panchayat* members in four districts of Rajasthan found that many women had been subjected to abuse and violence within the *panchayat*. "In Pyari Devi Balai's *panchayat*, Mokhunda, the *Upsarpanch* [deputy village head], Gisulal Ganna, ran the affairs of the *panchayat* in the beginning. When some scandals involving embezzlement came to light, Pyari Devi took over the control of the *panchayat*. Since then he went against her. He would hurl casteist abuses at her and practice untouchability with her. He would say: 'A low caste woman cannot be the *Sarpanch* [village head]; ever have your grandfathers become *sarpanches*?'". In its conclusions, the study commented: *"The 1993 Amendments to the Constitution had raised hopes that the gender and caste ridden society would lose some of its strength with the support of the state. But our association with the work of Women in Panchayati Raj Institutions made us realise that the road to such change was not that simple. We realised that the state, while agreeing to share political power with women through enactment, was yet unwilling at the grassroots for such a change. The society had a major role in denying real flow of power to women"*.

## Access to Justice: a Case for Negligence?

The area of accessing justice for women victims of violence in the community is one which brings into sharp focus continuing problems of discrimination at the grass-roots level in Indian society: where concepts of patriarchy, caste, community and honour have an immediate impact on victims and contribute directly to a situation of impunity for perpetrators. Given that the ability of women to access justice is part of the overall empowerment process essential to women's development and bearing in mind the priority being given to women's empowerment by the present government, Amnesty International believes that this crucial area must be addressed urgently by the state.

In its first periodic report to CEDAW, India acknowledged that *"A large number of women have not been able to fully avail the benefits under the Constitution and other legal provisions. There are several deterrents in the way of women seeking legal redress. Insufficiency of legal aid, procedural lacunae and delays, lack of basic knowledge about the law and procedures and long drawn out trials continue to hamper women's access to legal redress."* Amnesty International agrees that these problems are real for women attempting to access justice. However, these problems are also apparent for many others in India and are characteristic of an overloaded criminal justice system which mitigates against a range of marginalised groups in society. Amnesty International believes that the problems faced by underprivileged and marginalised women in accessing justice go beyond those identified above by the government. Notably these involve gender, caste and class discrimination within society, organs of government and the criminal justice system.

Even today, as we approach the 21st century, violence against women is usually treated as a marginal issue by the law-enforcement machinery in our country, whether it be the police, the prosecutors or the medico-legal fraternity or often even the judiciary. It is essential to sensitize this entire machinery to gender issues, particularly violence against women. Often, the police and other personnel are unaware of the legal safeguards for women and the amendments to laws relating to such safeguards.

## The Theory of Justice for Women

### The Law

The central government and state governments have taken several steps to protect woman through enactment of legislation and to prosecute those who perpetrate violence against them. The Indian Penal Code (IPC) has been amended several times in relation to crimes against women largely as a result of campaigns against violence led by the women's movement in the country.

Almost every campaign against gender based violence on women in the 1980s resulted in a new legislation providing protection to them. Each enactment resulted in making the punishment provisions more stringent, setting time limits for pending cases and extending compensation to the victims. Violence in its different dimensions has been sought to be tackled by legislative reforms, innovations in the structure and working of the police force, measures to sensitise the bureaucracy, media campaigns and new institutional structures

Section 375 of the IPC defines the offence of rape as sexual intercourse against the will or consent of a woman (punishable with between seven years and life imprisonment). Penetration is explained as "sufficient to constitute sexual intercourse". This has long been criticised for being too narrow a definition of rape. Section 354 of the IPC provides for punishment for "assault or criminal force to woman with intent to outrage her modesty", a wide-ranging provision which is commonly used in incidents of violence not amounting to rape (defined as penetration) but which invites a far lesser punishment of imprisonment of up to two years. The National Commission for Women and several women's organizations have been involved in attempts to establish a crime of "sexual assault" in its place – even drawing up a Sexual Assault Draft Bill, 1993 – but so far without success. In 1995 and 1996 numerous suggestions were made by lawyers and women's activists to strengthen legal safeguards regarding rape and other related issues in response to questionnaires on the criminal law distributed by the Law Commission of India. An Ad hoc Subcommittee of the National Commission for Women (NCW) conducted fairly widespread consultations about laws relating to rape culminating in a set of recommendations produced in September 1999. In March 2000, again after apparently widespread consultation, the Law Commission of India issued a Review of Rape Laws. The NCW also published a further study in August 2000, *Rape: A legal study,* again making recommendations for amendments to the law. In December 2000, Amnesty International delegates were told by officials of the Department of Women and Child Development of the Government of India that they were awaiting a final report on necessary amendments to the law from the NCW which would become part of the Empowerment Policy for 2001. It appears that the NCW had been asked by the government to consolidate its recommendations on laws regarding rape of women and children. However, it is not known what role the Law Ministry was to play in drawing up such legislation. Amnesty International is concerned that given the numerous discussions and studies that have taken place on this issue without a bill having been drawn up by government, draft legislation should be prepared and disseminated for discussion at the earliest opportunity with a time frame for its entry into parliament.

While the IPC provisions concerning rape are on paper available to women from all backgrounds in India, there are also special provisions in law which apply to sections of society, including women, who are deemed to be particularly vulnerable to abuses. Special protection exists in law for members of scheduled caste and scheduled tribe communities. The Scheduled Castes and Scheduled Tribes (Prevention of Atrocities) Act, 1989 was enacted in order *"to prevent the commission of offences of atrocities against the members of the Scheduled Castes and the Scheduled Tribes, to provide for special courts for the trial of such offences and for the relief and rehabilitation of the victims of such offences and for matters connected therewith or incidental thereto"*. Sub-sections of section 3(1) of the Act specifies "atrocities" against scheduled castes and scheduled tribes which are punishable with imprisonment of a minimum of six months and maximum of five years, and with a fine. While many of these atrocities are intended to protect men and women alike, some are specific to women (i.e. the assault or use of force against a women with intent to dishonour or outrage her modesty or using a position of dominance over a woman to exploit her sexually) or are atrocities to which women are particularly vulnerable — being stripped and paraded naked. Government officials have a central role to play in the implementation of the Act which contains a list of prescriptive measures, described as *"the duty of the government to ensure effective implementation of the Act"*. Listed in Section 21(2) are some of the measures which include the provision of legal aid, expenses for the witness and victims of atrocities, the provision of economic and social rehabilitation to the victims, the appointment of officers to supervise the action, periodic surveys, and special measures. The state government is instructed to designate one Sessions Court in each district to be a Special Court for trial of persons accused of offences under the Act.

The Scheduled Castes and Scheduled Tribes (Prevention of Atrocities) Rules, 1995 provide for reactive, preventive and promotional measures that can be taken in an effort to ensure that there is redress for the violations of the rights of scheduled castes and scheduled tribes and that such violations do not recur.

## The Administration

Special administrative measures as a means of ensuring implementation of legislative protections for women were apparent in both Uttar Pradesh and Rajasthan. *Mahila thanas*— "all-women" police stations established to encourage women to bring their complaints to police by staffing them with women police officers — had been established in both states. Both also had Crime Against Women Cells in their police departments where cases of crimes against women are investigated and monitored.

In Rajasthan Amnesty International delegates heard from government officials and activists about *Zilla Mahila Sahayata Samitis* (ZMSS) [District Women's Support Committees]. These were established in Rajasthan on 6 August 1997 as a result of pressure from the women's movement in the state who were concerned about implementation of legal provisions designed to protect women and provide them with redress. The Committees were designed to establish a forum at the district level which women could approach and which would address complaints at that level and in a comprehensive manner, dealing with several aspects of a situation at once: the criminal aspect, the welfare aspect and potentially the civil law aspect, ensuring that throughout the process the woman was assured justice. They are headed by the District Collector (the senior-most administrative official in a district) and consist of the district Superintendent of Police, a judge of the Family Court and representatives of non-governmental organizations from the district. The Member Secretary of each committee is the Project Director of the district Women's Development Program who operate under the government's Women and Child Department looking after women and children's development programs. The committees are provided with and collect their own funds to distribute to women in the districts. Complainants can come to these committees and hearings are held *in camera*. The committees review cases with officials from the local administration and police. However, Amnesty International is concerned that there appear to be no guidelines for the operation of these committees, or specialised training given to those involved. Women activists in Rajasthan claimed that the majority of the ZMSSs are "defunct". They also complained that those chosen to be representatives of non-governmental organizations on the committees were from amongst organizations such as rotary clubs rather than from grass-roots organizations who represented women and members of disadvantaged communities at the local level, thereby ensuring that they ceased to be a representative public platform. The State Women's Commission estimated that around 40% of districts in the state had functioning committees.

Amnesty International delegates were interested to learn during discussions with officials of the Department of Women and Child Development in Delhi subsequent to their visit to Rajasthan that the central government intends to replicate these committees throughout the country as part of its Women's Empowerment Policy.

## The National and State Commissions for Women

The National Commission for Women was established in January 1992 under the 1990 National Commission for Women Act. A statutory body, its aim was to check incidents of violence against women and to promote social, legal and economic equality of women. In addition to the NCW, several states of India have established State Women's Commissions (there is no formal relationship between the state and national bodies). As of March 2001, there were reported to be State Women's Commissions in 17 states.

The Rajasthan State Women's Commission was established in May 1999 under the Rajasthan State Commission for Women Act, 1999. The Chair, appointed by the state government, is to be an "eminent woman committed to the cause of women with sufficient knowledge and experience in dealing with problems of women". Its function is to inquire into "unfair practice" (the definition includes "mental or physical torture" of a woman), address inadequacies in laws, monitor enforcement of laws, inspect prisons, police stations, lock-ups, refuges for women victims of violence or other places of custody where women are held as prisoners or shelters and make recommendations for prosecution in individual cases. Between 1 April and 30 September 2000 the Commission received a total of 354 complaints, 154 of which were reported as "resolved".

Uttar Pradesh has no State Women's Commission. When Amnesty International delegates asked Home Ministry officials in Lucknow, they were not able to say when one might be established. In January 2001 it was reported that the National Commission for Women had directed the Uttar Pradesh government to establish a women's commission, alarmed at the number of complaints relating to atrocities on women received from Uttar Pradesh (the largest number from any state). The Policy on Women drafted by the Uttar Pradesh government states its intention to establish a Commission which will "work towards women's rights, relief against exploitation and also keep an eye on the implementation of the Policy". The Policy envisages task forces under the Commission in every district "to make available to the Commission, regular district level information on women's exploitation, domestic violence, misbehaviour towards women and also cases of non-compliance to laws". It will also have the function of reviewing laws. Uttar Pradesh has no State Human Rights Commission either. As an apparent alternative it has a human rights wing of the police department headed by an Additional Director General of Police to which all complaints against police are directed. However, when interviewed by Amnesty International delegates he appeared to be unaware of how special provisions for women victims of violence were operating in the state.

While the good intentions of the staff and members of the NCW and the State Women's Commissions are not doubted, they have suffered greatly from inadequate powers and resources. The Commissions have no powers to enforce or to exert pressure for the enforcement of their recommendations. In Rajasthan, recommendations are made on the basis of hearings, individual investigations or simply on the basis of the complaint. Many cases are simply "monitored". In many cases the Commission asks police to investigate and make recommendations on the basis of police reports. Amnesty International delegates were told that in only 168 out of the total number of the almost 1,000 complaints received by the Commission so far had hearings been held at the

Commission itself. In January 2001 it became apparent that as part of the Women's Empowerment Year, amendments would be made to the National Commission for Women Act 1990. In January 2000 CEDAW had recommended that the NCW's powers should be as wide as those of the National Human Rights Commission (NHRC) and include a complaints procedure. Media reports in January implied that the Commissions powers would indeed be enhanced along the lines of the NHRC allowing it to recommend initiation of prosecution proceedings against individual perpetrators following inquiry. Reports also indicated that a new Section 10(1)(e) of the NCW Act would empower the Commission to "take up cases of violation of the provisions of the Constitution, and of other laws relating to women, with appropriate authorities and recommend measures for the effective implementation of those provisions". No draft of the amendment Bill was available at the time of writing.

## The Practice of Justice for Marginalised Women

Attempts by women to seek justice through the criminal justice system are regularly forestalled. Although legislation exists, measures to ensure its full implementation – including communicating provisions to the public, training officials responsible for administering the legislation, providing legal support services to enable beneficiaries to invoke legislation, monitoring implementation and ensuring further development of legislation in response to the reality on the ground – have not been sufficient. Unless supported by male relatives or a strong social group, women victims of crime are at a severe disadvantage within the criminal justice system. Threats and harassment by perpetrators and their communities and social pressures which exist within families and communities force them towards compromise or withdrawal rather than pursuing justice. Gender biases which exist within institutions of redress are often exacerbated by ingrained caste and other biases against members of disadvantaged communities.

Not many of these cases reach the courts for trial, partly in view of the shame and honour involved and partly due to the existing difficult and complicated procedural laws. It was also noticed that the police are generally apathetic to the registration of complaints involving rape. Even in those cases which come up to courts for trial after going through all the investigations and medical examinations; our courts had not been sensitive to the trauma undergone by the rape victims, both during the actual commission of the offence and during trial in the courts. The courts are also oblivious of the social stigma and ostracism a victim of rape has to face throughout her life and all rapists to be acquitted on wholly irrelevant and flimsy grounds of age, religion, caste, status and other considerations. [National Commission for Women Annual Report for 1995-96]

## Registering a Complaint

Non-registration of crimes is a general problem in India. Political influence over the police and caste, class, religious and gender biases mean that it is extremely difficult for members of disadvantaged groups to file complaints, particularly against powerful individuals. A case cannot continue and a victim cannot receive justice if a First Information Report (FIR) is not completed and registered by police on the basis of a person's complaint.

A lawyer in Uttar Pradesh estimated that a maximum of 20% of cases of rape are registered and reach the courts. An activist working with *dalit* women estimated that only 5% of cases of violence against *dalit* women are registered. The under-reporting of cases was also acknowledged by officials with whom Amnesty International delegates spoke in both states.

It is clear that many women victims of violence in India do not approach police with a complaint because they know that they will be dismissed or further abused. Amnesty International delegates visiting Uttar Pradesh and Rajasthan in December 2000 were repeatedly told by activists working with women that the majority of cases were not reported to police for fear of dishonour or reprisals. Most women will only visit a police station with a male relative or will think twice about making a complaint without the support of a male relative. During a training program carried out by the United Nations Development Program in India in 1999, several police officials including one woman police officer, were sent in plain clothes to a police station to file a complaint. Out of

14 visits to file complaints in only two cases did the officials manage to file complaints after waiting 6-7 hours despite the fact that police are legally obliged to take down in writing a complaint of a cognizable offence. The woman police officer who tried to file a complaint of molestation was verbally abused by the Station House Officer, who refused to file her complaint.

In a study of women's participation in *Panchayats* carried out by the *Mahila Jan Adhikar Samiti* in Ajmer in 1999, it was found that "Of all the respondents who had to deal with the police in their four years of term 17.5% women said they experienced uncooperative attitude. But in the case of many *sarpanches* wherever there was sexist, casteist or other type of abuse or violence the women desisted from reporting to the police because they felt they would take the side of the powerful of the village. Ninety percent of the cases registered in connection with abuse/violence against women *sarpanches* were found to have been closed by the police. Most cases were claimed to have been closed because the investigation felt they were registered by the women for political rivalry."

As mentioned above, as a means of encouraging women to bring their complaints to police, many states have established *mahila thanas* (women's police stations). However, the majority of these are in large cities, thereby denying access to the most marginalised women in rural areas and there are few of them even in large cities. Rajasthan currently has nine *mahila thanas* and as of December 2000 was planning to establish a further three. This to cover a population of well over 44 million in the state. Uttar Pradesh's draft Women's Policy stated its intention of establishing *mahila thanas* in every district of the state. The *mahila thana* in Ajmer, Rajasthan was said to have been headed by a male Station House Officer until recently and there is no evidence that women police officers dealt significantly more sensitively with women victims or recorded a higher number of FIRs than men, given that they were provided with no specialist training. Women police officers working in *mahila thanas* have reported that investigations into complaints of rape are always carried out by male police officers although sometimes accompanied by women. Amnesty International knows of no systematic evaluation of the role of *mahila thanas* having been carried out by police or the administration as a means of assessing whether they are an effective means of providing an accessible and safe avenue of redress for women. Several women's orgnanizations, notably in Mumbai, have argued that *mahila thanas* marginalise women's issues and studies carried out by the Ford Foundation at the Tata Institute of Social Studies have reportedly identified several problems with them.

Crimes against Women Cells have also been criticised for not responding appropriately or effectively to cases of violence against women although the majority of crimes referred to these cells relate to violence within the family.

Police are reluctant to file FIRs citing offences under the Scheduled Castes and Scheduled Tribes (Prevention of Atrocities) Act, 1989, because the perpetrators — often powerful individuals within the community or even caste group to which police officers themselves belong — receive such stringent punishments. Amnesty International delegates were told that *dalits* and others are so reliant economically on upper castes that they are afraid to even think of filing a case under the Act because of the possible consequences. Several days prior to Amnesty International's visit to Lucknow in Uttar Pradesh, a *dalit* woman had reportedly been gang-raped by a group of men at gunpoint. Rather than registering an FIR the woman simply disappeared for fear of further consequences. Many *dalits* are not aware of provisions of the Act and their rights under it and it is rare for police to voluntarily inform them of those rights.

Many of the cases documented in this report demonstrate the refusal of police officers at the local level to file complaints brought by disadvantaged groups and particularly women and the problems members of these groups face in even approaching police. Well-known journalist P. Sainath during a visit to Rajasthan was told that there is an entry fee into police stations in Bharatpur district (Rs.225 [$5]) and more for filing a complaint. When Amnesty International delegates raised the problem of non-registration of FIRs by police, officials in Uttar Pradesh admitted that this was a general problem but maintained that they were dealing with it by issuing executive and departmental instructions to police to respond according to the law to complaints made by women and other sections of the community. However, they gave no indication that they followed up such orders with mechanisms for monitoring adherence.

In September 1999 the Ad hoc Subcommittee of the NCW recommended an amendment to the IPC to provide for punishment of a police officer who refuses to record a complaint relating to the commission of a cognisable offence. This proposed amendment — and the many others which accompanied it — has never been pursued.

The Scheduled Castes and Scheduled Tribes (Prevention of Atrocities) Rules strengthen the procedures in the Code of Criminal Procedure (CrPC) for the recording of an offence by the police, and specify that the officer-in-charge of a police station should record any offence under the Act, whether given verbally or in writing and give a copy to the informant, free of charge. Recognising the difficulties that a person may have in registering an offence under the Act, rule 5(3) states: "*Any person aggrieved by a refusal on the part of an officer in-charge of a police station to record the information... may send the substance of such information, in writing and by post, to the Superintendent of Police concerned who after investigation either by himself or by a police officer not below the rank of Deputy Superintendent of Police, shall make an order in writing to the officer in-charge of the concerned police station to enter the substance of that information to be entered in the book to be maintained in that police station.*" While many of the victims interviewed by Amnesty International delegates had pursued their complaints with higher authorities having been refused at their local police station, in many cases the directions of higher authorities continued to be ignored by police officials locally. Amnesty International did not come across a single case in which action had been taken against a police official who had failed to register an FIR or otherwise neglected his duties under the Act despite the fact that Section 6 of the Act provides for up to one year imprisonment for public servants wilfully neglecting their duty.

During Amnesty International's visits to Uttar Pradesh and Rajasthan, repeated concern was expressed about the failure of police to file proper FIRs in cases of rape and other forms of violence against women. Biassed handling of the original complaint by police can have disastrous effects on a case. Police were alleged to often record cases under section 354 IPC (*assault or criminal force to woman with intent to outrage her modesty*) which is bailable or section 376 read with section 511 (*attempt to rape*) both of which invite lesser penalties than section 376 (*rape*) which is also non-bailable, despite the fact that the victim clearly indicated that she was raped.

Lack of legal or even basic literacy on the part of complainants means that it is rare for them to detect that an inaccurate provision has been used until it is too late. Attempting to amend FIRs can also have serious consequences as complainants can be accused of changing their story for malicious motives.

## Problems of Evidence

Police are also accused of withholding and destroying evidence in many cases, often at the behest of the alleged perpetrators who might have caste or other community links with the police officers. Police also have the ability to delay the recording of medical evidence. It is not a legal requirement for police to send women who allege that they have been raped for an immediate medical examination. Much medical evidence is lost because this simple procedure is not followed. In one case that Amnesty International documented in Rajasthan when the victim asked about a medical examination she was told by police that she didn't need to have one until several days later by which time valuable medical evidence was lost.

Poor access to medical facilities necessary to document violence, including rape, is also a problem. Health centres are often scarce in rural areas leading to delays which mean that valuable evidence is lost. Obtaining sufficient evidence to prove rape — as strictly defined in Indian law and by the courts as penetration by the penis — can be very difficult. However, while prompt medical examination can provide strong, and in some cases irrefutable evidence, a victim's testimony also constitutes vital evidence. Contrary to the apparent view of many judicial officers in India, lack of medical evidence of sexual penetration should not refute an allegation of sexual abuse. According to the Istanbul Protocol, "even on examination of the female genitalia immediately after rape there is identifiable damage in less than 50% of cases [and lesions] in less than 30% of cases [of anal rape]". This underlines the importance of victim testimony as well as careful expert medical interview, examination, with the informed consent of the victim, and laboratory testing of specimens.

In the case of Narbada, when the medical examination did take place, police officers were present throughout and spoke to the medical officer carrying out the examination. This is in clear violation of the Principles on the Effective Investigation and Documentation of Torture and Other Cruel, Inhuman or Degrading Treatment or Punishment (Istanbul Principles — see above) which have been endorsed by the UN Special Rapporteur on Torture, article 6a of which states that "the examination must conform to established standards of medical practice. In particular, examinations shall be conducted in private under the control of the medical expert and outside the presence of security agents and other government officials".

In September 1999, the Ad hoc Subcommittee of the NCW recommended making the refusal or failure of a medical practitioner to conduct a medical examination of an alleged victim of sexual assault punishable with imprisonment of up to one year. It also recommended inserting specific procedural guidelines in the Code of Criminal Procedure for medical examination of victims of sexual assault. Neither of these recommendations have yet been taken up by the government and there are reports that many victims of rape are given cursory examinations by doctors with no attempt to document the testimony of the victim.

Reliance on the evidence of witnesses is also extremely problematic. It is common for witnesses in cases of violence against women to withdraw their testimony, often having arranged a financial deal with the accused. A lawyer in Uttar Pradesh estimated that around 25% of witnesses withdraw their testimony because of pressure placed on them by the accused or members of their community and noted that in cases regarding women this percentage would only increase because of the patriarchal pressures which exist in these contexts. It is also reported that in many cases witnesses give contradictory statements in court because they have been planted by police or defence lawyers.

## Time and Money

The length of time it takes to pursue a case of torture through the courts encourages victims to make compromises under pressure from perpetrators and often their own community or family. All lawyers and activists interviewed by Amnesty International spoke of the reluctance of victims to file cases because of the time and money involved. There are often significant distances between the village where a victim lives and the block [administrative unit within a district] court where a case is being heard. Money is lost in attending hearings not just on travel expenses but lost working hours for those women in employment and their male relatives who accompany them to the hearings.

The average time period taken for a case of rape to find its way from the Sessions Court to the Supreme Court was between 10-15 years [Gender and Judges: A judicial point of view, A preliminary Report based on research findings by a non-governmental organization Sakshi, June 1996]

The Scheduled Castes and Scheduled Tribes (Prevention of Atrocities) Rules provide for transport and other expenses for victims to enable them to attend hearings and in the case of women for an attendant to accompany them and covering of wages lost during days attending hearings. However, MARG's study, "Efficacy of the Enforcement System in Delivering Justice to Raped Scheduled Caste Women" found that many sections of the Rules had not been implemented in any of the fifty rape cases that were studied in Meerut and Banda districts of Uttar Pradesh, including provision for travelling and maintenance expenses. Often women simply do not have the money to pursue a case and having no economic independence, if their family do not support them in pursuing the case they drop it.

Amnesty International is interested to note statements in the draft women's policy drawn up by the Uttar Pradesh government which reads "The government will ask the High Court to undertake periodic review of crimes against women in the state and to set a time limit for settlement of cases relating to serious criminal offenses against women". It also talks of reaching decisions in rape cases with efficiency and promptness. "Officials found guilty of laxity in such cases will be punished and successful officials rewarded". In its Third Report covering the period 1994-95 & 1995-96, the National Commission for Scheduled Castes and Scheduled Tribes recommended that "Police should take timely and effective action in investigating the cases and submitting the chargesheet in the Court which would greatly help in curbing crimes. It is necessary that investigation on complaints are initiated soon after the FIR is lodged. It is also necessary to have regular monitoring and examination of cases which are closed without *challanning* [charges being filed in court], so that genuine cases are not closed".

Extract from a report on a series of attacks on women in Kanpur district of Uttar Pradesh by a *Sarpanch* (also the local landlord) including the rape of a *dalit* woman, Ram Rathi, in 1985. The extract is describing the perception of villagers concerning redress for the victims. The case against the perpetrator, which was pursued by Ram Rathi has been closed as he is reported to have killed the main witness. Above all, to get justice the judicial process is no less than the suffering of rape itself. Criminals will blame her as a characterless woman. She will have to prove that she was raped and the criminal has to prove that he has not raped. Questions and answers during arguments are no less than rape.

If it would be decided to tolerate this and fight till the end, even then the judgement is not made up of only the courage of a woman. A lot of money is required to have good advocate, to pay bribes to clerks, peons, servants, even to bribe the judge as it is said. Anybody needs a lot of money too for travelling from Pali to Kanpur court, Allahabad High Court and Supreme Court. Getting justice is a game of money. Krishna Pratap Singh [the accused] has sufficient money and means to escape from the punishment. Ram Rathi's husband is a labourer in a factory. Providing meals to his family is enough for him. Ram Rathi can get justice only from god.

It is clear that time and money involved in pursuing cases leads to a large number of women deciding not to file complaints or to withdraw complaints once filed. The long time periods allow victims to feel the effects of social ostracisation, harassment and intimidation and for witnesses to withdraw their testimony under similar pressures.

## Legal Support and Aid System in India

The legal aid system in India is entirely inadequate to deal with the number of people who require legal aid. This is particularly the case for women victims of crime. In three years of sitting on the district legal aid board, one lawyer that Amnesty International spoke to in Uttar Pradesh said that she was aware of legal aid being given in only two cases of violence against women. Under the Legal Services Authorities Act 1987, a wide range of groups including members of scheduled castes or scheduled tribes, women and children are all entitled to legal services. It is common knowledge that legal aid cases are given the worst lawyers and even if not taking legal aid, poor victims are at the mercy of unscrupulous lawyers who exploit their lack of knowledge of the legal system.

Constitutionally women have equal access to legal services but because of low levels of education, limited exposure to laws and legal procedures, social taboos and limited financial means, women cannot always utilize legal services... government has sought to remedy this condition by providing legal aid, legal literacy and promulgating the Family Courts Act.

MARG's study in Uttar Pradesh again found that in not a single of the 50 cases of women victims of rape studied had legal aid been provided to the victims as envisaged under section 21(2)(i) of the Act. Victims were merely given monetary relief of a few thousand rupees. The study concluded: "...we have seen that though on paper there are provisions for legal aid in the form of fees of lawyers, in reality the victims get no such aid. It seems either the Legal Aid Committee is not functioning at all or, people are not aware of its existence and procedures involved or, corruption amongst the lawyers has rendered it ineffective".

The draft women's policy of the Uttar Pradesh government states: "Women will be made aware of the various legal provisions affecting them, in their local language. For this, the government will set up camps at the village level, with the help of voluntary organizations and *Panchayats*... No fees will be charged from women for cases related to violence, property, divorce and maintenance. Women will be given free legal assistance on cases relating to violence and sexual exploitation". However, this policy is a draft policy and such provisions are far from being incorporated into law.

### Discrimination within the Criminal Justice System

As argued earlier, state institutions continue to reflect discrimination within society and Amnesty International believes that insufficient steps — both preventive and punitive — have been taken to address this. The effects of discrimination can range from direct connivance of police with perpetrators to inaction by police or members of the legal profession, to cursory treatment of trials by members of the judiciary.

### Women Demonstrating against Police Abuses

Police officers have their own caste and gender biases and often behave towards *dalits* and *adivasis* in a discriminatory way—acting within the norms of their social surroundings. The presence of caste biases within the police force was confirmed repeatedly to Amnesty International delegates by activists, government officials and police alike. Officials in Rajasthan also acknowledged that gender sensitivity is not institutionalised within the police force. Amnesty International delegates were told that a new syllabus was being developed with a topic on women for Constables, Sub-Inspectors and Deputy Superintendents of Police.

The state must train police and other state officials to separate their caste, gender and other prejudices from their duty to protect citizens if legislative and administrative policies are to have any meaning. The state cannot afford to overlook this problem any longer otherwise all its sincere efforts will be wasted. In its recommendations for the prevention of torture submitted to the Government of India in December 2000, Amnesty International referred at length to the need for reform of the police — emphasising amongst other things the continuing problem of political influence over the police which invites discriminatory behaviour. In its brief response to these recommendations, Amnesty International was disappointed to note that no indication was given by the Government of India that it would be taking action in this regard.

Reference has been made above to the problems within the police force in relation to registration and investigation of offences.

Amnesty International is concerned that discrimination and abuse within the police demonstrated by individual incidents of connivance, extends to the administration of policing and the manner in which crimes against women are viewed. Amnesty International delegates visiting Rajasthan were extremely concerned to hear of a large number of cases of violence against women which after the filing of an FIR were subsequently logged as found "false" after investigation. The labelling of these cases as "false" is itself a concern as it implies that women have falsely or maliciously filed the cases and plays into the hands of those who argue that women misuse legal provisions to wrongfully accuse men as a means of punishment. In fact, government and police officials explained in Rajasthan that it usually meant that the victim had reached a compromise with the perpetrator of violence, witnesses had turned hostile or there were other reasons for withdrawing the complaint. In these cases "Final Reports" were filed, indicating that a complainant had formally withdrawn a complaint. The Rajasthan government indicated that 30% of all cases of crimes against women in the state had been found to be "false" after investigation. As noted earlier, information was not provided by the government of Uttar Pradesh.

The case of Narbada, an *adivasi,* documented by Amnesty International delegates in Rajasthan clearly demonstrates the problems of discrimination faced by marginalised women throughout the process of trying to access justice through all stages of the criminal justice system. In Narbada's village in Udaipur district of Rajasthan — Samdhora — Rajputs (upper caste landowning caste) dominate, owning more than 50 acres. They practice untouchability in relation to the *adivasis* who are not permitted to take food or water from upper castes. Most of the *adivasi* villagers work for Rajputs as sweepers or agricultural workers and no-one dares speak out against them. However, Narbada and her uncle, when interviewed by Amnesty International delegates in December 2000, said that there were no previous incidents of rape of women by Rajputs in the village.

Narbada's family owns three *bighas* [2.5 *bighas*is the equivalent of one acre] of land. They do not work for the Rajputs. Narbada was married in 1999 and normally lives with her husband's family around 12 kilometres from Samdhora village. However, at the time of the incident she was staying with her mother for a holiday.

18-year-old Narbada testified that she was raped by a Rajput landlord on the afternoon of 10 March 2000. The incident took place about one and a half kilometres from her house when she went to buy a chicken in the upper caste area of the village. She was kneeling by a river and the Rajput threw her into the river and then raped her. Her attacker's mother reportedly heard Narbada's screams but did nothing to stop her son and when Narbada ran crying back to her section of the village his mother caught hold of her, beat her and told her not to go to the police.

Narbada told her mother and brother what had happened and they called her uncle. When they tried to go to the police station around 50 Rajputs stopped them. However, they went to the police station in Jhallara district on 12 March. An FIR was lodged but Narbada's uncle was not given a copy. He questioned the fact that they had filed the FIR under section 354 of the IPC [*Assault or criminal force to woman with intent to outrage her modesty*] rather than section 376 [*rape*]. One of the constables reportedly threw her uncle out of the police station saying: "who do you think you are". Police told her uncle that if he wanted a "true" FIR he would have to give them Rs.500 [$11] which he refused to do. Narbada and her uncle asked police for a medical examination but were told by police that this would be done only after an initial investigation. The two constables recorded a fresh FIR once the uncle was out of the police station. He was given a copy of the FIR the next day, 13 March. No case had been filed under the Scheduled Castes and Scheduled Tribes (Prevention of Atrocities) Act. The police constables were themselves Rajputs and are reported to be close to the accused who sells illegal alcohol in a shop which is a regular haunt of police.

On 15 March Narbada and her uncle went to Udaipur, the district headquarters, to see the Superintendent of Police (SP). Udaipur is 90 kilometres and a three and a half hour journey from Samdhora. They told the SP about the rape and their subsequent treatment at the police station. The SP recorded their complaint and ordered an investigation to be carried out into the allegation of rape. No action was taken against police officials who had originally refused to file the FIR and abused Narbada and her uncle. On 26 April the Deputy Superintendent of Police went to Samdhora to begin an investigation.

A medical examination was not carried out until 8 April at Bhopal District Hospital. Police constables who had earlier abused Narbada and her uncle went with them to the hospital. Narbada told Amnesty International delegates that the police officers were present when she was undergoing medical tests and x-rays and that her uncle was not allowed to stay with her. She said that the police spoke constantly to the doctors but she could not make out what they were saying. Narbada and her uncle were told that no medical evidence of rape was found during the examination but they were not given copies of the medical records.

After strong protests from local human rights organizations, the case was challaned in the special court for crimes against scheduled castes and scheduled tribes in Udaipur under section 376 IPC and sections 3(i) and 3(ii)v of the Scheduled Castes and Scheduled Tribes (Prevention of Atrocities) Act, 1989. On 20 May Narbada was told to come to the court at 10am to record her statement. The Public Prosecutor made her and members of her family who were present as witnesses wait for two hours after which he reportedly urged them to make a compromise with the accused and withdraw the complaint. He reportedly told Narbada and her family that if she pursued the case she would just do the rounds of the court and not obtain justice. Narbada and her family refused to withdraw the complaint. They waited until 4pm when the statements of Narbada's aunt and mother were recorded. However, there was no presiding officer or public prosecutor in the court when their statements were recorded by the clerk. Only the lawyer for the accused was present.

The accused, his mother and members of the Rajput community continued to put pressure on Narbada and her family to compromise. Her relatives were also reportedly threatened with detention by police as a means of putting pressure on her to compromise. On 11 October at midnight two police constables (including one of those who had originally refused to file the FIR) came to her parent's house and threatened her. They were drunk. They knocked on the door and asked her to come out. When she refused they went to her uncle's house insisting that she be sent to the Police Station. He refused and eventually the police went away.

On 6 October 2000 Narbada and her uncle gave their statements to the Additional Superintendent of Police, Udaipur, who is heading the investigation. However, no further progress has been made in the case. Narbada has not been provided with legal aid or received any immediate financial relief as required under the Scheduled Castes and Scheduled Tribes (Prevention of Atrocities) Act, but has been helped by a local union with legal fees.

Narbada's husband was initially supportive of her following the incident but has now indicated that he will not take her back. Although Narbada described villagers as supportive, she said that they had encouraged her to compromise with the Rajputs.

Section 15 of the Scheduled Castes and Scheduled Tribes (Prevention of Atrocities) Act provides for the state government to specify a public prosecutor or appoint an advocate. Amnesty International delegates were told that public prosecutors regard cases of poor women as easy money.

There is little communication with the victims and it is common for prosecutors to take money from the accused's side in return for putting pressure on the victim to compromise or withdraw the complaint. The judiciary is also blamed for failing to take sufficient care in cross-questioning witnesses and investigating officers during hearings. The draft women's policy of the Uttar Pradesh government says that "The government will make required changes in laws to ensure that court cases related to sexual exploitation of women are presided over by women judges only" and that "Persons associated with the legal processes to increase sensitivity towards girls/women will be provided training from time to time". A further problem appears to be the failure of prosecuting authorities to oppose bail (see also under Threats and Harassment below) which is routinely sought by the accused who often have the means to pay significant amounts of security in order to obtain bail.

Judicial decisions have also shown clear bias against women. In a now famous verdict given in November 1995, a lower court in Rajasthan commented that an incident of alleged rape could not have taken place because upper caste men would not rape a woman of a lower caste and acquitted the alleged perpetrators.

Bhanwari Devi, a *saathin* (village development worker) working to eradicate child marriage with the state-sponsored Women's Development Programme, was raped on 22 September 1992 in Bhateri village, Rajasthan, by five men of a higher Gujjar caste. The rape was widely seen as punishment for her actions in challenging accepted social and cultural norms including a particular child marriage which occurred in the village. Police had come to the village and attempted to stop the marriage, which had already secretly taken place, and the Gujjars held Bhanwari Devi responsible for the police intervention.

The police initially refused to record Bhanwari Devi's statement. She was also initially prevented from undergoing a medical examination. After much protest, the government ordered an inquiry to be carried out by the Central Bureau of Investigation. It finished its investigation in September 1993 but was reported to have subjected Bhanwari Devi to unnecessarily excessive questioning about the incident. It found Bhanwari Devi's allegations to be true and chargesheets were filed against five men. The trial began in a lower court only in October 1994. In a verdict given in November 1995, the Court found that the delay in filing her complaint with police and in obtaining a medical examination indicated that she had made the story up. Shockingly, it commented that the incident could not have taken place because upper caste men, including a Brahmin, would not rape a woman of a lower caste. The men were acquitted of the charge of gang rape but convicted of minor crimes.

Bhanwari Devi has been ostracised from the village community since the incident in 1992. Throughout, constant pressure was put on her to withdraw the case by members of the local community as well politicians.

Central and state government officials with whom Amnesty International delegates talked, all acknowledged that sensitisation of the judiciary was lacking, a central government official commenting that it had not been "mainstreamed". Officials of the Department of Women and Child Development in New Delhi told Amnesty International delegates that the government had set up a national centre for gender training and sensitisation at the Indian Administrative Service Academy in Mussoorie. However, they indicated that the centre had not yet started functioning having been approved a year previously. It was explained that this Academy would be the apex agency for mainstreaming gender in all government departments.

The law itself includes provisions which facilitate discrimination against women. Section 155(4) of the Indian Evidence Act provides that "when a man is prosecuted for rape or an attempt to ravish, it may be shown that the prosecutrix was of generally immoral character". This is in clear violation of Article 2(g) of the Women's Convention which requires state parties to repeal all national penal provisions which constitute discrimination against women. While successive Supreme Court judgements have ruled that the antecedents of victims are not relevant, lower courts continue to refer to these legal provisions in making their judgements and section 155(4) has never been repealed.

### Threats and Harassment

This report focuses on violence against marginalised groups, much of it perpetrated by those in powerful social, economic or political positions and able to exert enormous influence over victims and their communities as well as state institutions if threatened by criminal action.

Despite this, there is no protection program for victims or witnesses in India leading generally to a very high number of acquittals in criminal cases due to victims or witnesses withdrawing testimony and the resulting lack of evidence. In the case of women victims from marginalised communities, the odds are stacked against them and without some form of protection or removing them from the context in which they might be receiving threats it is not surprisingly rare for women to pursue complaints through the courts. In numerous cases documented by Amnesty International, victims received direct or indirect threats from perpetrators but received no protection from the state despite complaining to the authorities -- ensuring that perpetrators could continue to harass them and in several cases commit further acts of violence.

Interestingly, in 1995 the Supreme Court upheld the validity of the Scheduled Castes and Scheduled Tribes (Prevention of Atrocities) Act in its entirety in the face of a challenge to Section 18 of the Act which denies anticipatory bail (provided for in section 438 of the CrPC) to those charged under the Act. The Supreme Court argued that Section 18 "has to be viewed in the context of the prevailing social conditions which give rise to such offences, and the apprehension that perpetrators of such atrocities are likely to threaten and intimidate their victims and prevent or obstruct them in the prosecution of these offenders, if the offenders are allowed to avail of anticipatory bail". Amnesty International is concerned that the same fears about threats and intimidation have not been addressed by establishing victim and witness protection programs, recognizing that perpetrators of violence against such women exercise enormous influence over the victim, their community and sections of the administration, even from inside jail, and by extending these safeguards to all vulnerable members of the community who may not be covered by the Scheduled Castes and Scheduled Tribes (Prevention of Atrocities) Act.

Gangawati, a 25-year-old "Backward Caste" woman, was allegedly raped by an upper-caste Thakur [higher caste] on the evening of 31 May 1999 in her home in Lalua Nagla village in Badaun district of Uttar Pradesh. The village is dominated by the Thakur caste and Gangawati's house is surrounded by houses belonging to Thakur families. Her attacker [N] entered her house with a gun while her husband was away. Her nine-year-old daughter was present and witnessed the rape. After her husband returned and she told him about the incident they visited the Khader Chowk Police Station the next day to file a complaint. On their way to the police station, [N] reportedly threatened them with a gun saying he would kill them. The Station House Office (SHO) of Khader Chowk Police Station refused to file an FIR. A Police Inspector reportedly told the Circle Officer [police official] not to register a case against [N] as he was one of their caste — a Thakur — and useful to the police. The Circle Officer reportedly advised the family not to pursue the case and also told them that too many days had elapsed so that there would be no medical evidence.

Gangawati then went to the Senior Superintendent of Police of Badaun and requested him to order the registration of a complaint. An order was sent to the Khader Chowk Police Station but no complaint was registered by police at the police station.

On 4 July the SHO of Khader Chowk police station visited Gangawati's house after first visiting [N's] house and asked Gangawati to go with him to have a medical examination conducted. Fearing some trick and in light of the fact that he refused even to take her statement, Gangawati refused.

On 3 June 1999, Gangawati had gone to Lucknow (325km from Gangawati's village) and presented a complaint to the Chief Minister. She had also sent petitions to the National Human Rights Commission. Apparently as a result of these petitions, the Superintendent of Police (SP) of Badaun District was ordered to conduct an inquiry. An FIR (No.259 of 1999) was finally filed on 15 October 1999 accusing [N] under sections 376 (*rape*), 452 (*house-trespass*) and 506 (*criminal intimidation*) of the IPC. However, an initial inquiry carried out by local police dismissed Gangawati's claims and the case was closed for lack of evidence: no medical reports were produced and no statement was taken from Gangawati. The NHRC also closed the case on the basis of this police report.

However, in February 2000, Gangawati made a statement before the court of the Chief Judicial Magistrate, Badaun and the court reopened the case. Amnesty International understands that examination of Gangawati's clothes have now substantiated her claims of rape.

[N] was arrested on 13 April 2000. Immediately after his arrest his brother and several of his supporters threatened to kill Gangawati and her husband and other of their relatives. A complaint to this effect was sent to the SP, Badaun on 15 April 2000. The SP reportedly ordered the SHO to ensure the safety of Gangawati. However, on 29 April [N] was released on bail and threats against Gangawati and her husband continued to be received from [N] and also from the SHO. The prosecution reportedly raised no objection to the granting of bail.

On 12 May 2000 the National Commission for Women wrote to the Uttar Pradesh police asking them to protect Gangawati and her family and to transfer the SHO and other police officers accused of connivance from the area. No action was taken.

On 10 October 2000, Gangawati's husband, Suresh Chand, went to Khader Chowk Police Station to make a complaint about further threats. In a statement, Suresh Chand has given the following account of his encounter: "I told him [the SHO] that I was working as the district correspondent for Dalit Hitaishi, a national monthly newspaper published in Delhi and asked him to help me. [The SHO] stood up from his chair and said, "swine you recorded a case under 376 against [N] and you have got three policemen from amongst my staff into trouble, today, swine, I will kill you and dispose of you". Then [the SHO] searched my pockets. He removed seven hundred rupees I had in my pocket and removed my Dalit Hitaishi press card from my pocket, tore it up and threw it away. He also tore up my statement and threw it away and gave me a severe beating. He locked me in the cell and pointed a revolver at me and said, "swine, either settle with [N] or else I will call [N's] wife and have her register a case under 376 against you. And I will charge you with 3-4 cases and let you rot in prison". Then [the SHO] summoned [N] from the village in a jeep and said to him "look I have your enemy in my hand today. Do what you want".

Suresh Chand was beaten with a stick on the back and buttocks and threatened at gunpoint to withdraw the case of rape against [N]. His detention was subsequently recorded under section 151 of the Code of Criminal Procedure. Following this incident Suresh Chand went to Lucknow to appeal to a local Minister with influence in the area to intervene in the matter. The Minister reportedly told him that if he continued to pursue the case against [N] he would be sent to jail. On 18 November 2000, a criminal case of theft was filed against Suresh Chand. He was arrested but released on bail pending investigation of the case by police which is ongoing. Amnesty International has learnt that non-bailable warrants for the arrest of Suresh Chand have subsequently been issued — reportedly at the instigation of [N] — and that he is now in hiding. Gangawati also continues to receive threats from police officials and from [N]. Amnesty International was informed in March 2001 that further threats had been made to Gangawati and her daughter. They are reported to have left the village to live with relatives.

The National Human Rights Commission and the National Commission for Women are reported to have taken up their cases and requested information from the state government. However, as of mid-March 2001, both Commissions were said to be still awaiting a final report from the Uttar Pradesh authorities. Amnesty International delegates provided information about Gangawati and Suresh Chand's case to officials with whom they met in Uttar Pradesh in December 2000 and requested a response to the concerns raised. However, to date, no response has been received.

## Relief and Rehabilitation

The Scheduled Castes and Scheduled Tribes (Prevention of Atrocities) Rules, 1989 provide for compensation to be paid to members of those communities who have suffered abuses including Rs.50,000 [$1.073] to a woman who has had her "modesty" "outraged" or been sexually exploited and Rs 2 lakh to a woman who has been raped. However, MARG's study found that many sections of the Rules had not been implemented in any of the fifty rape cases that were studied in Meerut and Banda districts of Uttar Pradesh: there was no economic or social rehabilitation for the victims and there were serious delays in the sanction of monetary relief for victims.

A lawyer involved in numerous cases of violence against *dalits* and *adivasis* in Rajasthan told Amnesty International delegates that he had not come across a single case in which a woman was given immediate compensation and travel and maintenance expenses as set out in the Act. He did however refer to financial relief provided by the Chief Minister of Rajasthan from his discretionary fund or by statutory bodies such as the National Commission for Women. Amnesty International delegates learnt that the Rajasthan government had set up a rehabilitation scheme for victims of rape which provides them with Rs.10,000 [$215] in immediate relief if they need financial assistance. The Rajasthan government's welfare measures for scheduled castes and scheduled tribes include payment of Rs.100,000 [$2,147] for victims of rape from those communities. However, the Scheduled Castes and Scheduled Tribes (Prevention of Atrocities) Rules indicate that in cases of murder, death, massacre, rape, mass rape and gang rape at least Rs.200,000 [$4,294] should be given in compensation.

Rajasthan government officials with whom Amnesty International delegates spoke in December 2000 recognised the need for a cohesive rehabilitation policy for victims of rape and other forms of violence.

Many women victims of violence are in desperate need of relief and rehabilitation. Many need to be at least temporarily and sometimes permanently placed outside the community where the offence took place. This rarely happens. There are no efforts towards social rehabilitation of women victims of violence. They are left entirely on their own or subject to the mercy of their families and the social pressures inherent in that situation. Professional counselling of women victims is virtually unheard of.

Outside the formal criminal justice system, women in India can turn to other bodies for support and redress. There are a large number of active non-governmental and voluntary organizations which provide legal support and temporary shelter and economic support to women. However, given their localised nature, the lack of resources available and the vulnerability of such initiatives to pressure from families, police, community or state, these initiatives cannot wholly address the scale of the problem in a country the size of India. There is clearly room for discussion on ways in which the state can address the needs of abused women through supporting the work of voluntary sector organizations.

## Justice or Impunity?

One of the main factors in assessing whether governments have shown due diligence in addressing violence by non-state actors is whether those responsible for such violence are brought to justice. As can be seen above, a very high percentage of crimes against women go unpunished because cases are not filed, end in compromise and/or complaints are withdrawn. This is clearly so in cases where the victims are from marginalised communities and particularly vulnerable to discrimination, threats and pressure.

Figures produced by the National Crime Records Bureau (NCRB) under the Ministry of Home Affairs indicate a relatively high percentage of cases of crimes against women investigated by police in comparison to very low percentages for the number of cases processed through the courts. These percentages hide the fact that many incidents of violence against women do not reach the stage of registration because of the role of compromises, threats and harassment as well as direct refusal by police to register such cases.

According to the NCRB figures, in cases of rape overall, the number of trials completed within a year is extremely low. Of 58,655 cases of rape pending trial at the start of 1998, 48,685 remained pending trial by the end of the year. Only 16% of those cases went to trial during 1998 and only 4.4% of the 58,655 cases resulted in conviction. 83% remained pending trial. The percentages are similar for molestation (under section 354 IPC).

In its research undertaken in Uttar Pradesh and Rajasthan, Amnesty International found evidence of complicity of the police in covering up the crime in several cases of violence against women. While in several cases action has subsequently been taken to arrest the perpetrators, those state officials guilty of complicity invariably went unpunished. Transfer of officials was the only form of punishment which Amnesty International delegates heard of. Transfer is often temporary and delegates learnt that a common "punishment" is to be transferred to "police lines" for a period. This in effect means that police are removed from a community policing situation and placed within police accommodation and training areas, the primary punishment being that they are no longer able to exert power and influence including by obtaining bribes from members of the public as a means of supplementing their income.

Mohini Devi and her husband Laxman Singh are *dalits* who live in Guthakar village in Bharatpur district of Rajasthan. Mohini Devi recounted to Amnesty International delegates how she was raped in the early morning of 10 April 1999 by three of her neighbours while her husband was away. When her husband returned they attempted to file a complaint at the Wire police station nearby but they were stopped by the perpetrators who reportedly threatened to kill them. Laxman Singh took Mohini Devi to Sawai Mansingh hospital in Jaipur on 12 April 1999 for treatment for injuries sustained during the rape. As a result of the medico-legal report compiled by medical staff at the hospital, an FIR was filed (No.46 of 1999) alleging rape (under section 376 IPC) of Mohini Devi.

The investigating police officer is reported to have immediately put pressure on Mohini Devi, her husband and several witnesses (who saw the rapists running away) to withdraw their statements. On 24 April 1999 the perpetrators and several of their supporters from the village reportedly went to the home of Mohini Devi and Laxman Singh and forced Laxman Singh to sign a piece of paper withdrawing the complaint of rape. Attempts to complain to police about their being forced to withdraw the complaint were ignored by police. Human rights activists tried to put pressure on the authorities to order an independent investigation into the incident but no action was taken.

Mohini Devi was subsequently accused by police of Wire police station of making a false statement against the perpetrators at the instigation of one of the witnesses — Bhagwan Singh — who is also a *dalit* and member of the Bharatpur *Zilla Parishad* [District Council]. Mohini Devi did not pursue the case and no action was taken against police officials who appear to have been complicit in the cover-up of this crime. Shockingly, this complicity was repeated more recently when Laxman Singh and his brother were repeatedly attacked by upper caste members of the village — Gujjars. On the last occasion in October 2000, Laxman Singh's legs were beaten with iron rods and after developing gangrene, both of his legs were amputated. Local police from Wire police station consistently ignored complaints of threats and attacks filed by Laxman Singh and his brother and abused them for daring to file complaints against the Gujjars. No protection was offered to the *dalits* and the police reportedly told the Gujjars that if they killed Laxman Singh they would be protected. Although some of those responsible for beating Laxman Singh were arrested, they continued to harass Laxman Singh and his family members as well as Bhagwan Singh who gave his support to the family; they were released on bail in January 2001. In March 2001 police registered a case of rape against Laxman Singh's brother and Bhagwan Singh. Human rights activists allege that police and Gujjar villagers have falsely filed the complaint of rape as a means of pressurising Laxman Singh to withdraw the case and to harass Bhagwan Singh who has consistently supported the family. At no stage has action been taken to investigate the involvement of police in this series of incidents or to initiate action against them for unlawful activities.

### The Role of the Community

Members of the victim's caste community or their family members can place enormous pressure on women victims of violence to either compromise or not pursue justice at all through formal justice systems. Dominated by men, caste groups often consider that women victims of violence should suffer their ordeal in silence. In many cases, women who insist on pursuing justice are punished in some way — often by social ostracisation, but also by being abandoned by their husbands and his family — for what is seen as bringing further dishonour to the community. MARG's study referred to earlier found that "In almost all the cases we find that the victim has got no support from the village in fighting for justice. This as it is leads to psychological stress on both the victim and her family. People in the village do not forget such incidents especially when the official summons keep coming to the victim, and so the ostracization continues, increasing the psychological trauma."

Maya Devi, a 22-year-old domestic worker and member of a "backward caste" was raped by two backward caste and one *dalit* man in the late afternoon on 18 April 1999 in Bhadasa village, Kanpur district in Uttar Pradesh. The rest of her household were in the fields cutting wheat. Her children were playing outside the house. The men were constructing a wedding tent behind her house and attacked her when she was returning from fetching water from the well some way from the house. One of the men hit Maya and she fell down. They closed the door tied her hands behind her back and then all three raped her. She described to Amnesty International delegates how they kept arguing with each other as to who would have a go first.

*"All three of them tore off my blouse and stuffed it into my mouth. They then took off all my clothes, tied my hands behind my back and proceeded to rape me. After raping me they tied me up with more strings and then poured the bucket of water over me and started beating me. Then they pulled off my gold bangles, took out about 11,000 rupees from my husband's money box and ran away."*

When her husband, Chotelal Sahu, returned he found her in the dark house, unconscious and naked. Seeing that money had been stolen he immediately filed an FIR concerning the theft. He did not immediately report the rape but when Maya Devi regained consciousness the next morning and told her husband of the rape he took her to a nearby hospital — Ursula Kanpur Convent hospital — and filed a fresh FIR with police under section 376 IPC (*rape*). A woman police officer went to the hospital and looked through Maya's medical records. Maya subsequently recorded her statement in front of the local magistrate.

Following protests by women's organizations the accused were arrested ten days after the incident. However, they are currently on bail and are continuing to threaten Maya and her relatives. Maya has complained to police about the threats but no action has been taken. Maya and her family received very little help from villagers. Those who did sympathise are too scared to help. Maya's family have been told that they should compromise or they will be killed. When Amnesty International delegates interviewed Maya and her husband, he clearly wished to drop the case but she was keen to pursue it. One of the accused had previously been in jail for the murder of the local *sarpanch*.

In the face of a hostile and discriminatory criminal justice system, many communities look within to provide "solutions" to violence against women. During their visit to Uttar Pradesh and Rajasthan, Amnesty International delegates heard of several cases in which caste *panchayats* (councils made up of representatives of particular castes from a particular area) had sat in judgement over cases of violence against women. These *panchayats* are dominated by men and gender biases mean that even within the same caste women are often punished for bringing dishonour or forced to come to a compromise with the perpetrator. An activist in Rajasthan has commented: "Our experience in Rajasthan of combatting cases of violence against women in the last few years has shown that most institutions of justice at the village and community level have been used against women, the poor and *dalits*... On the other hand, the performance of the state institutions of justice like the courts and police has been as dismal." Reports of the judgements of these caste *panchayats* include women being forced to marry the man who has raped them as a means of "solving" the problem of lost honour and future economic dependence (due to lack of marriage offers) that confronts many victims of rape.

# Index

# Bibliography


Abbasayulu, Y.B.: *Scheduled Caste Elite: a Study of Scheduled Caste Elite in Andhra Pradesh*, Osmania University, Hyderabad, 1978.

Aggarwal, L. B.: *The Harijans in Rebellion*, Taraporewala and Sons, Bombay, 1934.

Ainapur, L. S.: *Dynamics of Caste Relations in Rural India*, Rawat Publications, Jaipur, 1986.

Aluwalia, B.K. & Shashi B.R.: *Ambedkar and Human Rights*, KK Publishers, New Delhi, 1981.

Ambedkar, B. R.: *Annihilation of Caste: An Undelivered Speech*, Arnold Publishers, New Delhi, 1990.

Anand, J. H.: *Dalit Literature is the Literature of Protest*, Dalit Solidarity, Delhi, 1995.

Ayrookuzhiel, A. M. Abraham.: *The Dalit Desiyata: The Kerala Experience in Development and Class Struggle*, ISPCK, Delhi, 1990.

Beteille, A.: *The Backward Classes and the New Social Order*, OUP, New Delhi, 1981.

Bhatt, V.: *The Harijans of Maharashtra*, All India Harijan Sevak Sangh, Delhi, 1941.

Briggs, G. W.: *The Chamars*, Association Press (YMCA), Calcutta, 1920.

Chatterjee, Partha: *Caste and Subaltern Consciousness*, Oxford University Press, Delhi, 1994.

Danda, A.K.: *Weaker Sections in Indian Villages*, Inter-India, New Delhi, 1993.

Dietrich, Gabriele: *Dalit Movements and Women's Movement*, Horizons India Books, New Delhi, 1992.

Ghurye, G. S.: *Caste and Class in India*, Popular Books, Bombay, 1950.

Gough, Kathleen: *Harijans in Thanjavur*, Monthly Review Press, New York, 1973.

Hocart, A. M.: *Caste,* Mathew and Co., London, 1950.

Jogdan, Prahlad G.: *Dalit Movement in Maharashtra,* Kanak Publications, New Delhi, 1991.

Kamble, J. R.: *Rise and Awakening of Depressed Classes in India,* National Publishers, New Delhi, 1979.

Khan, Mumtaz Ali: *Human Rights and the Dalits,* Uppal Publishing House, New Delhi, 1995.

Kosambi, D. D.: *Introduction to the Study of Indian History,* Popular Prakashan, Bombay, 1975.

Kuber, W.N.: *Dr. Ambedkar: A Critical Study,* People's Publishing House, New Delhi, 1973.

Omvedt, G.: *Dalits and the Democratic Revolution: Dr Ambedkar and the Dalit Movement in Colonial India,* Sage, New Delhi, 1994.

Punalekar, S. P.: *Dalit Women in India: Issues and Perspectives,* Gyan Publishing House, New Delhi, 1995.

Robb, Peter: *Dalit Movements and the Meanings of Labour in India,* Oxford University Press, New Delhi, 1993.

Sharma, B. D.: *Dalits Betrayed,* Har-Anand Publications, New Delhi, 1994.

Tripathy, R. B.: *Dalits: A Sub-Human Society,* Ashish Publishing House, New Delhi, 1994.

Webster, John: *The Christian Dalits: A History,* Indian Society for Promoting Christian Knowledge (ISPCK), Delhi, 1994.

Zelliot, Eleanor: *From Untouchable to Dalit: Essays on the Ambedkar Movement,* Manohar, New Delhi, 1992.

♦♦♦